W9-CHX-653

RUSSIA

EUROPE

Bikin River, Russia **16**

CHINA **4** Beijing, China

K2, Pakistan **2** **21** Northwest Chang Tang, Tibet

Mt. Everest, Nepal **1,6**

3, 20 Minya Konka, China

INDIA

Kathmandu, Nepal **5** **10** Gangkhar Puensum, Bhutan

AFRICA

18 Tsavo, Kenya

7 Borneo

19 Sabaki River, Kenya

Indian Ocean

AUSTRALIA

Life Lived Wild

Adventures at the Edge of the Map

Life Lived Wild

Adventures at the Edge of the Map

RICK RIDGEWAY

patagonia

Life Lived Wild
Adventures at the Edge of the Map

Patagonia publishes a select list of titles on wilderness, wildlife, and outdoor sports that inspire and restore a connection to the natural world.

© 2021 Rick Ridgeway

Photograph copyrights held by the photographer as indicated in captions.

Hardcover Edition
Printed in Canada on Roland Enviro 100 Satin FSC certified 100% post-consumer-waste paper.

Editor – John Dutton
Photo Editors – Cameron Tambakis, Jane Sievert
Book Designer – Annette Scheid
Project Manager – Sonia Moore
Photo Archivist – Taylor Norton
Production – Rafael Dunn, Tausha Greenblott, and Michaela Purcilly
Creative Director – Christina Speed
Publisher – Karla Olson

Hardcover ISBN 978-1-938340-99-4
E-Book ISBN 978-1-952338-00-7
Library of Congress Control Number 2021942105

Published by Patagonia Works

Excerpts from the poems of Robert Service by permission of his granddaughter Anne Longepe.

Excerpts from *The Selected Poetry of Robinson Jeffers*, edited by Tim Hunt. Copyright 2001 by Jeffers Literary Properties. All rights reserved. Used by permission of Stanford University Press. www.sup.org

Words and music for "Hey Jude" by John Lennon and Paul McCartney © 1968 Sony Music Publishing LLC, Copyright renewed. All rights administered by Sony Music LLC, 424 Church St., Suite 1200, Nashville TN 37219. International copyright secured. All rights reserved. Reprinted by permission of Hal Leonard LLC.

Maps and end sheets: Christina Speed

ENVIRONMENTAL BENEFITS STATEMENT

Patagonia Inc saved the following resources by printing the pages of this book on chlorine free paper made with 100% post-consumer waste.

TREES	WATER	ENERGY	SOLID WASTE	GREENHOUSE GASES
318	25,000	134	1,000	138,000
FULLY GROWN	GALLONS	MILLION BTUs	POUNDS	POUNDS

Environmental impact estimates were made using the Environmental Paper Network Paper Calculator 4.0. For more information visit www.papercalculator.org

FSC
www.fsc.org
MIX
Paper from responsible sources
FSC® C016245

1%
FOR THE PLANET
MEMBER

PREVIOUS SPREAD: Day two of our foot traverse across the uninhabited and unexplored northwest corner of the Chang Tang Plateau, Tibet. I am surveying that day's route during our self-supported trek pulling rickshaws, each with 250 pounds of food and supplies. **Jimmy Chin**

For Bella

Who heard these stories many times,
even if she was never able to read them.

Photo of Jennifer Ridgeway. **Terri Laine**

Day twenty-five of our foot traverse across the Chang Tang Plateau, northwest Tibet, when for each of those days calories out had exceeded calories in. That's me on the left and Conrad Anker, widely known as one of the world's strongest climbers, flat on his back. **Jimmy Chin**

Contents

Doug Tompkins, me, and Yvon Chouinard (l to r) on the summit of a previously
unclimbed and unnamed peak in what in 2008 was still the future Patagonia
National Park, in southern Chile. At first, we christened the peak Cerro Geezer,
but Doug later had the Chilean government name it Cerro Kristina to honor
Kris Tompkins, the force behind the final creation of the park. **Jimmy Chin**

Prologue

I once calculated that I have spent over five years' total time sleeping in tents, and most of that in small tents pitched in the world's most remote regions. I say that not to boast but to offer it as a measure of time spent deeply connected to wildness, because that connection has shaped the way I have lived my life, teaching me to distinguish what I call matters of consequence from matters of inconsequence.

I am seventy-two years old now, and I had my first significant adventure at age eighteen when I joined five friends and we sailed a small boat to Tahiti. My passion for adventure included both the ocean and the mountains, and later jungles, plateaus, and ice caps. I was obsessed with the way outdoor sports required both physical and mental skills, and how the sports were played not only in the arena of wild nature, but in those places on the planet so remote a few of them remained unexplored.

In my early twenties my companions were my accomplices, and we learned together from our experiences. In my late twenties I met Yvon Chouinard, who later introduced me to Doug Tompkins. They were both older than me, and now my companions also became my role models. Yvon and Doug had been climbing, skiing, and kayaking together since the early 1960s. In addition to outdoor sports, they had both started outdoor companies. Doug founded The North Face and sold that to cofound Esprit with his wife, Susie. In the early 1970s, Yvon started his own apparel business, which he named Patagonia, after the place where he and Doug had made a climb that, because of bad weather combined with steep rock and ice, had taken two months. Years later, looking back, Yvon would say that for both of them, the experience was a significant inspiration for what they did later in their lives.

"Going out into the wilds of the world at an early age," Doug added, "where nature was basically untouched, we got into our souls a sense of beauty."

Humans all strive to protect what we love, and protecting the beauty of wild nature from our species' aptitude to disfigure it would become a central focus for Doug and Yvon. I thought I was already doing an OK job taking the lessons I was learning in wild nature and applying them to my domestic life. As with any new friends, however, if you keep your antennae tuned you can usually pick up new ideas that give you new ways to go about your own life. One of the most important for me was a note card tacked to the wall behind Doug's desk at Esprit that said, "Commit and Then Figure It Out."

Doug was the one who came up with the Do Boys. He said he ran into the phrase in Japan, where Esprit had a design studio. It was the title of one of those comic books popular in that country, about a group of guys who go around having adventures, and as more friends joined us on more adventures, it seemed like a good name for our posse.

"We don't just talk about doing stuff," Yvon said. "We do it."

To a remarkable degree, the Do Boys were successful not only in outdoor sports but also in business. The professional side of our lives, however, was never the central defining attribute of who we were, and Doug and Yvon in particular disparaged the label "businessman." Many years after I had become a Do Boy—after I had successfully sold my company that licensed visual assets to advertising agencies and joined

Patagonia—I was at a business conference where I stepped into an elevator with another attendee, a pleasant-looking man in a nicely tailored suit.

"You work for Patagonia," he said, reading my nametag. His badge identified him as the Global VP of Sustainability at Coca-Cola. "I've met your colleague, Yvon Chouinard. We were on a panel together."

"That's great. Did you have a good conversation?"

"It's the only time in my professional life where in public someone has called me a 'business greaseball.'"

If business didn't define us, then how we used business skills to advance wildland and wildlife conservation did. In turn, our business skills were informed directly by the skills we acquired doing outdoor sports. In outdoor sports, as in business, we learned from our mistakes, but in outdoor sports, we knew if a mistake was too egregious we wouldn't get the chance to learn from it because we would be dead. In mountaineering—and in business—it's not about taking risks but managing risks.

In 1980, Yvon and I joined an expedition to attempt a remote mountain in eastern Tibet called Minya Konka. It was the first year China opened to outside mountaineers, and traveling through the People's Republic to the forbidden plateau of Tibet seemed reason alone for the adventure, never mind the climb. One day four of us, including Yvon and me, made a cache of food and gear at 20,000 feet and were descending to our high camp when we triggered an avalanche. We had failed to manage the risk, and all four of us were injured. One of us, Jonathan Wright, was injured so badly he died while I was holding him in my arms, trying to keep him alive. Jonathan was a close friend and, as a writer-photographer team, we were professional partners. The following day my companions and I buried him under a bier of flagstones a few yards from where he had died.

Back home, I tried to assess whether the rewards outweighed the risks. A couple of years later I was in a car with Yvon, on our way to go surfing. I still hadn't decided to return to mountaineering. We hadn't talked about the avalanche. I knew it made him uncomfortable, but I decided to bring it up, my need to talk about it overcoming his reticence.

"I think about the avalanche all the time," I said. "About Jonathan's death."

"So do I," he replied. "Every day."

That's all we said. We never talked about it again. Maybe we should have, but I knew that he knew, and he knew that I knew, that we had triggered the avalanche and Jonathan had died, and that fact would weigh on us for the rest of our lives. Two years after the avalanche I married, and at the wedding Yvon was my best man. My new wife, Jennifer, supported me when I decided to return to mountaineering and, as a writer, photographer, and filmmaker, to continue to go on adventures both as avocation and vocation.

For thirty years, Doug, Yvon, and I went on dozens of trips and adventures. Sometimes we brought friends, who became each other's new friends, and some of those friends would organize trips and invite us. If it was a kayaking trip, Jib Ellison often joined. Jib owned a successful sustainability consultancy built on a strategy of inculcating environmental responsibility in top executives; he was called the "CEO Whisperer." Peter Buckley had been Doug Tompkins's partner at Esprit, managing the business in Europe, and would sometimes join our outings if the trip was easy climbing, trekking, or sea kayaking. Same for Doug Peacock, the writer and environmental activist, and Tom Brokaw, the news anchorman.

On any of our adventures, the campfire conversations inevitably turned to the environmental crisis, or what Doug Tompkins preferred to call the environmental predicament.

"Crises are things that usually rally people to find solutions," he said. "Predicaments are a little more difficult."

Doug was at the vanguard of thinking about these things, and he always showed up with a list of new books for me to read. During my fifteen-year tenure at Patagonia, starting in the early

2000s managing the company's environmental commitments and its sustainability efforts, we developed the now-famous full-page ad we ran in the *New York Times* on Black Friday. It had a photo of one of the company's best-selling jackets and above it, in bold letters, the headline, "Don't Buy This Jacket." That ad is now used in the curricula of several business schools, crediting Patagonia with a campaign that advanced discussion of the unsustainable overuse by humans of the Earth's limited natural resources. In the late 1980s, however, near the end of his tenure at Esprit, Doug Tompkins had run an ad with a photo of one of their best-selling dresses and the headline, "Don't Buy This Dress." Of all of us, he could see farthest over the horizon.

In our popular culture there is a maxim that we succeed to the extent that we have mentors to guide our passages at pivotal transitions from one phase of our lives to the next. I was lucky to have had that guidance from Doug and Yvon and others in our posse. I was also fortunate to benefit from another of our core tenets: it wasn't just doing the adventure sports, it was working to save the places where we did the sports. For me, it has been a slow but steady progression from one focus to the other, and even though the transition has taken most of my adult life, I find abiding satisfaction in knowing that whatever years I have remaining, I will use them to do what I can to safeguard what remains of the wild places of my cherished home planet.

I'm not religious, but my wife did teach me to remain open to all possibilities, and if she and Doug are in some place where they are watching, I like to think they are nodding with approval.

Sacred Rice

With the trail slippery from the monsoon rain, Jonathan Wright, Ang Phurba, and I entered Thupten Chöling monastery in a cul-de-sac valley twenty-six miles from Mount Everest. The three of us were on a mission to seek a blessing from the high abbot, Lama Tuche Rinpoche. The blessing wasn't just for us, but for our American Bicentennial Everest Expedition. I was the youngest climber on a team hoping to become what back then would have been only the second American expedition to climb Everest. Jonathan was a cameraman on the film crew making a one-hour special for television and Ang, who spoke conversational English, was the climbing leader of our team of Sherpas.

We had left the rest of the expedition earlier that morning in the camp we had set up the previous afternoon at the end of that day's stage of the approach march. The team included my climbing partner Chris Chandler. Chris and I had started climbing together three years earlier, spending a season in the Peruvian Andes, where we succeeded in making a new route on a major peak in the Cordillera Blanca. Chris had started as my climbing mentor, but I learned quickly and now, on a rope team, we were equals.

The American Bicentennial Everest Expedition was one of the last of the old-school expeditions in the style of the first

Chris Chandler (kneeling) and I puzzle-out a potential route through the Khumbu Icefall. This is the most dangerous part of climbing Everest from the Nepal side. Today teams of Sherpas scout and maintain the route for clients paying guide services over $100,000. Back in the 1970s, we had to establish the route ourselves. **Johan Reinhard**

British teams that attempted Everest in the 1920s and '30s. We were approaching the mountain the traditional way, beginning at a trailhead a two-hour drive outside of Kathmandu. From there, the trek to Base Camp was 170 miles and would take a month. The size of the expedition was old school as well: 12 climbers, 44 Sherpas, and a little over 600 porters hired from the lowland tribes.

Six hundred porters! In Peru we had hired only a few burros and an *arriero* to wrangle the animals to our base camps. The Everest expedition seemed to have expanded under its own compounding inertia. It had an unusual genesis with three friends, all classmates at Harvard Law School, who, after graduation, pledged to fulfill their passion for adventure by getting together every year or two for a trip. They each had gone on to successful careers—one in real estate, one in international law, and one in the State Department—and they had held true to their pledge: skiing across Ellesmere Island, rafting the interior of Borneo, and climbing the Carstensz Pyramid, the highest peak in New Guinea.

Back in the 1970s, when China was closed and Nepal hadn't opened to hordes of guided climbers, the queue for an Everest permit was more than ten years. But the one friend who worked in the State Department got wind from a colleague in the US embassy in Kathmandu that a French team had failed to raise funds, and their permit was available. He got the permit through his diplomatic connections, but to climb Everest the friends knew they would need additional climbers, and ones with advanced mountaineering skills. They went to the annual meeting of the American Alpine Club, hoping to meet expedition climbers. Standing in line at the buffet, they introduced themselves to a guy with long blond hair who looked to be in good shape.

"I'm Chris Chandler. Nice to meet you."

By the time they got to the food, they had invited Chris to join their expedition, and Chris had recommended me. I was living in Malibu with some surfer friends and had been accepted into a Ph.D. program in cultural geography at UC Berkeley that was scheduled to start in a month. I had decided that I wanted to be a professor. To get into a good school, my strategy had been first to enroll at a university in Peru in cultural anthropology, with courses that included fieldwork in the Andes. When my courses concluded, I had stayed in Peru, where I met climbers, including Chris, who took me under their wing and initiated my apprenticeship in high-altitude mountaineering. The strategy had worked, and I had been accepted into one of the best schools in the world.

Then I got the call from Chris.

"I got us on an expedition to the Himalayas."

"The Himalayas? Wow! What's the peak?"

"Everest!"

"Everest?"

Chris heard the dismay in my voice. Everest! But what about school? My future as a university professor? My mother had been relieved that I finally seemed to be settling down. But Everest! I tried to think through the outcome of one choice over the other, but I needed more time.

"Give me a day," I told Chris, "and I'll tell you if I'm going."

We all arrive at forks in the road where the only signposts are constructed not from facts but from intuitions. I was twenty-six years old, and somewhere in my reading I had run across a quote from Saint Thomas Aquinas: trust the authority of your instincts. That sounded like good advice, and the next morning I called Chris.

"I might as well start at the top and work down," I told him.

* * *

We were two weeks into the trek to Base Camp when Jonathan, Ang Phurba, and I left the entourage, departing in the predawn from the tent city that was our camp. Our plan was to get the Lama's blessing and then catch up to the others. We didn't anticipate any difficulty, since our army of more than 650 people didn't move very fast.

Inside the monastery compound, I counted about a hundred buildings, seemingly living quarters for monks and nuns, all surrounding the central *gompa*, or temple. But there was no one around.

"Where is everybody?" I asked Ang.

"Time to make meditation."

"Does that mean we have to wait to see the Lama?"

"He knows we come."

We walked through the main door of the *gompa* into a courtyard to find three monks waiting. We followed them through a low doorway into a small, smoky kitchen. One monk motioned us to sit on a bench while another served us Tibetan tea made with yak butter and salt. In the corner an old monk sat cross-legged on a raised platform, staring at us through pince-nez spectacles. Around him, on several shelves, was an array of clocks: alarm clocks, wall clocks, cuckoo clocks, old pendulum clocks. All showed the same time: 8:50 a.m.

Another monk arrived and asked us to follow him. I considered asking if we could wait ten minutes so I could see what happened when the clocks sounded the hour—I was sure the old monk would break into a beatific smile—but thought that might be impolite. The monk escorted us back to the courtyard and then up a wooden staircase to a doorway covered with an exquisitely embroidered drape. We took off our shoes and entered.

The room was maybe twenty square feet and in one corner, sitting on a pillow, was the Lama. Ang Phurba prostrated himself, as did Jonathan. I followed suit. I knew this was natural for Jonathan; after going to college, he had spent many months in Nepal as part of a years-long overland journey across Turkey, Iran, Afghanistan, Pakistan, India, and Nepal, an experience that had changed his life. He had converted to Buddhism and had also taken thousands of photographs, a portfolio strong enough it later won him assignments for *National Geographic*.

My climbing partner Chris Chandler in the monsoon broadleaf forest on our 170-mile approach march to Everest Base Camp. **Rick Ridgeway Collection**

The Lama motioned us to sit. He next removed four small silver chalices from a cupboard and arranged them in a square-shaped mandala. Chanting, he opened one chalice and removed a pinch of yellow rice. We bowed as he pushed the rice into our hair. Then he took three pieces of folded paper and placed into each one a few grains of the rice. He refolded them, tied them with yarn, and handed one to each of us.

"We will sew covers on these," Ang said, "with the sacred rice inside. Then we wear around our necks. Bring good luck for the expedition. Also, rice stays in your hair for one day. Sacred rice of Chomolungma."

Chomolungma—Everest. The Lama opened another chalice and removed a pair of dice. I looked inquisitively at Ang.

"Lama now makes some prediction, to see if we have any accidents during the expedition. Very important. If no good for climb, Sherpas don't want to go to Chomolungma."

I considered what this meant: the Lama was about to roll the dice to predict our future, and if by chance the roll was bad the Sherpas would not go on the climb. And if they didn't go, the climb would be over before it started.

Resuming his chant, the Lama took the dice in his right hand and held them against his forehead. He closed his eyes and kept chanting. Ang seemed as nervous as I was. I looked at Jonathan. He had clasped his hands and closed his eyes and started chanting. The Lama opened his eyes, tossed the dice, then leaned forward to study them. The three of us leaned forward. The Lama didn't say anything.

"What do the dice say?" I asked.

"Wait and see," Ang replied.

Finally, the Lama leaned back and shook his head.

"Doesn't look good," Ang said.

"Doesn't look good?"

Ang didn't answer. I looked at Jonathan, who opened his hands in a gesture indicating what will be will be. I was wishing I had some of his equanimity.

The Lama then talked to Ang in hushed tones.

"Lama say there is one more thing to do," Ang said. "He will make a prayer to Miyolangsangma, the goddess of Chomolungma. He will tell the goddess that we will put up many prayer flags at Base Camp and have a big ceremony. Throw lots of sacred rice. Then Lama will look again to see if Miyolangsangma says things are OK."

The Lama resumed chanting, picked up the dice, and held them again to his forehead. This time his chant was even longer. He stopped chanting and threw the dice. He leaned forward to look at them, then leaned back and smiled and spoke to Ang Phurba.

"Lama says everything is now OK," Ang translated.

I looked at Jonathan and with my lips formed a silent whistle of relief. Jonathan smiled, and I got the impression that with his Buddhist training to accept the world as it is, he would have been OK whether the prediction had gone one way or the other. The Lama then spoke again to Ang, who turned to me and said, "Lama want to know why you want to climb Chomolungma."

I hadn't anticipated that question, and I was caught off guard. I knew the question was directed to me and not to Jonathan because he was a cameraman, so filming the climb was his job. But what was my motivation? So I could have adventures like meeting a high lama in a remote monastery? Because climbing was something I was good at? Because it was still there?

"Tell him I want to know what it feels like to stand on the highest point on Earth."

As Ang translated, I was already thinking that the answer was lame. The Lama looked at me without blinking, and I suspected he had the same thought.

* * *

The rest of the team had just begun the day's march when we caught up to them. I fell in line beside Chris, as I did most days—although I was enjoying getting to know everyone, especially Jonathan. For Jonathan, like me, interacting with remote cultures in remote parts of the world was as appealing as the climbs themselves. I knew that he valued our audience with the Lama as much as I had, and I wanted to talk to him more about the Lama's question—or was it a challenge to be honest with myself, about why I wanted to climb Everest?

My fascination with mountaineering—my mother would call it an obsession—had started when I was fourteen. My parents were in the process of separating—although I didn't realize that at the time—and I lived with my father on a 125-acre ranch in the Sierra foothills of California while my mother and younger brother had stayed behind in our small one-acre ranchette in Southern California.

My mother kept her job at the aircraft factory where she had worked her entire adult life while my father, at the new ranch, went from one job to another, a logger for a few weeks, working in a limestone mine for a few more. Looking back, I can see now that the organizing principle in my father's life was to avoid responsibility. There were other indicators I should have heeded that his marriage to my mother was in jeopardy: how he spent most of his time between his short-lived jobs sitting in a bar sharing off-color jokes with his barfly buddies, how there was nothing happening on the 125-acre ranch in the way of getting it ready for my mother and brother to join us.

It was a twenty-mile bus ride from high school to home, and one day I was sitting near the back as we crested a small hill just before the ranch. What I remember is not the remains of the house still smoldering in a heap around the brick chimney, but rather how as the bus slowed and then stopped, everyone turned to look at me. That included the bus driver, whose face asked the question he didn't need to voice.

I was sitting next to my best friend. We were on the football team together, and we spent most weekends at his parents' place, where they ran the village grocery store, and with his grandparents, who ran the village hardware store.

"Can I go home with you?"

"Sure."

"Bob"—we called our bus driver by his first name—"take me to Doug's house," I said, referring to my best friend.

I didn't see my father again for nearly two years. A couple of months after the house burned I got a postcard from him, mailed from the South Seas. It had a picture of a bare-breasted woman with a red hibiscus in her hair and a short message telling me that once he got back on his feet, he would send for me. I learned years later that he had burned the house down hoping to get the insurance money, but at the time I took him at his word that it was an accident. As for my mother—bless her now-departed soul—she gave me permission to stay with

Doug and his family for the rest of the school year, something I didn't fully appreciate until I myself became a parent of teenage children.

If my decision years later to go to Everest instead of grad school was a fork in the road, deciding to move in with my best friend's family was another one, and looking back on it now I can see how going down one road as opposed to the other would have led to an entirely different life. When I joined Doug's family there was insufficient space in his bedroom for both of us, so we were allowed to move into the family's Airstream trailer. I worked in the grocery, stocking shelves and operating the cash register. I had my own "house" and my own job, earning my own keep, even though, truth be told, my mother folded a twenty-dollar bill in the letters she wrote me each month. In my mind, my independence was probably greater than it actually was, but it gave me an abiding satisfaction.

Things of course weren't entirely bucolic. Doug cut off the end of his thumb in the salami slicer, but once the blood was cleaned up and his parents recovered they continued to give us more responsibility. The bigger setback was the letter I got from my mother saying that she was divorcing my father. I sat on a log next to the Airstream and cried while Doug held his arm around me. Once more, against all the evidence, I had allowed myself to believe that once my father had completed whatever "self-recovery" he was making on that island in the South Seas, my parents would get back together.

My mom had given me a subscription to *National Geographic*, and before my father had burned our house down I had sat in our living room in front of the fire—the only heat in the house—and read in the October 1963 issue the cover story about the first American ascent of Mount Everest. Inside, there was a photograph of Jim Whittaker, the first American to reach the summit of the world's highest mountain, standing on the crest wearing a down jacket and down pants, holding his ice ax adorned with the small flags of the United States and the National Geographic

Society whipped by hurricane winds. I had said to myself, *I want to be THAT guy.*

Doug's parents vacationed each summer in a rental cabin on an alpine lake higher in the Sierra. It would be my last summer in Northern California, and I was excited to join them. Across the lake there was a peak called Thunder Mountain with a steep-sided face. I told Doug I wanted to climb up the steep side. We knew better than to ask his parents for permission to go on anything more than a long hike, so we figured we had just enough time to climb it and get back before dark. We jogged along the trail that circled the lake, then followed game trails through the woods to the base of the peak and started climbing. We made steady progress until just below the summit we encountered a ten-foot-high step of vertical rock.

"I've got an idea," I said.

Doug squatted while I stood on his thigh and then stepped onto his shoulders. He stood and I grabbed the edge at the top of the vertical step.

"OK, now I'm going to hold on," I told Doug, "and you climb up on my legs and arms."

Doug was heavier than me, and it took everything I could muster to hold on. On the summit I was elated, but Doug was worried about getting back to the cabin before dark. We started down, pausing at the top of the ten-foot step.

"Let's jump," I suggested.

We each launched, taking care to land on our feet to avoid rolling down the rest of the precipice. We got back to the cabin before dark. Sitting on the porch with his parents, we looked up at Thunder Mountain in the last light of the day.

"*That* was a good hike," I told Doug.

* * *

Of the forty-four Sherpas on the American Bicentennial Everest Expedition, twenty-one of them were deemed high-altitude climbers. This was the team that Ang Phurba led, and they were paid a higher rate than the rest of the Sherpas, who would carry loads to the lower camps. All except for Pasang Kami, or PK, as everyone called him. He was the *sirdar*, the overall leader of the entire Sherpa team.

He was also my favorite. He was slightly built, with thick glasses that made him look like a professor. I watched amused as each morning he stood on a rock or a camp chair with clipboard in hand and called out the day's duties in an authoritative voice that belied his thin stature. He was one of those leaders who gained respect from his team through the power of his intellect. When you talked to PK, it felt like he knew what you were going to say before you said it.

One day on the approach march I had the opportunity to hike with him. He told me he had a trekker's lodge and general store in the Sherpa village of Namche Bazaar that his wife ran while he was away on expeditions and treks. He had traveled to Europe and the United States, hosted by Westerners he had guided.

"What's the most impressive thing you saw in the United States?" I asked.

"Disneyland," he answered. "It was something like a dream, that didn't seem real. Maybe someday I can take my children there."

A few days later I was hiking with another Sherpa, Nima Norbu. Nima also owned a trekking lodge in Namche Bazaar. Nima had attended Tribhuvan University near Kathmandu; he spoke three local languages, was fluent in English, and spoke passable Japanese. He had been helping the film team, and they had told me he was a quick study, learning to operate the sound recorder—positioning the microphone on a boom pole and leveling the input tracks—and to load 16mm film magazines inside a changing bag.

I asked Nima if, like PK, he had been to the United States. He said he hadn't but that his sister was going to go to college in Seattle, and he hoped to visit her. I then told him that PK had said that the most memorable part of his visit was seeing Disneyland.

"That's not what he told us," Nima replied.

Nima then said that PK had told everyone in Namche that he had visited a small city in the American Midwest, staying in a house owned by a couple whom he had guided on a trek. One morning he got up early to go on a walk, and as he passed a house with a large front window he saw on the other side a number of old people sitting in chairs staring back at him. Perplexed, he had asked his hosts about the house, and they explained that it was a home for old people.

"PK had a hard time understanding that," Nima said. "How you could send your mother or your father to another home instead of keeping them in your own home. I think maybe that was the thing that made the most impression."

* * *

A week later I was once again hiking with Nima, ascending a lateral moraine connected to the nearby Khumbu Glacier. We would arrive at Base Camp the next day, and as we approached the crest I saw six chorten—small Buddhist shrines—silhouetted against the indigo sky.

"They're for the six Sherpas killed on the Japanese expedition a few years ago," Nima said.

"What happened?"

"They were in the Khumbu Icefall and stopped to have lunch." The icefall is the most dangerous part of climbing Everest—it's a jumble of ice blocks called séracs that shift and collapse as the glacier inexorably moves over the steep underlying bedrock. "An avalanche came," Nima continued, "and wiped them out. All of them. This spot here, it's where their wives came to get their bodies."

We stopped and faced the chorten. Nima clasped his hands and bowed. Neither of us said anything until Nima broke our silence.

"I was on the expedition. They were all close friends."

After a while I asked, "If it's so dangerous, why do you think Sherpas like this work?"

Pasang Kami, *sirdar,* or leader of the Sherpas, directing placement of prayer flags at Everest Base Camp. **Rick Ridgeway Collection**

"Some prefer working on treks. It's not as dangerous, but you don't make as much money."

"And the Sherpas on this trip? If they made as much money, they would prefer working someplace else?"

"Yes. Especially if they could be home, with wives and children."

"What about us?"

"You?"

"Why do you Sherpas think we climb?"

"I don't know," Nima laughed. "But we do talk about it. Maybe you people have too much money and you don't know how to spend it. You wear good clothes and you drive nice cars. Maybe when you have a holiday you don't know what to do, so you go to the mountains."

"But doesn't it seem odd to spend your holiday and your money doing something very difficult and very dangerous?"

"Well, if you really want to know what we think," Nima said with another laugh, "we think it is kind of silly. But you people seem to like it."

* * *

Clouds of incense boiled up from boughs of smoldering juniper stacked on a stone altar. Sherpas jostled so each could breathe in the smoke. Nearly all were chanting. Nearby, another group of Sherpas decorated a thirty-foot pole with prayer banners and tied two long lines of prayer flags to the end of the pole. It was our second day in Base Camp, and the Sherpas were having the ceremony that the Lama had prescribed to win the favor of Miyolangsangma.

Several bottles of *chang*—local rice beer—made the rounds. The chanting increased in volume. It seemed to reach a crescendo just as the pole was raised, and then gave way to shouting and cheering as each Sherpa reached into the Lama's bag of rice and tossed the sacred grains into the air.

Four days later, Chris and I stopped at the altar to breathe in the juniper smoke. Jonathan came along to film, as did another Sherpa in his late fifties who was the oldest and most venerated on the team of climbing Sherpas. We were scouting a route through the Khumbu Icefall. Others behind us would fix ropes and install ladders across the crevasses so that the Sherpas could ferry supplies to the upper camps.

It was dark as we left Base Camp, navigating by the beams of our headlamps. At dawn we stopped to rest. We all lit cigarettes, except for Jonathan, who didn't smoke; back in the sixties and seventies, most of the high-altitude climbers I knew smoked, the warmth of the tobacco providing comfort that—at least we thought back then—offset any health hazards.

Across the valley the snow on cone-shaped Pumori turned soft pink. The Sherpa drew on his cigarette, then slowly exhaled. The smoke rose slowly into the still, cold air.

"Look, sahib," he said. "Much view coming now."

Our challenge was finding the safest way through the icefall, although any route was only slightly less dangerous than another. I belayed the rope as Chris led, and when it paid out, I followed him and he didn't stop to belay me; the older Sherpa and Jonathan, on another rope, followed us. We wound around and among the house-sized ice blocks, placing bamboo markers into the snow every twenty yards or so.

In four hours, we neared the top of the icefall. The Sherpa led up a thin snow bridge spanning a deep crevasse. On the other side he set up a belay. Chris followed while Jonathan filmed. Chris was halfway across the snow bridge when suddenly there was a loud rifle-like crack deep in the crevasse. The snow shook as though there was an earthquake. We were surrounded by séracs fifty feet high. The blood rushed to my head and my stomach tightened.

"Up or down?" Chris yelled.

"Up!" I shouted.

Jonathan jammed the camera in his pack and we climbed as fast as we could, even at the risk of bunching up on the fragile bridge. In another fifty feet, we were above the séracs. We collapsed on the rim, breathing hard. The Sherpa started chanting.

"This road no good," the Sherpa said. He reached in his pack and took out a handful of sacred rice and threw it across the crevasse.

"We lucky this time."

* * *

Chris Chandler was my climbing partner and also my best friend, and Jonathan was emerging as someone I sensed would also become a close friend even though he was very different from Chris and, as a consequence, was becoming a different kind of friend.

Chris was a natural athlete, six feet tall, solidly built, and, with Nordic features and blond hair he wore in a ponytail, uncommonly handsome. He lived in Seattle, where he was a doctor working in a hospital emergency room. I earned money for my expeditions painting houses, and I was conscious that Chris had a profession and I did not. Not that he ever emphasized it; in fact, he prided himself on wearing secondhand clothing, driving old cars, and living in low-rent apartments. He encouraged me to think twice about trading the liberty of my odd-job life for what he considered the chains of responsibility attendant to a professional career. I told him that even though I had traded my chance to become a professor to join the Everest expedition, and even though I didn't know what I was going to do after the expedition, I knew that even if I went back to painting houses, I wasn't going to make my living as a handyman long term.

Chris was only a year older than me, but he had been married and divorced and had two young sons, both in the custody of his ex-wife. He didn't like to talk about it, but he had confessed that he struggled to make alimony payments. He was also hesitant to talk about his kids. Our friendship was based more on doing things, while my friendship with Jonathan was developing around our mutual pleasure in talking about things, especially his commitment to Buddhism. It wasn't that he was naturally voluble; in fact, he was quiet and reticent, but I was interested and he was willing to explain his apprenticeship in Buddhism, including the story of his original trip to the Himalaya three years before when he had dropped out of college to travel overland by low-fare bus from Europe to India and Nepal. He was twenty years old and spent two weeks meditating in a Buddhist monastery, an experience that he said was the most influential of his life.

"I used to be short-tempered," he told me, something I found hard to imagine, given his preternatural calm.

After his stay in the monastery, he was in a Sherpa house when he stood and smacked his head on a beam and nearly

After Chris and I, with support from others on the team, established the route through the icefall, a team of Sherpas was assigned to maintain it as the séracs shifted and the crevasses expanded and contracted. **Johan Reinhard**

knocked himself out. He cursed the beam with a string of exple-
tives until he noticed his Sherpa hosts giggling. With his head
aching, he suddenly felt as though he could see himself through
their eyes and he started laughing with them. They then stood
and pretended to hit their heads on the beam, pointing to it and
cursing, making everyone laugh even more. From that day on,
every time he felt a rising anger or even a minor exacerbation,
he remembered the beam, until finally he stopped being angered
or even annoyed by life's inconveniences.

Memories can be like movies—sometimes you can't remember a plot as well as you remember a scene. After establishing
the route through the icefall, one morning Chris, Jonathan, and
I left Base Camp to carry equipment to the site of the next camp,
where we paused to rest before going back down. It was still early
morning, and we gazed across the valley of the Khumbu, framed
on one side by the high pass of the Lho La where wind created
a cloud that blew off the leeward side like a banner in the Hall of
Valhalla. We were in the lee of the surrounding mountain walls,
however, and where we sat there was no wind. Jonathan was quiet
and Chris was fidgety. Reaching in his pack, Chris retrieved his
ball of hash, loaded his pipe, and lit it. Then Jonathan reached
in his pack to retrieve his camera. Holding it in both hands, he
positioned his elbows on his knees and remained as steady as
a statue while he took a photo of the Lho La.

"I think that's the best mountain photograph I have ever
taken," he said quietly.

Four years later, Jonathan's wife gave me a framed print of
that photograph. I have kept it above my desk for forty-five years.
It is faded, but I can still see Jonathan's signature, a stylized
om mani padme hum. When I look at the photograph, I sometimes think of the three of us that morning, each in our own
way grateful for the privilege of bearing witness to the majesty
of the wild world. In the years that followed, all three of us
would remain loyal to our passion for climbing high mountains
in remote places, but I alone would survive. I remember Chris's

grin, the way he tried to laugh away the burdens of his life, and Jonathan's smile, the way it reflected how he had learned, at an early age, to avoid an attachment to gain or fear of loss.

* * *

For the next three weeks Chris and I alternated with other climbers on the team pushing the route through the great ice valley known as the Western Cwm, then up the Lhotse Face to the South Col. The expedition leader announced the summit teams, and Chris and I were selected for the second bid. Chris was disappointed because he believed there wouldn't be sufficient oxygen for a second attempt. I thought there would be, and because Chris had a sore throat and cough, I felt an extra day or two would give him time to recover.

There were additional supplies to carry to the upper camps, and feeling guilty about leaving this task to the Sherpas, I decided to help ferry two bottles of oxygen. Chris stayed in Camp II to rest. When I returned later in the day, one of the other climbers met me at the edge of camp.

"There's been a last-minute change in the summit teams," he said.

I went to the cook tent and saw Chris in a corner, looking down. At first, I thought he was still sick. Then I learned one of the climbers on the first team had become ill, and Chris, feeling better, had been asked to take his place. He looked at me, and our eyes held.

"It's kind of tough," he said, "after being together the whole climb."

Early the next morning, Chris and his new team left camp, including Ang Phurba, the leader of our Sherpas who were high-altitude climbers. The second team, which I was on, left two days later. I was still confident I had a good chance to make it, but it was hard to believe it would be without Chris. As I climbed the fixed ropes up the Lhotse Face, I could see Chris and his partners—three red dots—slowly advancing to our high camp above

Chris Chandler on the summit of Everest, in extreme wind holding onto a survey tripod placed by a Chinese team the previous year. **Bob Cormack**

the South Col. I could also see the plume of snow like a great banner boiling off the summit pyramid—not only see it but hear it, like the sound of heavy surf on a distant beach.

That night the wind buffeted our tent. The next day there was no sign of Chris and his team, but in the late afternoon a radio call from Base Camp reported that through the telescope they could see two red dots scaling the Hillary Step, just below the summit. One of them must have turned back, and we soon learned it was Ang Phurba. When he reached us, he said his oxygen regulator had frozen and, not being able to keep up, he had turned back. He took the regulator out of his pack and threw it down in disgust.

"Me and my team finished," he said.

I realized his desire to reach the summit was as strong as any of the rest of us, and I suspected it was because of the prestige it would have brought him, as well as the guarantee of high-level positions on future climbing expeditions. Meanwhile, Base Camp reported that two red dots had reached the summit. Now, the concern as the day ended was whether Chris and his partner could descend in the dark to the lone tent at high camp, at 27,500 feet.

Sometime during the night, I woke from a dream. It was a vision of Chris, old and hunchbacked, his face and beard sheathed in ice, emerging from a storm cloud, hobbling toward me with one arm extended. I lay in my sleeping bag and between gusts I could hear the distant roar of the wind off the summit. The next morning, there was no sign of anyone at high camp. We ascended the fixed rope and finally, just before noon, we saw two climbers—two tiny dots—leaving high camp. Two hours later, Chris and his partner reached us. We hugged tightly. His eyes were a combination of exhaustion and jubilation. He patted me on the head and told me I too would make it. I wasn't so sure. All morning my breathing had been labored and now I could hear congestion in my windpipe. Was I getting pulmonary edema, the potentially fatal accumulation of fluids in the lungs that sometimes happens at high altitude? Chris and his partner left, continuing their descent, and I soon told my partners that I also needed to go down.

As it turned out, that was the end of the expedition. Chris and his partner had reached the summit, so the expedition was considered a success. A week later we were hiking down from Base Camp when we passed a group of trekkers who stopped us to get Chris's autograph. Jonathan and others on the film crew recorded the scene while I stood to the side, off camera. When the filming finished, Jonathan walked to me and smiled.

"How are you doing?"

"I'm OK."

Later, thinking back on that scene, I would realize that Jonathan knew me well enough to know what was going on in my head, that I was reconciling how Chris had reached the summit while I had not.

"Someday, we should come back to the Himalaya," Jonathan said. "You and me. We'll go to a monastery and spend a couple of weeks there, meditating."

* * *

The next day we reached the Sherpa village of Kumjung, where we planned to have a celebratory party. The Sherpa Nima Norbu asked if I wanted to stop and chat with an old man, then in his eighties, who was the last living Sherpa who had been on the early British expeditions back in the 1920s. I immediately agreed, anxious to meet a man whom I knew only by reputation. We entered his house and he stood to greet us. He was more than six feet tall, with a straight back and broad shoulders, and he served us tea while he and Nima talked.

"He says it is very good we have a successful expedition," Nima translated. "He tells me that the expedition job is very good, and it's good that I follow this work even though it is dangerous. But he says that's why we get paid so much."

"Ask him why he thinks we sahibs come here to try and climb Everest," I said.

Nima asked the old Sherpa.

"He says it's because you make much money, become famous, write many books."

"Tell him that many sahibs climb mountains like Everest because they like adventure, that they like to be away from cities and buildings and trek and climb in remote places where few men have been before."

Nima translated, and the old Sherpa laughed and gave his answer to Nima.

"You don't expect me to believe that, do you?"

The amulet containing the sacred rice the Lama of Thupten
Chöling monastery gave us. I kept the amulet with me
during the climb, "for good luck," as the Sherpas told me.

Chapter Two

The Knife-Edge

Before Edmund Hillary and Tenzing Norgay made the first ascent of Everest in 1953, the peak had long been thought of as a British mountain, since the British had made most of the early attempts. In a similar way, K2, the second-highest mountain on Earth, was thought of as an American mountain. Americans had made two attempts in the 1930s, including one that got within a few hundred vertical feet of the summit, and another in 1953. The Italians made the first ascent in 1954, however, and then, because of border conflicts with China, the Pakistan government closed the Karakoram Range—the western extension of the Himalaya where K2 is located—to foreigners and it didn't open again until 1974.

In 1975, the Americans tried and failed again to climb K2. The leader of that attempt, Jim Whittaker—the first American to climb Everest—got a permit to try again in 1978, and he invited Chris Chandler to join the team. Just as Chris had done on the Everest expedition two years before—when he convinced the leaders of that climb to add me to the roster—he talked Jim Whittaker into adding me to the K2 team.

For me, the invitation was a mix of excitement and foreboding. I remembered when I was fourteen years old reading that article in *National Geographic* and seeing that photograph of Whittaker on the summit, holding his ice ax in victory, and

The northeast ridge of K2, the knife-edge. I'm in the foreground with Lou Reichardt behind me as we approach Camp IV at about 23,000 feet. You can just see the tents at Camp III at the far end of the knife-edge. **John Roskelley** saying to myself, *I want to be THAT guy.* Now I was invited to join an expedition led by *THAT* guy.

At the same time, I remembered that day on Everest, struggling to get to the South Col, when each breath had been painful. Even though my problem had turned out to be a lung infection, I was worried that if I returned to high altitude—to 8,000 meters—would something similar happen, this time with more grave consequences? And K2 was supposed to be much harder and more dangerous than Everest.

But I couldn't say no. Not to an opportunity like that. In addition, it would give me another chance to climb on a big mountain with Chris. I imagined Chris and myself standing on the summit of what was said to be the most difficult high-altitude mountain in the world.

* * *

Just like the Everest expedition, the K2 climb was going to require a long walk to Base Camp—110 miles each way—and half of it on glaciers with no trails. And as with Everest, we hired an army of local porters, this time from a tribe called the Balti. Unlike the Everest expedition, however, there were no Sherpas in the western end of the Himalaya whom we could hire as high-altitude porters. We did retain four men from the Hunza district, who had some climbing experience, to help us carry gear to the lower camps. Other than that, on the climb itself we would haul all the gear.

Our plan was to attempt the unclimbed northeast ridge. A team of Polish climbers had attempted but failed to climb the route two years before, and they were said to be among the toughest climbers in the world. As if that wasn't enough to give us pause, while on the approach march, we passed a British team coming down who had attempted and failed to climb the west ridge. They too had on their team some of the best climbers in the world, and one of them had been killed in an avalanche.

Jim Whittaker, leader of the K2 team, was the first American to summit Everest. This photo ran in the October 1963 issue of *National Geographic* and inspired me to become a mountaineer. Original Kodachrome by Nawang Gombu, courtesy of Jim Whittaker Family Collection

We established an advanced base camp at 18,000 feet, halfway up a pocket glacier that led to the northeast ridge. It felt great to be climbing again in the Himalaya, and doing it with Chris. My only disappointment was that Chris seemed to lack the enthusiasm he'd had on Everest. After we established Camp I at the base of the northeast ridge, four of us were asked to scout the route to Camp II, but when my wristwatch alarm sounded Chris was reluctant to get up, and we were delayed over a half hour while he slowly dressed. Later, while I belayed him, Chris picked a questionable route up a spur, loosening rocks that hit me several times, and, losing patience, I cursed at him and we got into a shouting match. A few days later we were carrying supplies to Camp II. Chris spent the day ascending the ropes we had fixed in place with Cherie Bech, whose husband was also on the team. At the Camp II position Chris unloaded his pack and revealed that he had carried only a single oxygen bottle, and another climber got into an argument with Chris, accusing him of not working hard enough.

Meanwhile, I started spending more time with John Roskelley, one of the most experienced climbers on the team. As a climber, I had noted both his athletic grace and his strength. We knew from reports by the Polish team who had attempted our route that higher up we would have to traverse a knife-edge ridge that was a half mile long. It would be the most technically challenging section of the climb, and Jim Whittaker was already talking about having two rope teams alternate one day after the other to lead across the knife-edge and fix ropes: John and another very strong climber as one rope team, and Chris and me as the other.

I knew Chris was having trouble with his ex-wife—divorce, alimony, child custody. We didn't talk about it, but I assumed that the problems were weighing on him, and may have been the reason for his apathy. I also knew that those who Jim Whittaker selected to go to the summit would be the ones who had not only worked the hardest and climbed the best, but who had the most verve.

I thought, *Maybe that's why I felt guilty yelling at Chris for knocking down rocks, criticizing him for being slow, faulting him for not carrying enough weight. Because I know he's not going to be chosen if he doesn't go the extra distance. And he and I are a rope team. I'm feeling guilty because I know I want to start climbing with Roskelley. And that doing that would be abandoning Chris.*

* * *

With Camp II stocked with supplies, several of us occupied it in order to stage our push to Camp III, which we intended to position at the beginning of the knife-edge. The next day it started to snow, however, and we stayed in camp. The snow continued the following day, and we had to make a decision: if we stayed in Camp II, we would acclimatize more quickly, but we would also be eating the food and burning the fuel we had worked hard to carry to that position. It made sense to stay if the storm was short, but if it was long, it would make more sense to descend to Camp I. We decided to give it one more day.

We woke to more snowfall, so we started packing personal gear in order to descend—all except for Chris and Cherie, who said they were staying. We tried to convince them to descend with us, but they said it made sense for two people to stay, to shovel snow and prevent the tents from getting buried. The storm continued for four days, five days, six days. Each day Jim Whittaker tried on the daily radio call to coerce Chris and Cherie to descend; each day Chris and Cherie countered, saying it made more sense to stay.

I was now sharing a tent with John, and we were getting along well, keeping each other in good humor. One day I had been staring at the tent walls, counting the squares in the rip-stop, when out of nowhere John said, "I apologize."

"For what?"

"For not being a girl."

We laughed, but we both knew that it seemed likely that something *was* happening between Chris and Cherie, and with her husband on the team it could blow up into an altercation that might jeopardize the expedition. When the storm cleared, Chris and Cherie descended to break the trail in the new snow, making it easier for those of us ascending to Camp II. When we passed them, one of the climbers going up confronted Chris for not coming down when Whittaker had ordered him to.

"He never *ordered* us down. He said it would be nice if we came down, but he made it sound like we could come down if we wanted to. And we didn't want to."

"And what about you and Cherie?"

"Do I have to clear it with *you* before I choose my friends? That's my business, not yours."

"It's my business—it's everybody's business—when it affects the team."

I stayed out of it other than suggesting to Chris that he talk to Whittaker and make sure he wasn't mad, and maybe to Cherie's husband, to make amends, if that were needed. Chris said he would. I was uncomfortable getting more involved in the matter than that, a reticence consistent with my tendency to avoid conflict, even as my rational side knew that avoiding conflict was seldom a good recipe for resolving it.

* * *

With the storm gone we were ready to resume the climb, and Jim Whittaker announced a new plan: John Roskelley and I would lead the first, and most difficult, section of the knife-edge. The morning John and I left Camp III, the sky was cloudless and there was no wind. In a half hour we reached the beginning of the knife-edge, a serrated blade a half mile in length, its sharp crest forming the border between Pakistan and China.

"I'm not sure I have my visa," John said as he set up the first belay.

John belayed the rope while I crabbed sideways across the flank of the ridge. The front points of my crampons and the tips of my two ice axes were my only connection to the steep ice. Every fifty feet or so I would turn an aluminum screw into the ice, clip my rope into the anchor, then continue. When I was 200 feet out, I placed two screws and tied off the rope. John crossed

The "Snow Butterfly." This is the photo John sent the entomologist that put us in the record book for the highest recorded sighting of a butterfly. **John Roskelley**

using mechanical clamps called jumars, and then I belayed while he led the next pitch. The altitude was 23,000 feet. We both felt strong, and we were in sync, pausing only to exchange a nod or a grin.

By midafternoon we had fixed over a thousand feet of rope. I was hanging from two ice screws, belaying John. Under me, the slope fell away steeply for thousands of feet before joining a glacier that extended into the sere expanse of the plateau of northwest Tibet known as the Chang Tang. I paid out the red rope, watching it gently undulate up and down on the ice as it reacted to John's movements. I saw a butterfly land next to the rope. It was piebald orange and black, like the painted lady butterflies at home. I used to catch butterflies like that when I was a kid, in my cheesecloth net.

A butterfly? At 23,000 feet? I yelled to John and he called back that there were more butterflies where he was. I looked around and saw two, three, four more. Soon there were dozens, hundreds of them across the slope, a cloud of butterflies migrating on an air current, carried higher and higher over the snows of the Karakoram. John took several photographs of them. I described the butterflies in *The Last Step*, my book about our K2 expedition, and forty years later an entomologist who read the book would contact us, and John would send him the photographs, and the entomologist would identify them as *Vanessa cardui*, and John and I would go on record for having made the highest-altitude observation in history of a butterfly.

* * *

A little more than a week later, with the route fixed across the knife-edge, Camp IV was established, and Jim Whittaker announced the first summit teams. John and I would be on one team, and two other climbers on the other. The second team did not include Chris. I glanced at John, and he gave me a barely perceptible wink. Chris stared at the tent floor, and we didn't make eye contact.

Before we could make a summit attempt, however, another storm hit. Once again, we rappelled to advanced base camp. The storm cleared, and we ascended the ropes, digging them out of the new snow, excavating our collapsed tents as we re-established the camps. We pushed the route to the next camp, and another storm hit, and again we descended. That storm lasted a week. We went up again, and after several days of hard work we reached our previous high point.

We had now been at or above 18,000 feet for fifty days. Tempers continued to flare. Members of the group began to refer to the four of us selected to make the first attempt as the A-Team, calling themselves the B-Team. I assumed this was simply a recognition of the order of the summit attempts, until a member of the B-Team told me *A* stood for assholes.

It was late August, and the period when we'd have any hope of good weather in the Karakoram was closing. Then an unexpected area of high pressure formed over the western Himalaya, delivering a short window of Indian summer. As the four of us on the A-Team made our final preparations for an eleventh-hour attempt, we fell into disagreement over the best route to use for the summit bid.

The other two, Lou Reichardt and Jim Wickwire, thought it made sense to traverse under the summit pyramid to join the Abruzzi Ridge, the route taken by the two previous expeditions that had succeeded in climbing K2. John and I wanted to ascend straight up the headwall at the intersection of the northeast ridge, a route that would be more difficult but, in our opinion, more elegant.

Unable to compromise, we attempted to finish by the two different routes. Lou and Jim (whom we also called Wick) began their traverse toward the Abruzzi Ridge. John and I climbed a long slope to the base of the headwall, where we set up a high camp. The next morning, we started up the headwall, but soon encountered unstable and dangerous snow conditions. We had a walkie-talkie, and our colleagues at advanced base camp told us that through their telescope they could see Lou and Wick reaching the summit.

John and I decided to abandon our direct finish, traverse to the Abruzzi, and follow Lou and Wick. Our packs were so heavy and we were so weak that we decided to abandon some of our gear, leaving our pickets and snow flukes. John pointed out that without anchors, it made no sense to rope up because if one of us slipped, we would both die. And so we abandoned our rope too. We still had one oxygen bottle each and, uncertain if we could climb K2 without oxygen, we decided to keep the bottles.

By late afternoon, we reached Lou and Wick's camp. With our ice axes we slowly cut a platform into the angled snow slope for our own small tent. I could only make a few cuts before I had to rest—it was our third full day at 8,000 meters. We pitched our tent and waited for Jim and Wick to return from the summit. It got dark. We had a whistle, and, leaning out of the tent every five or ten minutes, we blew it. We scanned the slopes with our headlamps, using them as searchlights to guide Lou and Wick to safety. Finally, Lou arrived and we pulled him into our tent. He was shaking, too cold to speak clearly. We tried to give him a cup of hot chocolate, but there was so much ice in his beard we couldn't get the cup to his lips. We tore the ice out—pulling out clumps of hair—until he could drink the hot chocolate. When he could speak, he told us Wick was behind him, and was probably going to bivouac.

It was forty below zero. Our two small tents were at the 8,000-meter contour. It seemed doubtful that Wick would be able to survive. John and I stayed up melting snow and filling our water bottles. It was just past midnight by the time we had everything staged. We had an hour to sleep before we had to wake and get ready to leave.

"I think we're more likely to be on a body detail than a summit bid," I said.

John didn't answer.

* * *

We started the stove at 1:30 am, first warming water, then our leather boots and wool mittens. We tried to drink as much hot liquid as we could, but it was impossible to hold a warm mug of cocoa—the heat so comforting to cold fingers—without thinking of how desperately Wick was in need of it. Was he still alive? Had he somehow survived the forty-below temperatures with no sleeping bag?

At 3:30 am, we crawled out of the tent, putting the last items in our backpacks, including one bottle of oxygen each.

"Good luck, you guys," Lou called from the next tent. "I have a feeling Wick will be okay."

We set a steady pace, as much to warm our bodies as to make progress. By 4:30 am, we were several hundred feet above camp. I was just a few steps behind John, zigzagging up the slope. I was thankful for each switchback because it allowed me to change my ice ax from one hand to the other. My fingers were numb, and I tried to convince myself they weren't frozen. At first light we stopped to rest.

"Wick might be moving by now."

"I hope so."

"If he's in bad shape we'll have trouble getting him down without a rope."

"If he's bad, we won't be able to get him down."

John was only a few feet above me as we started up a narrow couloir slicing through a rock band at about 27,000 feet. I looked directly into the teeth of his crampons. Only the front points were on the ice and rock, so that the remaining sharpened steel points—ten on the bottom of each boot—poised above me like an executioner's ax. I did not want John to slip.

I waited for him to make the several moves necessary to pass the steep bottleneck. When he was above the difficult stretch, it was my turn. I found two good handholds and, using my arms to balance, leg-pressed my body up, moved my hands to higher holds, and lifted one boot, then the next. Between my legs, the couloir fell away steeply to the Abruzzi shoulder. Ten thousand feet below that, I could see the Godwin-Austen Glacier.

The hold is solid, I said to myself. *Fingers numb but grip it, firmly. No, lift my leg, high. Hard with wool underwear and two layers of pile and the nylon jumpsuit. OK, now put my crampon front points carefully on that small bump in the rock. Wait, first put my ice ax through the shoulder strap of my pack—got to keep both hands free. Balance. Breathe. Dust the snow off that handhold, bump it, make sure it's solid. Move slowly, stay in balance, each move has to be perfect, don't waste energy. Don't fall. You are NOT wearing a rope.*

The gusts of wind lifted spindrift, small snow devils backlit by morning sun. But the wind was easing, and the sky was cloudless. It was turning into a perfect summit day—if only we knew that Wick was alive. I estimated it to be 7:30 a.m. Where was he? If he had tried to down climb last night and fallen, we would never find him.

Funny how I don't feel any emotion. Snap out of this. Pay attention, focus. Two more moves and I'll be above the bottleneck.

I couldn't see John but expected he had moved left, probably to wait for me before we had to traverse a steep section of ice-covered rock. At the top of the bottleneck, I looked for him.

There he is, but wait? There's two people. John and someone standing above him, legs slightly apart, arms down, not moving. It's Wick. Is he frozen?

John climbed up to Wick, who lifted an arm in greeting. As I neared, I could hear their conversation.

"I bivvied on a small flat spot just below the summit. Pretty cold."

"Frostbite?"

"I think so. Hard to tell."

"Can you make it down? By yourself?"

"Yeah, I'm doing OK. I've got the hard part behind me—that traverse over there."

Wick pointed with his ice ax to the steep ice-over-rock section in front of us. The bottleneck was hard, and it was not good news that the next section was even harder. There was ice in Wick's beard and his eyes were sunken, but I could see in them his determination.

"Good luck, you guys," he said.

"Be careful, Wick. You still have the couloir, so go slow."

"Don't worry. I'll be OK."

John patted him on top of his cap. It was a simple gesture, yet that pat on the cap, the first human contact in over fourteen hours, had nearly brought him to tears. It was something he said he would remember for the rest of his life. We wouldn't know until nearly a week later, once we were down, that Wick was fighting for his life against frostbite, frozen lung tissue, and a diaphragm that had stopped working properly.

* * *

"Let's go on oxygen," I said.

The traverse looked as hard as Wick had suggested, and it seemed like a good idea to attempt it with the benefit of the oxygen we had worked so hard to carry up. We took off our packs, and John set his bottle in the snow then put his pack back on.

"What are you doing?"

"Leaving the oxygen. I'm going without it."

I looked at my own twenty-pound bottle.

"There's no way I'm hauling that thing to the top," John said, pointing to his. "I can get up without it."

I knew he was right. *He* could get to the summit without it. And Lou had made it yesterday without oxygen. I also knew they were both stronger than me. Could I do it without oxygen? The only climbers who had been at this altitude without oxygen for any length of time were Peter Habeler and Reinhold Messner, a few months before on Everest—the story going around was that they had suffered brain damage.

"I'm going to use mine."

"OK."

John waited while I removed the regulator, screwed it on the bottle, and opened the valve. Full pressure, no leaks. I shouldered my pack, secured the second-stage selector valve to a drawstring on my shoulder strap, then tried to secure the mask tightly on my face. But I couldn't get the mask adjusted. Without a firm seal, the oxygen would escape.

John watched with growing impatience. I removed the mask and adjusted the straps. I took it off and turned it upside down. Then right-side up.

"I'll see you up there," he said.

I watched John start across the traverse, moving more easily without the weight of the oxygen bottle. He placed his crampons on the snow-laced rock with precision, keeping his hands securely on holds until his feet were solid, only moving one hand or one foot at a time, always keeping three points of contact.

He moved with the confidence that comes from decades of experience. Crossing a section of steep ice and rock, he held his ax with one hand on the head and one on the shaft and placed the pick on the ice between rocks. I was reminded of old sepia photographs of the great French alpinist Armand Charlet, known for his balletic precision. Charlet had influenced my friend Yvon Chouinard, who in turn had introduced French ice-climbing techniques to North America. John was all the more graceful because he had no rope. Feeling as if I were in a dream, my eyes looked beneath him, where I could see the zebra stripes of the glacier two miles below.

Focus! Get this oxygen to work, or you'll never catch up.

I tried and failed again to get the mask to fit securely. I looked up. John had disappeared around the corner. He would now be moving up the long snowfield leading to the summit.

This is crazy. I had this thing adjusted days ago. Imagine my IQ score right now. Even a half-wit chimpanzee could do this. How long have I been fiddling with this thing? Five minutes? Twenty? Put this strap through this other loop. Try that. No, that doesn't look right. Where is John by now? He climbs faster than me anyway. What can I do? Try and climb without oxygen? K2 without oxygen?

I had been climbing well up to that point, moving with confidence up the bottleneck. Without the oxygen, I should be able to repeat John's graceful steps across this next section. But what would happen higher up? On Everest, I had been just short of the South Col when the pain in my lungs had forced me to descend.

I needed to decide fast. I was getting cold. John was getting farther ahead. My only chance was to abandon my oxygen bottle. I put on my near-empty pack, took my ice ax, and started across the steep section, concentrating on each foot- and handhold.

* * *

An hour later I was still struggling to catch John, but the gap was closing.

It's only 200 more feet. Maybe less. I have to lift my boot. I can't. I've come this far, I have to. John is ahead of me, not that far. He's still moving, so I can too. He has broken more trail than me. It's my turn. He's stopped. He's hunkered over his ice ax. I've got to reach him. Ten steps, then rest. OK, breathe, breathe, step, breathe, breathe, step. No good, have to stop, getting dizzy. Only four more steps, I made it!

"You OK?" John asked.

"Slow. Hard to breathe."

"Can you lead a little?"

"I'll try. Need to rest a minute."

"We're close. Maybe a hundred and fifty feet."

"If that's the summit. If not . . ."

"Don't worry. We got it now."

John is right. We have it now. Keep remembering that. We are too close NOT to make it. Lift a foot. Ankles hurt but ignore it. Lift another foot. Careful with your crampon placement. What's that noise? And those voices? Like there are many people around me, like on a crowded train with everyone talking. Echoes, noises, voices. A din, like a million voices. But that's crazy, there is no one around, only John, just below me. Lift a foot. Look at that crescent in the snow up ahead. That's my goal. Lift a foot, another. Have to get to the crescent. Breathe, breathe, breathe. Dizzy again, don't panic, breathe it out. There, it's going away.

"You OK?"

"Have to rest. Tried going too fast. Dizzy. Hallucinating."

"I'll take the lead."

Rest while John climbs. He's stronger than I am. How can he do it? He's doing most of the step-kicking. Need to do more of my share. But we are close. Maybe that's the summit ridge? Fifty feet? John is almost there. Now his head is even with the ridge. What does he see? How far is the summit? He isn't saying anything. Do we still have more to go? Can I do it? Yes, lift a foot, then another. Now John is only ten feet away. Breathe a few times so I can speak.

"How far?"

"Fifty feet. A fifty-foot walk."

* * *

No wind, no clouds. Blue sky, just deep-blue sky and brilliant sun and warmth through the parka, but also a strange cold. Nothing quite real. Below the world seems to fall away in all directions. Snow peaks below me, a sea of snow peaks. Glaciers traveling to the distant horizon. Quiet, other than a kind of ringing. Maybe that's the sound of silence? Someday when you're an old man you'll want to recall this moment, so try to remember it. It must be important.

At 28,250 feet, there was not a breath of wind. The sun shone through the cloudless atmosphere. We could see the curve of the Earth. To the north and east, two distant peaks stood somewhere in the wild vastness of Chinese Turkestan; to the west, the peaks of Hunza, Shangri-la; to the west and south, the great Karakoram, an endless sea of peaks and glaciers; away to the south, the singular Nanga Parbat; closer, the Gasherbrums; and below us, the summit of Broad Peak, the twelfth-highest mountain in the world.

Twenty feet below the summit there was a flat rock bench, and we descended to it to rest. The rock was warm, and I lay back and my breathing slowed and I closed my eyes and drifted into half consciousness. I opened my eyes and said to myself again, *Remember where I am, the second-highest point on Earth. I must remember this.* Then I had an idea: I could chip off a few rocks and take them home. To help me remember. I removed my climbing hammer and started hitting the rock.

"What are you doing?"

"Souvenirs. Rocks from the summit. To remember it. Also, Christmas isn't far off. I'll give them away, as presents."

My fingers were frostbitten in the cold predawn of summit day, but eventually the dead tissue fell off, and I had no permanent damage other than a slightly rounded end of one finger. **Dianne Roberts**

"Good idea."

John and I sat on the rock, beating on it.

"We should take some pictures," John said.

"Oh yeah, I forgot about that."

I lay on the rock while John took my photo.

"We've been up here almost an hour," he said.

"An hour?"

"We should take a couple more photos on the summit and head down."

We climbed back to the high point. I recalled the way summit photos normally looked: the climber stands, ice ax above head, flags waving in victory. I had no feeling of having conquered anything. We were two tiny humans on top of the world's most awesome mountain, and the mountain was indifferent. I held my ice ax across my waist, shoulders down, and stared into space. John took the photo, and we started our descent.

My K2 summit photo. "There are no conquerors ...," Barry Bishop said after reaching the summit of Everest on the first American ascent, "... only survivors." **John Roskelley**

Men Against
the Clouds

I met Yvon Chouinard in the early 1970s, when I was living in
Malibu, and I started going up to his place in Ventura to surf.
He lived in a small cottage on the beach with his wife, Malinda,
and their two young children. We also started climbing together
in the Sierra, where we made ascents testing the climbing gear
he manufactured at his company, Chouinard Equipment. I told
Yvon that I was getting tired of Malibu—of all the posers and
the pretension—and he told me about a fisherman's shack on
the beach that might be coming up for sale. I was finishing my
book on K2 at the time, and I sold it for just enough money to
make a down payment. So in 1979, I moved into my new shack
near Yvon's place. Shortly after, we traveled to Alaska to climb
Denali, an expedition that cemented our friendship.

Once back from the summit of Denali, Yvon received an
invitation to join an expedition that had secured a permit to
attempt Minya Konka, a 24,800-foot peak on the eastern margin
of the Tibetan Plateau. It was 1980, and the People's Republic of
China had decided to open the country to international mountaineering, and an American team led by Al Read, who ran
the Exum climbing school in Grand Teton National Park, had
secured the permit. Al needed additional funds to cover the
expedition's cost and wanted to make a pitch to one of the television networks. During the Everest climb I had helped the film

crew (including Jonathan), and afterward I had gone on more expeditions organized for the purpose of making adventure films, including climbs and explorations in the Amazon and Antarctica. Yvon knew all this and recommended me to Al as someone who might help secure a television deal and, at the same time, be a strong addition to the climbing team.

I was excited when Al invited me to join the climbing team, and I was just as excited when he made a deal with ABC to film the expedition. Then ABC offered me a job as field producer to support the director and his film team. And, as if that weren't enough, the director then hired Jonathan as one of the cameramen.

Jonathan and I were increasingly close friends, and the two of us planned to be a writer-photographer team. We had developed relationships with executives at the National Geographic Society—Jonathan when the TV division had hired him to shoot stills for a show about a climbing expedition to Peru, and me when I had helped with my journal notes for a feature story in the magazine on our K2 climb. That story had been well received, and I was thrilled when it came out because there was a photo of me on the cover that John Roskelley had taken.

With those qualifications, Jonathan and I won an assignment from *National Geographic* to do a story on the newly chartered Sagarmatha (Mount Everest) National Park. After the Minya Konka expedition was over, we planned to travel overland to Lhasa and then continue to Kathmandu and on to Everest. It was a dream come true, and we began to plan future projects that included running rivers in Borneo and skiing mountains in Antarctica.

* * *

All of us on the climbing team and the film crew were as excited about the travel part of our adventure as we were about the climbing part. The mountain had been climbed only twice: an American team had first climbed it in 1932, and a Chinese team had made the second ascent in 1957. We would be the first Americans allowed in the area since those who made the first ascent, and the only information we had to plan our trip was their account in a book they wrote called *Men Against the Clouds*.

Beijing, or Peking, as it was still commonly called in those days, was just emerging from the Cultural Revolution. Everyone wore Mao suits, and there seemed to be a hundred bicycles for every automobile; the background noise of the city was the tinkle of handlebar bells. From Beijing we traveled for four days in a private railroad car pulled by a steam locomotive to Chengdu, the capital of Sichuan. Chengdu was the home city of the new Chinese leader, Deng Xiaoping, and he was using the city as the launching pad for his plans to create a market-driven economy.

In Chengdu there were signs of change. Some women were starting to grow long hair—something we had not seen in Beijing—and a few were even bold enough to wear clothes other than Mao suits. Always one to enjoy a little mischievousness, Yvon, when we registered at our Communist-era hotel and completed the guest information cards, wrote in the blank for occupation that he was a "capitalist."

"Ah, Mister Chouinard," our Communist Party liaison officer said, reading our forms. "You are a capitalist. Very good, very good. This means you are also very rich?"

"Yes," Yvon replied. "Very rich."

"Aw, that is very good, very good."

Those of us on the expedition seemed to be the only foreigners in the city. When we ventured out of our hotel, we drew such crowds that we were quickly pushed apart. For Yvon and me, as the two shortest guys on the team, it was even more of a challenge to keep sight of our companions. At one point, after losing Yvon, I climbed a lamppost to see across the sea of heads and noted that the knot of people was densest about fifty feet away. Forcing my way through, I found Yvon struggling like a rugby player pushing against a scrum.

Jonathan Wright was my close friend and professional partner. We were a writer-photographer team, with projects in the pipeline as far out as we could see. **Edgar Boyles**

From Chengdu, we drove four days eastward in a minibus, leaving Sichuan Province and entering the Tibet Autonomous Region. We were now in the homeland of the Khampas, the Tibetans who had most fiercely and famously resisted Chinese occupation. The road switchbacked to the plateau, and we drove through a small village where we saw graffiti depicting Chinese war planes dropping bombs on a village with people's limbs flying through the air. We asked the bus driver to stop, and when we tried to take a picture our Chinese liaison officer grew upset and said photographing the graffiti was not allowed.

At the end of a dirt road, our Chinese hosts and their Tibetan translators arranged with villagers for the rental of horses to porter our equipment. Unlike the approaches to Everest and K2, this trek was only going to take about five days. On the second day, however, the film director, who had been suffering from dysentery, said he was too weak to keep going. Since I was the field producer, it made sense for me to take over directing the film until he could recover and catch up.

The next day we followed the horses laden with our equipment to a pass above tree line that defined the drainage on the west side of Minya Konka. It was snowing and we were unable to see the peak, but the descent down the snow-covered slope looked dramatic, and I had the idea to have the climbers join the Tibetans herding the horses so I could get everyone in a single frame.

I positioned the two cameramen one above and one below the trail, but when the climbers got close to the horses one of the animals spooked and slid on its back a hundred feet down the slope. It was unhurt, but some of the team looked upset.

"We shouldn't risk injuring a horse just for the film," Al said.

"Or for somebody's fucking drive to get a film credit," another team member added.

The film's director and most of the climbers lived in Jackson, Wyoming, and were close friends, so I suspected that part of their issue with me was their disappointment that the director had gotten sick. I suspected that the other part was that they didn't agree with my approach to making the movie.

My involvement in filmmaking had started on Everest four years before. The trip had been filmed for a CBS special directed by Mike Hoover, an adventure documentary filmmaker who would in the years ahead win several Emmys and an Oscar. One day at 24,000 feet on the Lhotse Face, I had volunteered to help the film crew—including Jonathan—record a scene. Waiting for one of the cameramen to get in position, I gazed down the Western Cwm and across the glacier to Pumori. The soundman was next to me, and Jonathan was nearby. We were all doing the same thing: climbing the side of the mountain to get our scene, enjoying the stunning scenery on a day of stunningly good weather. But there was one difference: they were getting paid.

Back in California I called Mike Hoover and told him I wanted to get into the film business.

"One of the most important things is having good ideas," he said.

"I've got lots of those," I answered.

In fact, in my home office I had a three-drawer filing cabinet that I had labeled, bottom to top: Ideas, Good Ideas, and Great Ideas. In the middle drawer was a folder about the Guiana Shield, an expanse of quartzite rock across the upper Orinoco that in places had eroded into flat-topped, vertical-sided mountains called *tepuis*. I wrote a proposal to climb one of them, and Hoover—who liked to be called by his last name, and who in return often called people by their last names—sent it to one of the networks. A few months later we were off to the Amazon, with Hoover directing and me leading the climbing team and helping organize the climb and the film production.

I watched Hoover carefully set up every scene. Part of the discipline was imposed by the simple arithmetic of how many—or, more accurately, how few—cans of film we could carry in our backpacks. Every shot had to count. The other part was Hoover's conviction that a good documentary didn't just happen. One of his closest friends had made *Endless Summer*, the early '60s surfing film that had been a major hit. Hoover knew that didn't happen just because the filmmaker followed a couple of guys who were going around the world surfing wherever their whims took them. It was a story carefully constructed to have goals, with built-in obstacles to reaching the goals, and characters you wanted to hang out with as they overcame the obstacles in order to reach the goals.

"It's basically what the Greeks figured out a few thousand years ago," Hoover told me.

What Hoover hadn't taught me, however, was how much easier it was when you got everybody on board with your ideas, all pulling in the same direction.

* * *

We arrived at the ruins of a monastery that had been destroyed a few years before by the Red Guards. It was as far as the horses could go, so we set up camp and then a few of us explored the debris of the desecrated monastery. Jonathan called Yvon and me over to the most intact section of what was left of one of the walls. It had been painted with frescoes depicting various Buddhas and bodhisattvas, and all except one had been smashed to pieces.

"It's interesting," Jonathan said, "that this is the one Buddha to survive."

"Who is it?"

"Maitreya. The Buddha of Things to Come."

"You think there's a message?"

"Yes," Jonathan replied, turning to me with the faint smile that defined his countenance. "It's to remember that the first fact of existence is impermanence."

We spent the next day sorting gear into loads that we would backpack farther up the valley until we found a location suitable for Base Camp. We had a leisurely morning, and I took the opportunity to explore the hillsides behind the monastery, hoping I might see interesting birds. With the monastery no longer inhabited, the only people venturing this far into the mountains were a few herders taking their yaks to seasonal pastures, and the area was resplendent with wildlife; we had seen musk deer in the forest, Himalayan tahr on the hillsides at higher elevations, and one of us, while alone on the trail, had encountered an Asiatic black bear, also known as the moon bear due to a white crescent on its breast.

In 1980 my interest in wildlife was focused mostly on birds. But that would evolve over my lifetime, guided by mentors—especially the eminent wildlife biologist George Schaller—to include a deep appreciation for all forms of wild creatures that inhabit our planet.

My fascination with birds was the result of personal history. When I was eleven years old my parents sold our World War II-era tract house outside of Long Beach, California, and moved to a one-acre ranchette in Orange County, just south of Los Angeles, where we were surrounded by orange groves. My grandfather on my father's side came with us, moving into a storage shed that he and my father upgraded, adding a kitchenette, toilet, and shower. My grandfather took me under his wing, and I spent most of my time in his shed-now-apartment.

My grandfather and I built a large chicken coop, and one day I saw a ring-necked pheasant pacing along the wire-mesh fence. I opened the gate, circled the cage, and shooed him in. I convinced my grandfather to buy a girlfriend pheasant for my captured bird. Within two years, the two of us were raising hundreds of ringnecks a year, selling them to hunting clubs. I started adding other species of pheasants and it turned into an obsession. I studied my dog-eared copy of *Pheasants of the World* as though it were pornography. Eventually I had ten species, and I could tell visitors to my zoo details about the native habitats of each one, remote places in the mountains of the Himalaya and the jungles of Asia.

On the steep hillside above the monastery the forest was dense. I stalked slowly through the understory, and in the leaf litter under the dark shadow of a rhododendron I detected movement. I focused my binoculars and saw the shadow-shapes of birds the size of large roosters that I recognized by silhouette as eared pheasants. From my childhood studies I knew that there were three species of eared pheasant in the world, all occurring in China, and I knew that two of them could be found in this region, the blue eared and the white eared pheasant. I was also familiar with the blue eared pheasant because I had seen a pair of them when I was a kid in the collection of another pheasant fancier. I had wanted to buy the pair for my zoo, but he was asking seventy-five dollars, more money than I could afford.

I estimated there were perhaps a dozen birds in this flock. They moved furtively, staying in deep shadow or hidden behind low bushes. Then in better light I saw the black crown of one bird's head, and then the dark patch on another's wing. I remained motionless, hoping for a better view, but the birds knew I was there and, presumably because they had been hunted by locals, they crept away, never fully revealing themselves.

That was okay. I remembered studying both species in *Pheasants of the World* when I was a boy. I had also studied the map of their habitats, places in the eastern Himalaya that to me back then had seemed so mysterious that I would have doubted anyone who told me I might someday go there and see the birds in the wild.

* * *

With packs loaded, we hiked along the top of a lateral moraine until we made our way to the base of a spur descending the same ridge that the Americans had climbed in 1932. We set up a Base Camp, and after spending a couple more days ferrying supplies from our cache adjacent to the ruins of the monastery we began ascending the spur.

We established our Camp I on a snow ledge at about 18,000 feet. We still had another 2,000 vertical feet to get to the top of the spur, and two days later, while others shuttled food and gear to Camp I, Yvon, Jonathan, and I, along with another friend named Kim Schmitz, left to backpack supplies to where the spur joined the summit ridge. Our plan was to cache our loads at a place that we felt would be a suitable site for Camp II and then descend back to Camp I. It was October 13, 1980, a day that even now, all these decades later, I remember in vivid detail.

It was 9:30 in the morning by the time we got out of Camp I. I drew the first lead, post-holing up the slope above camp. Then

I took this shot on the trek to Base Camp, only a moment before one of the horses spooked because I had asked the climbers to mix with the Tibetans so I could film everyone in one scene. It was the beginning of tension between me and some of the climbers, and also the beginning of several days of wet snow. Both were portents of challenges to come. **Rick Ridgeway**

Kim took over, then Yvon. At noon we stopped next to a crevasse for lunch. Yvon bit off a piece of cheese, then turned to Jonathan.

"Whenever you're on a glaciated section," he said, "always stop at the edge of a crevasse when you take a break. That way you'll know you haven't stopped on top of a hidden one. Same for setting up camps."

"Thanks," Jonathan replied.

As a cameraman, Jonathan had never done much lead climbing, and had asked us to give him pointers whenever we thought of anything, and Yvon was always obliging to anyone who wanted to learn. We finished lunch and then kept climbing. Soon our options narrowed to a steep section of chest-deep snow, so we had no choice but to tackle it. I led and Kim followed. To get footing I had to pack the snow first by pressing my torso into the slope, then my knee, and finally my boot. No matter how careful I was, I still knocked snow down on Kim.

"Sonofabitch!" he yelled.

"Sorry, I can't help it."

"I wasn't cursing you. Just the snow down my collar."

I returned Kim's smile and kept climbing. In another hundred feet the snow firmed. In a clearing between clouds we could see an area of large séracs where the shifting glacier had cleaved into blocks. I stopped and studied our options.

"Two ways," I yelled. "Up the middle through the séracs or off to the right."

"Looks a little better to the right," Yvon called.

While Kim moved up to take the lead, Jonathan stepped aside and took several photographs. I paid out the rope, then followed Kim as he angled up the side of a sérac that then turned into a long, steep slope. The heavy packs and thin air made the effort debilitating, but we still maintained a steady pace. I tried not to look up but instead to focus on the steps in front of me, hoping I might achieve a state of self-hypnosis.

"Heartbreak Hill," Yvon called out.

The rope on my waist went taut. I looked up, and Kim had stopped to wait patiently while I caught up. It was all I could do to match his speed, and he was the one punching the steps. I was tempted to unrope and go at my own pace, but there were still crevasses in the area. We had roped up earlier in the morning when we crossed the first crevasses above Camp I. That was before we got into the soft snow, but footing had still been difficult, with about four inches of new snow on top of the older surface. Several times my boot skidded on the interior layer, leaving a streak in the new snow. I knew that meant avalanche potential. I wondered what Kim and Yvon thought, but if they had been concerned, they would have said something. Still, I noticed that whoever was leading had stayed on the edges of the crevasses and close to the sides of the séracs, avoiding the wider slopes.

Kim kept leading until the slope eased and I took over kicking steps for a long time. I was hypnotized: one foot up, breathe a few times, and then move the next foot. Jonathan yelled, "Rick, you need relief?" Ahead I could see a flat spot on the edge of a crevasse, and I made that my goal. When I reached the flat, I plopped down, leaned back against my pack, closed my eyes, and breathed heavily; the altitude was now 20,000 feet, and I wasn't fully acclimatized. In a few moments the others arrived.

"Good effort," Yvon said.

Kim kept going without pause, lifting his legs and pushing steps into the soft snow. When the rope caught up and tugged on me, I had no choice but to peel off my shoulder straps so I could stand, then saddle my heavy pack and follow. Ahead, in a glimpse between clouds, we sighted the top of the ridge only a hundred yards farther. Then the wind strengthened to thirty miles per hour, and the clouds raced over the snow and obscured our vision. Through another fleeting hole in the clouds, I saw that the best route was to the side.

"Traverse left . . . to the crest . . . out of the wind."

In a few minutes we were on a flat bench sheltered in the lee of the ridge. We unshouldered our packs.

"Good place for the tents."

"Welcome to Camp II."

"Wuuwee," Jonathan exclaimed. It was his favorite expression, and even though he said it calmly—almost to himself—I knew it revealed his excitement. We looked toward the summit ridge, now obscured in clouds, but we knew from studying the 1932 photographs what it looked like.

"Two more camps and we can make the summit," I said.

"Ten days, if we have luck with the weather," Yvon added.

We rested a few more minutes, then picked up our empty packs and headed down to Camp I.

We made good time, slowing to test bridges over crevasses or, as Kim preferred, broad jumping them. In only a few minutes we were back at Heartbreak Hill. We down climbed, belaying each other with our ice axes as anchors. When the angle eased, we decided to glissade. We slid down on our butts, laughing and yelling, the rope going taut, pulling one, then the other. I felt like a kid in a giant sandbox of snow. In only seconds we were at the bottom of the steep part and on our feet again, continuing on in jumping steps.

We were moving fast and our spirits were high. We arrived at the hill above Camp I. We could see our three yellow tents, and on the trail through the snow leading into camp, three figures. That would be our comrades, moving up to camp. Everything was on schedule and according to plan. We decided to make another glissade. Yvon went first, then me, then Jonathan, then Kim. I heard Kim give a whoop, and I answered with a "Yahoo!" and remember thinking, *Those guys coming up will get a kick out of watching us slide down.*

Then it happened.

* * *

I was right behind Yvon, and we quickly gained speed. Snow built around me and flew in my eyes. It was hard to see, but I didn't need to see. Since Yvon was first, all I had to do was follow his track.

This is great, I thought, *we'll be down in a few seconds. The rope is tugging on my waist, though. Yvon must be going awfully fast. But wait, he can't be going faster because he's making the track. That's funny. All this snow is building up around me. There's too much snow. Something's wrong. We've got to be careful; we'll load the slope. We have to stop glissading. Now, stop! Stop! Oh my God, it's too late.*

It was as if the snow had started to boil.

No way to get out now. It will stop, just below the tents. Has to. No, we're gaining speed. No, no. There's someone beside me. Jonathan? Kim? Can't tell. Someone yelling, "Oh Christ, here we go!" Think fast. We can't get out, but we might stop. If we stop, I will be buried. Remember what they say, "If you're in an avalanche, start swimming to stay on top." Try to backstroke. You're still on top, stay there. Backstroke, hard. It'll stop. Oh no, losing control. Can't, have to stay on top. No, I'm flipping.

I made a complete cartwheel, snow, sky, snow blurring across my vision.

Tumble up, down, up. Then in. Oh my God. I'm buried under the snow. Everything still moving fast. Curl up tight, like you're supposed to in a plane crash. Trap air in front, have an air pocket when it stops. That way I'll last long enough for those guys to dig me out. Those guys coming into camp, they were watching. They'll know what happened and dig us out. Air pocket, curl up. I'll make it. Must still be going fast. Can't breathe. I need air. Spots in front of me, black and white. Am I still alive? I must be.

Suddenly my face surfaced. I sucked air as fast as I could, then backstroked until my chest, then my knees, pulled out. Around me the snow was heaving and pulsing as if it were alive. To the side an outcrop sped by in a blur. Then in front, past my feet, I saw the slope steepen then disappear over an edge. Suddenly time slowed. I breathed deeply and exhaled deeply, and in that brief second, I managed to calm my thoughts. I looked ahead as the entire slope of snow we were riding, the tons and tons of snow, pitched into space.

Died October 13, 1980. Thirty-one years old. Buried in Tibet.

* * *

Inside the snow again. Curl up in the airplane-crash position. Ice blocks punching my back, then my arm. Hard on my arm. Am I dead? My arm hurts. It's OK. Listen, Mom, Dad, Brother, everybody—I know you love me, and I love you, but listen, it's OK, this isn't that bad.

Hit again. Still alive? Dead yet? Pain . . . I feel pain! Must be alive because I feel pain! I'm still buried. Open my eyes. White snow in front of my face, moving in and out, shifting ice blue, shifting and moving. Any moment now, any second, one final blow.

I'm on top again. Suck in the air as fast as I can. Can I survive this? Maybe, so breathe fast. If I go under again, I'll need air. Pull my arm out. Good, now the other arm. Legs out. Ice moving all around me, pulsing, breathing ice. Noise, the noise of the ice. To the side, rock cliffs whirring past. Must be in the gully, going down the rock face.

Think fast. Made it this far. I can make it. Maybe. Have to fight! Swim! Breathe fast, stay on top! There's Yvon in front of me, right in front. His head is up too. Wait, it's slowing. The avalanche, it's stopping. It's stopped!

Get out! Can't move, the rope is tight on my waist, can't get out. Knife? My pack? Where is it? Oh my God, the snow is moving again. It's going to start again. Get out, quick! God no, here we go again! There's the lower cliff. We're slowly sliding toward it. Pull, pull as hard as I can! This rope, can't get loose from it! Cliff is getting closer! Wait . . . it's slowing again. Slowing, slowing, it's stopped. Now get out, fast. Out of the rope. There, I can slip it off. Slide the loop down my legs, over my boots. OK, now to the side, crawl if you have to, careful so the snow doesn't start sliding again. Probably have fractures,

73

so go slow but quick. Slow and quick, like this. To the side, crawl, yes, keep going. To that rock. The rock is safe, off the snow. There, I made it. I'm safe. OK, breathe, breathe again, again, alive. God, I'm alive . . .

* * *

I sat panting, unable to do anything until I caught my breath, anything except to repeat to myself that I was alive. I had to be injured, but where? I felt my legs, then my arms, my ribs, my back. Bruises, probably bad ones, but apparently no broken bones.

What about the others? I saw Yvon below me at an angle, thirty feet away. He was buried to his waist, but he was working slowly to free himself. There was blood running down his face. I looked up and saw Kim. He was staring at me. Our eyes held, and his were round, like an animal that knows it is about to be killed. Blood was trickling from his mouth, staining his teeth. Then he screamed. An animal scream that made me look away.

Jonathan was closest, only a few feet from me, at the edge of the ice. He was head down, and the rope around his waist stretched tightly to where it disappeared into the ice, now set hard as concrete. He was mumbling something, but I couldn't hear what it was. I didn't move but continued to lie on the rock thinking that we were all alive and we were all going to get out of this. My breathing slowed. *What to do next?* I was OK, but the others seemed hurt. I needed to help them, but who first?

Yvon was still buried to the waist, leaning back on the snow as if he had given up trying to get out. Blood was running out of the corner of his mouth. He still had his glacier glasses on. *How could that be?*

"Yvon, are you OK?"

"Where are we?"

Kim screamed again. He was on one knee, trying in a frenzy to stand up. Maybe he thought the ice was going to move again?

The day after the avalanche we tried to carry Kim out on a jury-rigged stretcher, but it was too painful on his broken vertebrae. We gave him morphine, and he walked the remaining three days to the trailhead. Rick **Ridgeway**

"I can't breathe!" he yelled. There was panic in his voice. "Get the rope off!"

He started pulling the rope where it disappeared into the ice. He pulled like a madman, screaming as he yanked on the rope. "I can't breathe!"

Help Kim first.

I stood and stepped toward Kim, looking down at Jonathan. He was moaning. "Jonathan, are you OK?" He mumbled again, but I couldn't understand him.

No, help Jonathan first. His head is downhill, and he doesn't seem to be able to move.

I bent down and looked in his eyes and said, "Jonathan, we're all alive. We all made it. Everything is going to be OK." He didn't answer, but our eyes held. "Don't worry," I said. I had to get him upright but had to be careful in case his back was broken. He was heavy, but by lifting slowly with my arms under his head and back I straightened him out. "OK, buddy, that should be better." He still didn't answer, but our eyes held again. Then Kim screamed, "I can't breathe! The rope. Get the rope off!" I told Jonathan, "Hang on, I've got to help Kim. He can't breathe. I'll be right back. Everything's OK."

When I reached Kim, I told him to stop pulling against the rope. "Can't breathe. My back. I'm hurt. Can't breathe!"

"Relax. Take the strain off the rope so I can untie it."

Kim collapsed on his knees. I coaxed him to move a few inches to relieve tension on the rope. But the knot was too tight to untie.

Should I keep working on it, or help the others?

I looked down. Yvon had nearly dug himself out, but then he leaned back again on the snow. He seemed dazed.

"Yvon, are you hurt?"

"What happened?"

"Are you OK?"

"Where are we?"

I turned back to Kim and managed to untie the knot. "OK," I told him, "now I've got to help the others."

I stepped down the avalanche debris to Yvon.

"Are you hurt?"

"I don't think so. What happened?"

"We were in an avalanche. Stay right here. I've got to help Jonathan."

When I got to Jonathan, I bent down to ask him how he was doing, and my stomach tightened. His eyes had rolled back in his head. I put my ear to his mouth. He wasn't breathing. I put my fingers on his neck. His pulse was quick and strong. I held his head in my lap and placed my finger on his tongue and breathed into his mouth, once, twice, three times. Nothing. Again: once, twice. Nothing. Then I saw his chest rise and fall. He had started to breathe again.

He's going to make it! Things will turn out OK. We're all going to get out of this alive.

Then his breathing stopped. I breathed into his mouth, once, twice, and again he started breathing on his own. But there was a sound inside his chest.

No, no, this isn't going to happen. We've all got to come out of this OK. We're all still alive.

He breathed three times and stopped, and I breathed again into his mouth. He breathed, stopped, I breathed into him, and again he started to breathe on his own. His pulse was still strong. I had to keep him going until the others arrived. The others.

Where are they? They saw us go down, so they're coming to help. But they should have been here by now. Or maybe the avalanche was so wide they'd been swept away too. They could be buried in the snow.

I stood up and looked around but there was no sign of anyone else. Yvon was now on his feet, staring at me. Kim was crawling off the ice, still crying in pain. Our red rope wove in and out of the jumbled blocks of ice like an intestine from a gutted animal. I turned back to Jonathan. He had stopped breathing once more, and once more I started mouth-to-mouth. His chest rose, fell. I breathed into his mouth and his chest rose, held, fell, then rose again on its own . . . then stopped. I watched, waited, then put my mouth again to his mouth. I felt his neck. His heart was still beating.

Yvon walked over and stood a few feet away. He was unmoving, like a scarecrow. There was blood on his face.

"Are you sure you're not hurt?"

"What happened?"

"We were in a big avalanche. We just fell fifteen hundred, maybe two thousand feet. I don't know . . . a long way. We're alive. But Jonathan is hurt bad."

"What mountain is this?"

"Yvon, go help Kim."

Yvon looked toward Kim, who was now off the ice, lying on his side, doubled up and moaning.

"What mountain did you say this was?"

Yvon then started toward the place where he had been buried. I was afraid he would walk off the cliff that was only yards away.

"Yvon, don't walk around. Come over here. Help Kim."

In a daze, he turned and started back toward me. I needed help. *Where were the others?*

"Help!" I shouted. "Down here. Help!"

There was no reply, and I called again. Yvon was again standing near me.

"Where are we?"

"Minya Konka, Yvon."

"Where?"

"Minya Konka, in Tibet. China."

"What are we doing in China?"

I turned back to Jonathan. Each time I breathed into him there was a gurgle in his chest. I waited. His head rested on my knee. I moved my fingers through his hair and watched his face. His lips had lost color. Then all of a sudden his face paled, as though some part of his being had evaporated, and he looked different. I held him in my lap and continued to run my fingers through his hair. I bent and kissed him on his forehead and set his head down and folded his arms on his stomach so he looked comfortable. Yvon stood watching. He didn't say anything, and I didn't think he understood.

"Yvon, Jonathan just died."

Jonathan Wright on the train from Beijing to Chengdu. Reading his journals, I found an entry quoting his Buddhist teacher S.N. Goenka, "Your name or your person, which is dearer? Your person or your goods, which is worth more? Gain or loss, which is the greater bane?" **Rick Ridgeway**

The Door in the Mountain Wall

The day after the avalanche I left camp at first light, before the others were out of their tents. I wanted a few minutes to be alone with Jonathan. When I got to his body, I saw that the day before the others had covered him in a blue bivouac sack. I pulled it back. His knees were bent and his arms crossed over his chest. His pack lay partially under him where I had placed it to keep him warm. I opened it, looking for something to take back to his wife.

I found his camera damaged but with the film intact, and put it in my pack. Then a few feet away I saw his baseball cap, which had somehow stayed with us the entire distance of the avalanche. He had worn it every day. Sweat had discolored the rim where he had marked his initials and a stylized *om mani padme hum*, and bloodstains made me unsure whether I should give it as a remembrance to his wife.

Looking around, I noticed a rock promontory in relief from the slope. The surrounding slate was suited for constructing a platform, so I started building a bier. The others arrived, and in silence we worked together. The sun rose higher, and I took off my jacket. When the platform was complete, we lifted Jonathan's body to our shoulders, two on each side. He was frozen and heavy and the footing was difficult. I heard the clink of the flat stones under my boots. I felt the cold of his body on my shoulder and

After we tied prayer flags between two glacier wands,
I placed the final stone on Jonathan's grave. **Edgar Boyles**

the heat of the sun on my face, and from my sweat I could taste salt on my lips.

We laid him on the platform. His bent knees fit perfectly inside the slight curve of the tumulus. We covered him with stones, and between two bamboo wands at the head of his grave we hung prayer flags. The flags fluttered in the breeze. Above us, the west face glacier tumbled to the moraine. From its snout the meltwater began its journey to the Yalong, the Yangtze, and the East China Sea.

* * *

We left Base Camp, following the same trail out that we had taken in. Kim had a foam sleeping pad trussed around his torso to stabilize injuries, which we would later learn included cracked vertebrae and a damaged knee. He walked slowly, a ski pole in each hand. The team's doctor had given him morphine, but the pain was still evident on his face. The sky was clear and there was only a light breeze. At the pass where we'd had the mishap with the horse that spooked and slid down the slope, we turned and had our last look at Minya Konka.

"These mountains are too high," Yvon said. "Fuck these mountains."

In three more days we reached the trailhead. Our vehicles were scheduled to arrive the next morning to take us back to Chengdu. From there we would catch a flight to Beijing, and then home. We slept on the concrete floor of the village schoolhouse. That evening it snowed, and I imagined Jonathan's grave buried for the winter. That brought to mind a conversation with one of the camera crew before we left Base Camp, when he told me that some of the team members were blaming Yvon and me for triggering the avalanche, and that further, they were holding me in even more contempt for my singular focus on making the film and reaching the summit for the sake of the movie, both of which they viewed as my pursuit of personal glory.

I woke before the others and quietly sat up and propped myself against the wall of the schoolroom. Another member of the team woke and, also taking care to make no noise, dressed and walked outside. Like many on the team, he was a guide in the Tetons, and I had been told he was the one who in particular was blaming me. But I didn't feel any more responsible for the avalanche than any of the others. We had failed to manage the risk, and it was a failure on all of our parts.

Outside I heard the dawn chatter of a flock of laughing thrushes. I looked at my teammates, each burrowed in his sleeping bag, which together looked like a scattering of colorful cocoons. While I didn't feel singularly responsible for the avalanche, they had a good point about my focus on the film, which I knew to them may have appeared monomaniacal. The laughing thrushes continued their chatter and I thought, *Maybe the birds are mocking me.*

My teammates started to wake and sit up. One of them, Edgar Boyles, a close friend of Jonathan's, was reading Jonathan's personal journal, something he knew Jonathan would have allowed. Edgar had told me that Jonathan had made frequent references about me, about our growing friendship and our partnership as a writer-photographer team. Apparently, there were no entries about my egoism, but I knew that didn't mean it wasn't there, or that it wasn't something I needed to deal with. I remembered that day coming down from Everest Base Camp when the trekkers had stopped Chris Chandler to ask for his autograph, and Jonathan had spotted me standing to the side, feeling sorry for myself, and he had walked over and told me that the two of us would come back to the Himalaya and go into retreat in a Buddhist monastery. He didn't say more than that, but he didn't have to, because I knew he meant a retreat to think through what was and was not important in our lives.

The memory made me smile. I wasn't sure I would go on a retreat in a Buddhist monastery, but I knew I owed it to Jonathan to integrate into my life some of the ways he had lived his. When Edgar finished reading Jonathan's journal, I would ask to borrow it, and I would also ask Jonathan's wife if I could have copies of Jonathan's earlier journals that recorded his many journeys to Asia, the place in the world he loved above all others, the name of which he chose for his baby daughter.

The laughing thrushes continued to laugh. *They're not mocking me*, I thought. *They're just doing what thrushes do.*

* * *

I was hiking on a trail high in the Himalaya. There were no people and no trees, and the land was open until I reached a mountain wall. It was a vertical rock wall and it was featureless. I hiked along the base until I arrived at a door inset into the wall with nothing around it except smooth rock. I tried to open it, but it was locked. I knocked, but no one came. I pounded on it, but still there was no response. I put my ear to the door, but there was no sound from whatever or whoever was on the other side.

I opened my eyes, and for a moment I wasn't sure where I was. There was sufficient light through the thin curtain covering the window to vaguely illuminate the pale-green walls of the hotel room, and even though the window was closed, I could hear the chime of bicycle bells. I was in Beijing, on the way home from Minya Konka. I lay in bed and thought about the dream. It was the second time since the avalanche that I had had the dream, and I wondered what was on the other side of the door, or, for that matter, why I had had the same dream twice.

I got up and walked to the window and saw that even though it was just getting light, there were already hundreds of bicyclists pedaling to wherever it was they were going to begin their day's duties. As for me, we had an extra day to see the city before we caught our flight home. I dressed and went downstairs to have breakfast. Some of my teammates were there, but they continued to give me a cold shoulder. Outside, the sky was blue and the air was cold and clean. We boarded a minibus for our tour, and one of the stops was the Beijing Zoo.

While the others viewed the big mammals, I stayed in the aviary, looking at the pheasants. There were seven species, including golden pheasants, silver pheasants, Lady Amherst's, Reeves's, and Temminck's tragopans. They were all native to China. There were also blue eared and white eared pheasants. I compared the two, and from its black cap and dark tail feathers and dark wing primaries I was able to confirm that the birds I had seen on the hillside above the monastery at the base of Minya Konka had been white eared pheasants, *Crossoptilon crossoptilon*.

On the drive back to the hotel in the minibus, I watched the sea of people pedaling their bicycles. All the people wore the same Mao suits, and all the bicycles were the same model, and all had the same handlebar bells that made the same chime. I was thinking about the pheasants, about my backyard zoo when I was a kid and how I had dreamed of someday getting to the remote places in China and Asia where the birds were from, and how impossible that had seemed at the time. Now I had been to some of those places. Would I see more of those places in the future? Would I continue to go on adventures? When someday I was an old man, what would be the stories of my life, looking backward?

Then I had the idea that maybe as an old man I would again take up raising pheasants. That made me smile. I continued to look out the window and suddenly I realized what was on the other side of the door in my dream: it was a path that wound in a circle back to my childhood.

* * *

After my father burned the house down and took off to the South Seas, and after I had finished the school year living with my best friend in his parents' Airstream, I returned to Southern California to live with my mother while I finished high school. I was shocked by the change the area had undergone in the brief three years I had lived in the northern part of the state. Our one-acre ranchette where I had my backyard zoo was gone, incorporated into a fenced compound for a building supply company. The town where I had gone to elementary school—a village named Olive that had had a one-room bank, a small grocery, a blacksmith shop, and a drugstore with a fountain that made Coke with mixing syrup—was also gone, subsumed by tracts of nearly identical houses incorporated into Orange and Anaheim as the two cities expanded their borders like growing cancers.

I had spent some of my preteen years in the chaparral bordering the Santa Ana River hunting quail and rabbits with my single-shot .22; the riverbed was now a concrete channel. I had a Honda 90 motor scooter, and I started ditching school and riding into the San Gabriel Mountains above the Los Angeles Basin to hike to the top of Mount Baldy. Years later, as I thought through the impact of witnessing the desecration of the rural and wild areas where I had grown up, I would see how my sojourns into the mountains in search of solace was the origin of both the magnetism with which wilderness pulled me into it and, later, the resolve to do what I could to protect it.

At a little over 10,000 feet, Mount Baldy is the highest peak in the San Gabriels, and there was one section called the Devil's Backbone that was steep on both sides. I had hiked to the summit twice in spring and summer, but then I tried it in winter, when the Devil's Backbone was coated in ice. I made it to the summit and back down, but realized I could easily have slipped, and that the consequence could easily have been dire. What I needed was boots, crampons, and an ice ax just like Jim Whittaker had in that photograph of him standing on top of Everest.

Our local sporting goods store did not have crampons and ice axes, but it did have copies of a magazine called *Summit* that had advertisements for stores that did have climbing gear. There was one called Highland Outfitters not far away, in Riverside. I was then a senior in high school, and I had upgraded my Honda scooter to a 1949 Chevy panel truck. I drove with a couple of my school buddies out to Riverside, and we bought boots, crampons, and ice axes, along with a book called *Freedom of the Hills*—the only thing on the shelves with anything resembling a tutorial on how to use our new equipment.

We drove to the trailhead leading to 11,500-foot Mount San Gorgonio. It was a slow slog through wet snow, and we camped halfway to the summit, the first time any of us had slept on snow. I used the last hours of sunlight to climb a slope above our army-surplus tent, and after reading the appropriate section in *Freedom of the Hills* I made several mock slides down the slope, arresting my "fall" with my ice ax. My friends, complaining of the cold, stayed in camp the next day as I went on and climbed by myself to the top of the highest peak in Southern California.

As a high school graduation present, my mother enrolled me in Outward Bound, which she hoped would provide more mountaineering guidance than I was getting from my dog-eared copy of *Freedom of the Hills*. I drove my Chevy panel truck to the Oregon Cascades, and for the next month I gained some basic mountaineering and rock-climbing skills.

Earlier that year, I'd had to select a college or university. My SAT scores weren't that high, and we couldn't afford much, so the elite schools were out of reach. Meanwhile, my father was in Hawai'i working for a military contractor on optical systems to track downrange ICBMs. I missed my dad, but he had burned our house down and abandoned me and left my mother. By then I had a drawer full of postcards from the South Pacific of bare-breasted women, all with messages hoping I was doing well, and that he was looking forward to seeing me again. And then there was Hawai'i. "The Islands," as my father referred to them in his postcards, sounded like a fantasy in all ways except they lacked mountains I could climb. Still, the Islands were surrounded by the ocean, and in high school I had taken up surfing.

In the fall of 1967 I went to my first classes at the University of Hawai'i. I continued to surf, but I also met a neighbor who had a sailboat in the harbor, and soon my new passion for sailing eclipsed surfing. At the end of my freshman year I joined five other guys on a thirty-six-foot sloop that we sailed to Tahiti.

My last move to the summit of the South Sister during my Outward
Bound course in the Oregon Cascades, in 1967. **Rory Sheridan**

I was nineteen years old, and it was my first big adventure, and
I was hooked. I returned to Hawaiʻi to continue school, but I also
continued to sail around the Islands, and I made another long-
distance voyage to French Polynesia, and from there to Mexico
and down the coast to Panama.

In Panama I met the owner of an eighty-two-foot Alden
schooner. He and his first mate, both in their midthirties, invited
me in on a scheme to buy .22 shells from a contact at the rifle
range in the Canal Zone. The plan was to sail to Colombia and
trade the ammo to natives who lived in the highlands. They
explained that the natives had rifles that they used for subsistence hunting, but they didn't have ammunition. Apparently, they
also worked in emerald mines, and they pocketed some of the

gemstones, so the scheme was to trade the ammo for emeralds. The boat owner and his mate then planned to sail the schooner to Fiji, where there was an international gemstone trade run by Hindi merchants. After selling the emeralds to the Hindis, they were then going to use the cash to buy an island and start a resort, taking tourists on excursions in the schooner.

While I have all my life considered myself an entrepreneur, it took a while to develop the skill to scrutinize the viability of a business plan. We ordered 50,000 rounds of .22 shells, but our contact said it would take a few weeks to get that much ammo. So we sailed the boat to a resort island off the coast to wait. On the beach, we met three young women who accepted our invitation to join our cruise. One day one of the young women, Candace, and I were working on the boat while the others were in the Canal Zone buying supplies for the long passage to Fiji when a Panama navy patrol boat pulled alongside us.

Candace and I were arrested. She was taken to the women's prison and I was thrown in the holding tank of the men's prison with several dozen others, mostly drunks. I wasn't sure how serious of a situation I was in. One of the drunks was a young kid who cursed at the guards. Eventually he fell asleep, and in the early hours of predawn the guards came in and hauled him away. They brought him back an hour later. He was beaten, badly, and by dawn he had died. The guards came back and dragged his body by the arms out of the holding tank.

* * *

Two days later I was transferred to a cell on the second floor. There were eight others in a space maybe eight feet wide by twelve feet long. The two most tenured inmates—a Creole in his early thirties and a wiry mestizo who looked to be in his midtwenties—slept in bunk beds against the wall, and everyone else slept on cardboard. There was no toilet, but the cell faced a corridor that had a latrine at the end. I soon learned that the drill was to hold your arm out of the bars and yell *Llave!*

("key" in Spanish) and the guards would signal when you had permission to leave. The cell doors were actually left unlocked—so you just walked the corridor to the latrine—but the corridor itself had double-locked doors, and the guards followed you with their rifles partially raised.

The second day after my transfer two guards came to my cell and ordered me to go with them. They escorted me to a small room where there were two other men in civilian clothes who I assumed were interrogators. There were three chairs and a small desk. They motioned toward one of the chairs and told me to sit. I tried to calm myself with the fact that there were no visible electric wires or whips or any signs of blood splatter on the walls.

"Where is the marijuana?" one said.

"We are not going to hurt you," the other one added.

I didn't know a good cop from a bad cop, but I had already decided my strategy was to tell them the truth. There was no crime in that—unless there was some offense in ordering a few thousand rounds of .22 shells.

"You traded ammunition for marijuana. Where is the marijuana?"

The interrogators repeated their alternating threats and assurances, and I repeated the same story, saying again that there was no marijuana. After what seemed like an interminable amount of time, the guards took me back to my cell. My cellmates didn't ask what had happened, and I didn't offer. The next day the same two men came back, and after another hour of giving them the same answers, I was again returned to my cell.

When I had been arrested, I was allowed to take with me a small stuffsack with a few belongings: my address book, pen and paper, and a pipe and tobacco that I had enjoyed during night watches on my long-distance sailing passages. I had left my stuffsack on the lower bunk bed when I left for the interrogation, and now it was gone.

"Where's my sack?"

No one answered.

"Which one of you took my sack?"

"What sack?" the wiry mestizo said. He occupied the lower bunk, and even though he was young he called the shots.

"My small red bag."

He shrugged his shoulders and, following his lead, the others ignored me. I sat on the lower bunk; I'd learned it was OK to sit on the bunk during the day, but when it was time to go to sleep, you had to sit on your cardboard and give the bunk to its owner. But it was not going to be OK if I did nothing about my missing sack. It wasn't the contents; it was about what would happen if I didn't do anything about its theft. I had no idea how long I was going to be in prison. A week? A month? A year? If I was stuck in this lower rung of hell, I knew that doing nothing about my stuffsack would be the beginning. The beginning of abuse, of bullying, of . . . ?

I sat on the bunk, hands folded, arms resting on my knees, eyes looking down. I could see the legs and feet of my cellmates. They resumed talking, standing at the one window with its columns of metal bars, stepping with desultory repetition to the one door with its columns of metal bars. Could I find the courage? In school I had never been in a fight. I had never taken up boxing. Other than scraps with my little brother when we were kids, I'd never punched anyone. Could I do it now?

I could see the feet of the ringleader walk from the window to the door. When I knew his back was to me, I pushed off with as much force as I could muster and drove his head as hard as I could into the barred door. I cocked my arm and drove my fist into the side of his head. I could hear the yells erupt from the others, and I cocked my arm again, but they were on top of me and punching me and yells came from the other cells and I could hear whistles blow and feet running.

"*Basta!*"

The guards were in our cell telling everyone to get on their feet. As the guys got off my back, one of them whispered, "As soon as you go to sleep, you are dead."

I got to my feet. The guards had their rifles at the ready position, fingers on triggers.

"*Que pasa!*" one demanded.

"They stole my sack," I said. "A small sack, with my things."

"So what," another guard replied.

"Where's the gringo's sack?" another guard said. He was a large man and overweight, and I had the sense that he was the lead guard.

"No one stole anything," the ringleader said dismissively. He had a small cut on his head, and I was disappointed that it wasn't bigger.

"Give me the gringo's things," a voice said.

Everyone turned, including the guards. It was a prisoner from the opposite cell, standing outside the cell door. He was about fifty, a mestizo with close-cropped gray hair and black eyes whose shirt was always carefully tucked into his pants. I had already noticed that each day, when we were escorted to the concrete courtyard for our hour of recreation, everyone nodded when he passed and said deferentially, "*Buenos días*, Magellan."

"Give me the gringo's things," Magellan said again.

The ringleader lifted the mattress on his bunk to expose a cut in the stuffing. He pulled out my stuffsack and handed it to Magellan.

"I want the gringo in my cell," Magellan said to the head guard.

The guard nodded and led me across the corridor to Magellan's cell.

"That took guts," Magellan said.

I shook my head, too rattled to reply.

"I like men with guts," he added as he drew on his cigarette. He then turned and introduced me to my new cellmates.

I was never able to discern the source of Magellan's influence, but it was manifest in the deference all the prisoners gave him. Even the guards treated him with respect, never ordering him around like they did the rest of us or motioning with their rifle barrels for him to move more quickly up and down the stairs on our way to the cafeteria for our skimpy meals.

Whatever the source of his influence, I welcomed his protection, because the danger was real. One night there was an attempted breakout, and the guards shot and killed four men trying to scale the walls around the prison. For me, the worst part was the uncertainty of how long I would be in prison. After a month, however, I was released when the guy who owned the Alden schooner forfeited the boat to the Panamanian generals. Candace was freed the same day, and we had a celebratory dinner with her girlfriends.

Candace told me that in her prison she was treated fairly, until one day she was escorted to the office of pock-faced Manuel Noriega. His proposition was straightforward: sex for freedom. So was Candace's reply: go fuck yourself.

The next day I wrote my mother, explaining why she hadn't heard from me for a month. I mailed it from the Canal Zone, where I knew the Postal Service would have it to her in a few days, but then decided to spend some of what little money I had to call her, so I could explain what had happened before the letter arrived.

"Richard!" she said after I had said hello. "I haven't heard from you . . . is everything OK?"

I told her I had been in jail, and I could tell by the way she said "Oh . . ." that she was shocked, and I could hear she was in tears when I told her I was OK, and that a letter would arrive soon with the details, and I couldn't talk for too long because it cost too much, and I was thinking of going to South America but that I would be very careful not to break any laws.

Now that Candace was freed, her friends wanted to return to the United States, but Candace still had more than seven months before she started law school, and she didn't want to spend it back in the States.

"I'm going to South America," she said to me. "You want to come?"

Over the next two months, by combination of hitchhiking and low fares on cheap buses, we traveled through Colombia and Ecuador. In Peru we arrived just as an intense El Niño started, and we had to flee a coastal city as it was flooding. We spent more money than we wanted on a DC-3 flight to Lima. By then, including my time sailing through the South Pacific, I had been traveling for over a year.

"I want to stay in Lima for a while," I told Candace. "Take a few classes at the university, and then maybe go to the mountains and see if I can meet some climbers. I need to get back into mountaineering."

It was a hard decision. I wanted to travel with Candace to the southern parts of South America. But if I enrolled in the university, I might get credits that would help me get into graduate school so that someday I could become a professor. I was in love with Candace, but she wanted to be just friends, albeit a deep friendship. I had had to learn how to make it a different kind of love, and though it took me a while, I managed to do that, and that meant a lot to Candace. Over the years, I would learn how important it was to me as well.

We said goodbye in Lima, hugging each other tightly. I watched her get on a cheap bus by herself, pack over her shoulder, no fear of traveling alone. She sent me aerograms from Bolivia, Chile, and Argentina.

When I finished my semester at the university, I bought a cheap bus ticket to a small town in the Andes at the base of the Cordillera Blanca, where I knew mountaineers convened to plan their ascents. My mother had shipped me the boots, crampons, and ice ax I had bought while in high school. I met several climbers, including Chris Chandler, who took me under his wing. I returned to the Peruvian Andes for the next two years, and by then I had made several new routes and first ascents, and I was a seasoned mountaineer. Chris then got me on the American Bicentennial Everest Expedition, and that led to the invitation to join the American K2 Expedition, and that led to the invitation to attempt Minya Konka.

Jonathan's photograph of Khumbutse, a satellite peak of Everest, that he took while he, Chris Chandler, and I were resting at Camp I on Everest. This is the photograph with his signature I've had on the wall of my studio for forty-five years. Jonathan Wright

Chapter Five

Matters of Consequence

On the way home from Minya Konka, I flew from Beijing to Tokyo and then to Los Angeles, but before I could return to my fisherman's shack on the beach, I traveled to Aspen for Jonathan's service. I went for a walk with his wife and their baby daughter, Asia. We sat on a rock next to a stream, and I told Jonathan's wife, with the baby in her arms, about the avalanche that had killed her husband. There was snow on the bare branches of the aspen, and occasionally the snow fell and hit the ground in faint thumps that punctuated the purl of the stream. Asia was asleep, and I noted that while the baby had her mother's eyes and hair, there were other features that looked like her father.

Back in my fisherman's shack, I listened to the waves on the beach and wondered how it had happened that I was there and not buried next to Jonathan. Was it some slight deviation in my path compared to his path as we rode the avalanche down the mountain? I spent most days walking the beach. I was alone, but I didn't feel lonely. It was winter and the shorebirds were down from their summer breeding grounds in the High Arctic.

A month later, Jonathan's wife called to ask if I would do her and Jonathan's family a favor. It was about the project Jonathan and I had underway with *National Geographic*, to do a story on the recently created Sagarmatha (Mount Everest) National Park

Jennifer and I in 1982 shortly after we married, in front of
my surfer's shack "just south of Montecito." **Lear Levin**

97

with me as writer and Jonathan as photographer. Jonathan had already made one trip to Nepal to take initial photographs. Would I be willing to go back with another photographer to complete the story?

* * *

Nicholas DeVore was a contract photographer with *National Geographic* who had done many stories for the magazine. He also was a childhood friend of Jonathan's, having grown up with him in Aspen. He was so inscrutably odd, however, that I didn't know what to make of him. His sexual orientation was ambiguous, yet he was tough outdoors and seemed to relish harsh conditions. In the city, however, he liked to wear pancake makeup. Then there were the five tuxedos he traveled with, each in a different pastel.

In late March 1981, less than six months after the avalanche on Minya Konka, Nicholas and I checked into the Yak & Yeti hotel in Kathmandu—he had insisted we stay in the best hotel in the city. He also said we needed to go to the bank. Nicholas had $20,000 in traveler's checks that he had convinced *National Geographic* he would need for things like a helicopter to get aerials.

"And Sherpas," he said as we converted the checks to rupees. "We can't have too many Sherpas. And a cook, and assistant cook. We have to have a fully appointed camp. Table and chairs. Tablecloth. Fresh flowers. Have to have fresh flowers, every day."

Leaving the bank, I judged we would need another Sherpa just to carry the rupees. We stored the bills in the safes in our two hotel rooms—they wouldn't fit into just one—and then went to Durbar Square and the Asan Bazaar to mix with the vendors and barkers, the beggars, the sadhus; to smell the spices and incense blended with the aroma of shit from the sacred cows walking the streets; to watch the tourists glance furtively at the pagodas with their carved friezes depicting princesses and princes copulating in multiple positions; to take in the novelty of the sudden appearance of an elephant with a *tika* on its forehead, its mahout urging the mammoth pachyderm through the crowds. Nicholas was grinning as he reloaded cannisters of film into the two cameras around his neck. I was grinning too, to be back in what Peter Matthiessen called the "Oriental rumpus" of Kathmandu, with Jonathan's childhood friend, who seemed just as bizarre as the scenes he was photographing.

The next morning I had breakfast with Pasang Kami, PK, the Sherpa *sirdar* from our Everest expedition. Seeing him across the table was like reuniting with an erudite uncle whom you haven't seen for five years. He reported he was doing well, managing fewer climbing expeditions and working with his wife on his lodge for trekkers and adjacent general store in Namche Bazaar.

"Chris Chandler and his girlfriend Cherie were here last week," he reported. "Or maybe wife? We had dinner."

"I don't think they're married," I said. "But Cherie and her husband were both on our K2 climb, and it was . . . complicated."

"Yes, I know about that," PK said. "The Himalayas are a big range, but gossip goes quickly from one end to the other."

"What were Chris and Cherie doing here?"

"They were on their way to attempt Yalung Kang—you know, the west summit of Kanchenjunga. Just the two of them, with some Sherpas to help carry the loads."

I told PK how Chris and Cherie had built a boat with plans to sail it around the world. I was writing *The Last Step*, my book about K2, and Chris had told me he didn't want me to refer to his friendship with Cherie. I went to Seattle to talk to him. We sat on the deck of his boat, and I told him his affair with Cherie was so central to everything that happened on the expedition that there was no way to tell the story without including it. I pledged to be as accurate as possible, but Chris hadn't spoken to me since.

"Maybe I should try again," I said to PK. "I could write him a letter."

"That's a good idea. I will give it to him when they come back through Kathmandu."

"Their climb sounds dangerous. Just the two of them."

"That mountain has lots of avalanches," PK said.

I stared at my breakfast, not saying anything. PK, perhaps sensing the reference to avalanches was what had made me pause, was also quiet. Then I looked up and said, "I'm not sure if I'll go back to mountaineering. It's Jonathan's death, but it's also being in the avalanche myself. I don't know, maybe for a full minute I thought I was dead too."

PK sipped his tea and didn't respond, but looked at me through his eyeglasses with the scrutiny that I had come to associate with his ability to see behind what people were saying, with what I had concluded was a wisdom uncommon even among his Sherpa brethren, who in the main seemed to have a preternatural ability to see things as they are.

"I'm thinking I might give it up," I said.

"That's a good idea," PK replied. He offered his hand, and I shook it. He was the first person I had told about my uncertainty whether or not I would continue to climb, and I wondered if giving the consideration voice to someone I respected would influence my choice.

"It's a hard decision," I said. "I think about K2, never giving up. Sticking with it, storm after storm. It's been a big lesson for me."

"You're still young. You can get married and have children and figure out other things to do."

I smiled and nodded. I wasn't sure about the getting married part. Not that I wasn't open to the possibility, but it seemed like it depended on happenstance beyond my control. I was awkward around women. In high school I only went on one date, and I was so nervous she had never returned my calls even after multiple attempts to ask her out again. After college I had joined a small band of rock climbers in Southern California that included as many women as men, and that felt natural, but maybe that was because we had climbing in common. It was the same for many of my male climbing friends. Yvon had once told me how he had grown up in northern Maine in a French-Canadian family that moved to California for his father's health. "When you're a teenager who can't speak English that well and you're five foot four," he once told me, "it's pretty hard to get a date. The only thing left is to climb rocks."

At least the climbing part, however, *was* in my control, and one thing I had realized just in the few days I was in Kathmandu was that I could still experience the travel part of going on mountaineering expeditions, as well as the satisfactions of meeting characters like Nicholas whom I might otherwise never encounter.

* * *

Nicholas and I had two more days in Kathmandu before we left for the Everest region. I wrote the letter to Chris Chandler, telling him I still hoped we could get together someday to talk through our differences. I left it at the office of a trekking agency that represented PK's lodge, with instructions to give it to PK so he could give it to Chris. I then spent the day arranging our trekking permits and authorization for a flight over Everest so Nicholas could get aerials.

In the afternoon Nicholas and I met in the lobby bar at the Yak & Yeti. I noticed two tables away a beautiful woman who appeared to be about my age, sitting alone. I had seen her earlier in the elevator. She wore jeans, a white T-shirt that looked like it had been pressed, and gold earrings, and she had brunette hair that looked like it had been cut by someone who knew what they were doing.

"She's pretty cute," Nicholas said.

"Who?"

"The girl you're staring at."

I was sure Nicholas could see me blush, but that only egged him on. He signaled the waiter and asked him what the woman was drinking.

"Gin and tonic, sir."

"Get her another one and tell her it's from my friend here."

When the waiter delivered the drink, the young woman looked at us, and Nicholas waved to her to come over. She picked up her drink, and we stood to introduce ourselves. She said her name was Jennifer.

"Are you on vacation?" Nicholas asked.

"No, I'm actually on assignment for Calvin Klein. I was in Thailand, buying silk. Then I caught a flight home—back to New York—but there was a long layover in Delhi, so I checked into a hotel. Then they didn't wake me, and I missed the flight. You know, Pan Am 1, that goes around the world?" she said, making a circle with her index finger.

"So, you came to Nepal?"

"It's going to be three days before the plane comes back around. I was in the lobby trying to figure out what to do, and I saw this sign in front of the travel office that said, 'Visit Kathmandu.' You know, the Cat Stevens song? Well, here I am."

I could see by his grin that Nicholas loved that story. We told her about our *National Geographic* assignment and our upcoming trek to the Everest region.

"You should come with us!" I blurted, surprising myself at my own brashness. I was usually shy with women at first. I had a girlfriend back in California, but that was both exacerbating and distracting me from the introspection of trying to decide whether or not to go back to mountaineering.

"We travel in style," Nicholas said, clearly in agreement with my proposal. "You'll have your own tent and your own Sherpas."

"I only have these heels," Jennifer said, pointing to her kid-skin pumps.

"We can get some boots here," I said. "There's a whole section of the city where they sell trekking supplies."

"That's very nice of you, but the farthest I've ever walked is from a cab to the front entrance of Bergdorf Goodman."

I could see that Nicholas loved that answer even more. If we couldn't convince Jennifer to come with us, at least we could talk her into dinner.

"Yak steak," I said, "at Boris's restaurant. You'll love it."

I had met Boris five years earlier when I came to Nepal with the Bicentennial Everest Expedition. Boris was a White Russian who, with his mother, fled the Bolshevik Revolution in 1917 and ended up with a dance troupe touring Europe and then eventually Asia. He settled in Calcutta and started Club 300, a favored nightspot for Asian glitterati, including the king of Nepal, who invited him to move to Kathmandu. Boris opened a restaurant and hotel in an eighteenth-century Rana palace, and the Yak & Yeti became the country's premier hotel. Since I had first visited, however, Boris had expanded, adding an expensive wing, and his partner had then used the debt to force Boris out. He had recovered—sort of—and had recently opened a new restaurant.

Boris met us at the door, raising an approving eyebrow at Nicholas, who had selected for the evening a powder-blue tuxedo. Two other friends were waiting for us: Al Read, the leader of our Minya Konka expedition, and his wife, also a Jennifer. As we sat down, I knew it was likely that we would talk about the Minya Konka expedition and Jonathan's death, and if that happened, I hoped it wouldn't be awkward for Jennifer-the-guest. Instead, the evening turned to levity when Al, who had just landed after a long flight from the States, fell asleep and face-planted in his borscht soup. He jerked his head upright, and as his Jennifer cleaned him with her napkin, I could see the other Jennifer grinning but also shaking her head with a *Where did these people come from?* expression.

* * *

After Al recovered from his borscht bath, we talked about the avalanche and how Jonathan's widow was doing with their baby daughter, Asia, and I could see Jennifer-the-guest was listening quietly. I had brought a copy of *The Last Step* to give to

Jennifer, with her leather Hartmann garment bag, suitcase, and cosmetic box, arriving at the Yak & Yeti hotel in Kathmandu where we first met in the lobby bar. All of us have that experience when the path of our life crosses another's and, like a boat rounding a navigation marker, we are forever on a new course. **Jennifer Ridgeway Collection**

another friend in Kathmandu, but in the taxi back to the Yak & Yeti I told Jennifer I wanted to give it to her. At the hotel, I went to my room to retrieve it, and then knocked on her door. Her room was tidy, all her clothes carefully folded and placed in her leather Hartmann suitcase. I gave her the book. She thanked me. I was relieved that she didn't ask me to inscribe it—I wasn't sure what I would say.

"I'm sorry about your friend Jonathan."

"It's been a rough six months since he died. Losing him, but also nearly getting killed myself. I don't know if I'm going to go back to climbing, especially the high peaks."

I could see she was crying.

"Your story . . . well, it's so similar to what happened to me."

"To you?"

"I haven't talked to anybody . . . I don't even really know you."

"You don't have to say anything if you don't want to . . ."

"Even the timing. Of your avalanche. It's so close to the . . ."

"To the . . .?"

"To the tidal wave."

We both remained standing as she told me how she had been married to a Mexican who, like me, was a sportsman who loved adventure. His twin passions were polo and sailing. She told me how they had met in Puerto Vallarta, and how he had invited her to go sailing, and how eventually they married, and how a few years later her husband decided to sail his boat around the world, and how she joined him for parts of the cruise.

She told me how they were sailing across the shallow passage between Australia and New Guinea when there was a major earthquake that triggered a tidal wave. Jennifer was never a good swimmer, and her husband made her wear a life jacket whenever she was out of the cockpit. She was on the afterdeck sunbathing when the wave hit. It broke the boat apart and it sank. The Australian Coast Guard sent a helicopter to fly over the area, in case any boats had been caught in the tidal wave. Jennifer regained consciousness in the hospital. She was told later that of the dozen people on board the yacht, only one other had survived, and he was not her husband. She was pregnant, and she lost her baby.

There was nothing I could say. I held her and she cried. I gave her my address and phone number and told her I hoped to see her again. I kissed her on her cheek and said good night.

* * *

Two months later Jennifer called. She was in Beverly Hills, doing a trunk show for Calvin Klein, and was wondering if she could come up and visit. When we had met in Kathmandu, I had told her I lived in a house on the beach "just south of Montecito," which sounded better than "just north of Oxnard." The "house" had only one bedroom, and the shower was outside, and the walls were a single layer of plywood nailed between posts buried in the sand.

But it was on the beach, in the same colony of houses where Yvon and his wife, Malinda, lived. Yvon had torn down his shack to build a real house, and during construction his family was living in their log house in Jackson, Wyoming. When Yvon was in California to work at Patagonia and its sister company, Chouinard Equipment, he stayed with me, sleeping on the sand in front of my shack. That summer I had another houseguest, a Japanese climber named Naoe, who was a sales rep for Yvon's climbing hardware business. Naoe was also sleeping on the sand.

"It might be easier if you fly up," I told Jennifer. "I can pick you up at the Oxnard Airport."

I told Yvon and Naoe that a woman named Jennifer who I had met in Kathmandu was coming to visit. I was going to put her in the bedroom, and I would sleep with the boys on the beach.

"Great," Yvon said. "We can take her out to dinner. I know a sushi place in Oxnard that has fresh sea urchins."

It never occurred to me that Jennifer might find it odd that I had my two climbing buddies with me to pick her up. Oxnard was a small regional airport, and when we got there the agent said the flight was cancelled and they were driving everyone up in a bus. It was happy hour at The Red Baron—the airport bar— so Naoe, Yvon, and I took advantage of the dollar margaritas. When the bus arrived, we wandered out of the bar and stood in a line to greet Jennifer. She was still wearing her runway dress and heels that made her look six feet tall. I am only five foot five, and Yvon is a little shorter than me, and Naoe, a little shorter than both of us. She would tell me later that her first thought was that she was being met by three drunk dwarfs.

I opened the passenger door of Yvon's old Toyota station wagon as Jennifer, careful with her dress, got in. There were oily

Nicholas grooming with his pocket rescue mirror, preparing for the day's stage on our trek to Everest Base Camp. **Rick Ridgeway**

parts from the machine shop in the back, but we had cleared out the front seat. She would tell me later that her second thought was that her dress had to be worth at least four times as much as Yvon's car.

This was 1981, and though the sushi craze was getting off the ground in California, it did not yet encompass, as acceptable fare, raw sea urchins. That is all we ordered, however, and Yvon, Naoe, and I, now switched to tall Kirins, consumed piece after piece of what Yvon told Jennifer were the sex glands of the sea urchin.

When we arrived at the shack, the three of us proudly showed Jennifer her room. She thanked us, and then retrieved from

her Hartmann suitcase a bottle of Mumm Champagne in an
insulated sock and two carefully wrapped Waterford cut-crystal
champagne flutes.

"I brought this for you," she said.

"Wonderful," I said. "Thank you so much. I've got two more
wineglasses. Enough for everybody!"

* * *

The next day I drove Jennifer to the Los Angeles airport. She
asked me if I had decided whether or not to return to climbing.
I told her that I was going rock climbing with Yvon in Wyoming
later in the summer and explained that rock climbing was not
as dangerous as mountaineering, especially high-altitude mountaineering. I confessed I was struggling with the decision, but
I didn't tell her that part of the struggle was because climbing
mountains was *the* main thing I did. It was not only the way
I defined myself, it was also the way I imagined others thought
about me. I knew intellectually it would be wiser to use other
personal attributes to define who I was, but I knew emotion-
ally that when you get really good at something because you've
dedicated so much of yourself to it, it's really hard to turn your
back on it. Especially when you are just entering your thirties, and especially when it's a sport that takes time to develop
not so much the physical skills but the mental discipline, and
consequently a sport whose best practitioners most often reach
the top of their game only when they are well into their thirties.

I dropped Jennifer off at the airport and told her I promised
to stay in touch, and she said the same. A month later I went to
Jackson to join Yvon and his family. We were on a rock climb in
the Tetons when he said, "Whatever happened to that girl who
visited us, Jennifer?"

"I think she's back in New York."

"You have her number?"

"Yeah."

"Call her up and invite her out."

Jennifer arrived two days later. Yvon loaned me his car, and this time I was alone when I picked her up at the airport. She was in jeans, just like when I first saw her in the elevator at the Yak & Yeti. She had her two Hartmann suitcases, a large and a small one. I wasn't sure if she traveled with a lot of stuff, or if she was just prepared to stay a while. At Yvon's house, I showed her to the guest room. It was called the Jeffers Room because it had a single iron-frame bed that, years before, a friend of Yvon's had stolen out of an abandoned cabin in Big Sur that had belonged to the poet Robinson Jeffers. The friend gave the bed to Yvon, and he kept it because Jeffers was one of Yvon's favorite poets and Jeffers had written many of his poems in the cabin, and one of them was on the wall of the guest room.

I set her suitcase on the chair in the small room with its small bed and its big window looking across an open meadow past the forest to the Grand Teton. My bag also was in the room; I had been staying there. I wasn't sure what to say, but Jennifer was gentle with me and I was gentle with her. I think we sensed our mutual fragility.

That night, with moonlight on the peaks, I lay in bed having no way then of knowing for sure that I was holding the woman with whom I would spend the rest of my life. But I was thankful that I was holding her in the bed in which Robinson Jeffers had slept in the cabin where he had written some of his poems that had guided me like beacons, including the one in a frame on the wall next to the bed:

> *I entered the life of the brown forest*
> *And the great life of the ancient peaks,*
> *The patience of stone.*
>
> *I felt the changes in the veins*
> *In the throat of the mountain,*
> *And I was the stream draining the wood*
> *And I was the stag drinking*

And I was the stars, boiling with light, wandering alone
Each one lord of his own summit

And I was the darkness outside the stars, I included them,
They were part of me.

I was mankind also, a moving lichen on the cheek of
a round stone
They have not made words for it,
To go beyond things
Beyond hours and ages

And be all things in all time . . .

I would find out in the years ahead just how much Jennifer believed in omens.

* * *

Three weeks later Jennifer came to visit, staying with me in my surfer's shack. In the morning, still wearing her ivory-colored silk nightie, she went to the open kitchen to make our breakfast. I heard an "Ohh!" that I assumed was her reaction to one of the mice that lived under the cabinets, but walking into the room I saw her arms spread open in what appeared to be delight.

"Everything okay?"

"I opened the espresso coffee and the smell just burst out!" she exclaimed, waving both hands excitedly.

Two days later we flew to Seattle to join Jim Whittaker on a cruise on his sailboat on Puget Sound. When I mentioned the invitation to Jennifer, I assumed that she might decline because I knew she had not been on a boat since the sailing accident that had killed her husband and her unborn child. She said she felt ready.

It was a two-day voyage. It was mid-September, and the days were cloudless and warm, and we wore T-shirts. The breeze was light, but the spinnaker was full, and off the starboard beam we could see Mount Constance in the Olympics, and there was a ray of sunlight reflecting off the east-facing snow. We sat next to each other, our shoulders touching and our backs against the mast. A Bonaparte's gull flew by and I wondered if it was as content as I was.

"Today is the anniversary of my accident," Jennifer said. "It was two years ago today."

"Are you OK? I mean, being back on a boat?"

"I am. In fact, I'm happy, even joyful. For the first time since the accident."

"I'm the same. For the first time too, since the avalanche."

A month later I asked Jennifer if she would marry me, and she accepted. She moved into the beach shack, tidying it up to an extent I never imagined possible. She seemed to accept the outdoor shower after I built a shoulder-high enclosure around it, although there was an awkward moment with a UPS delivery-man. She had never imagined herself in the life she was now living, and I had surprised myself, always assuming that if I ever married it would most likely be to someone who also was "an outdoor person."

"I'm happy to go with you on your trips," Jennifer had offered. "But only to the last hotel, as long as it has room service."

We married on Valentine's Day in 1982 at the Biltmore Hotel in Santa Barbara. Her parents were there, beaming with pride and relief their daughter had found her way again, even if they were baffled by this tribe of climbers and surfers, some of whom were scaling the walls of the hotel to get better camera angles. Yvon was best man, and Nicholas, this time in a pink tuxedo, had applied an extra layer of makeup for the occasion.

Jennifer had worked most of her life in the apparel sector, starting when she was a teenager growing up in Portland modeling swimwear for Jantzen. Yvon had introduced her to Kris McDivitt, Patagonia's CEO, and soon Jennifer had a full-time

I proposed to Jennifer two months after I got to know her, she scheduled the wedding for four months later, and we had our first child eight months after we married. As the ceremony commenced, Yvon Chouinard, my best man, leaned in to me and whispered, "There's a rumor circulating the bride is with child." **Dianne Roberts**

job in what was called the company's Creative Services department, a fledgling in-house advertising agency. Jennifer also had a new friend: Kris was one of Jennifer's bridesmaids. That fall we had our first daughter, Carissa, and Kris was with us in the delivery room.

Shortly after we married, Jennifer's father, whom she was very close to, died unexpectedly, and her mother moved in with us, to help care for Carissa, just as Carissa—and later our additional two children, Cameron and Connor—gave her new purpose. My wife's mother would live with us for the next twenty-five years, and she and I became like mother and son, and we never once had a cross word between us.

I continued to work in film, photography, and writing, focusing on subjects that had to do with adventure; my business card said, "Adventure Capitalist." My work required frequent travel, and even with Jennifer's mother helping care for Carissa, that was an added burden on Jennifer that we sought to balance as best we could. A few months after our wedding, I was invited to join two businessmen, Frank Wells and Dick Bass on a mountaineering trip they were planning. They had a dream to take a year off from their professional lives and, even though they didn't have much mountaineering experience, see if they could become the first to climb the highest mountain on each of the seven continents.

"It would mean going back to the high mountains," I told Jennifer. "I'm not sure I should do that, especially now that we have a family. It's too risky."

"But it might be more risky *not* to go."

"More risky?"

"Maybe more loss. *Not* staying true to who you are. *Not* getting to know Frank and Dick."

"I've only met Dick once, but I'm getting to know Frank. He might become a good friend."

"You need to stay open to getting to know new people. You never know where that can lead you."

It was the first of many instances in the years ahead that would confirm for me the adage that two parts can be bigger than their sum, even if the parts were so different. She was the urbane sophisticate and I was the outdoor pragmatist. After we had children, she introduced them to museums and art, and I took them camping and hiking. Yet we had in common our mutual experiences when we had nearly died, and when those we had loved or been close to had died, and we built our marriage on that.

We both loved books and poetry, and shortly after we were married she found my copy of *The Little Prince* and said it was one of her favorite books, and she asked me to read it to her. I got to the part where Saint-Exupéry is trying to fix his airplane, and the Little Prince keeps interrupting him to talk about flowers, specifically about why some flowers have thorns. Saint-Exupéry loses patience and says, "Can't you see I am very busy with Matters of Consequence!" The Little Prince is shocked. "Matters of Consequence?" Saint-Exupéry looks at the hammer in his hand, at his greasy fingers, at his broken airplane, and the Little Prince says, "You mix everything up. You confuse everything!"

"Can you read that part again?" Jennifer asked.

That became our shorthand. Accepting Dick and Frank's proposal to join them in trying to climb the highest mountain on every continent *was* a matter of consequence. Then there was the time shortly after we married when we were standing in line at the airport and the guy in front of us was yelling at the clerk because his flight was delayed and Jennifer turned to me and said, "Does that seem like a matter of consequence?" And we both started laughing.

My copy of *The Little Prince* that I read to Jennifer and later gave to her with an inscription from me.

The Boldest Dream

My involvement in what eventually would be called the Seven Summits started when I received a letter with the embossed logo of Warner Brothers and under that "Frank Wells, President." Frank explained how he and a friend, Dick Bass, an oil-and-gas man from Texas who also owned the Snowbird ski resort in Utah, wanted to climb the highest mountain on each continent. He said that no one had ever climbed all seven mountains, adding that the logistics—especially getting to Vinson Massif, the highest point in Antarctica—were likely to be as daunting as the climbs. Frank had learned I'd been to Antarctica. Would I be willing to meet?

After talking to Jennifer, I wrote back proposing that I also invite Mike Hoover to the meeting. After I had become Hoover's filmmaking apprentice, I had helped make the television show about our ascent of the rock spire in the Amazon, and then I had gone on to join him filming other adventures including, in 1979, a two-month climbing and skiing exploration to Antarctica. Mike was as informed as anyone on the challenges of getting to the frozen continent, including the remote interior where Vinson was located.

When I arrived at the Warner Brothers gate in my rusting Fiat station wagon, the guard directed me to a parking area adjacent to a small, palm-lined street behind the original building, now headquarters for the studio's senior executives. I circled the parking area, but all the spots were taken. Back

Dick Bass (left) and Frank Wells, neophyte mountaineers who were an odd-couple partnership that nevertheless would make mountaineering history. **Rick Ridgeway**

on the narrow street there was an empty space, but the name on the curb said "Clint Eastwood." I decided to take a chance. I was gathering my maps off the passenger seat when there was a knock on my driver's-side window. It was Clint. In the rearview mirror I could see his Mercedes 500SL. I rolled down the window. He looked directly at me, eyes narrowed. The only thing missing was the straight-rimmed cowboy hat.

"I think you've got my parking place."

"Sorry, Mr. Eastwood. The lot was full."

Then, playing my trump card, I added, "I'm late for a meeting with Frank Wells."

"Tell him I said hi."

So much for the trump card. After the delay finding another space I was in a real rush. My flip-flops slapped on the stairs as I made my way past photos of Bette Davis, John Barrymore, and Errol Flynn to Frank's second-floor office.

"Thank you so much for coming," he said, pumping my hand. There were a dozen people in his large office huddled over a table covered with what looked like storyboards for the next *Superman* sequel.

"OK, meeting's over," Frank said, addressing the others. "I've got some important business."

He was tall, with an angled face and a wide grin showing a line of perfectly shaped white teeth with a small gap that seemed to add to rather than detract from his rugged appearance. My first impression was that he and Clint would make a good pair. I unrolled my maps and was reviewing the expedition I had been on to Antarctica when Mike Hoover arrived. He and Frank were about the same height—about six foot four—and stood eye-to-eye as they shook hands. I had the same thought about Hoover fitting in well with Eastwood, although I knew he and Eastwood were already friends, having met on *The Eiger Sanction*, for which Hoover had worked on the second unit.

"You have much experience climbing," Hoover said. It was both question and demand, which was typical of Hoover's style, more appropriate to directing armies than small climbing expeditions.

"I climbed Kilimanjaro when I was in college," Frank replied.

"That's it?"

"I plan to take some lessons."

"You probably don't have a chance. Especially on Everest."

"I'm in pretty good shape. I play tennis every weekend, and I'm starting to jog."

"How many push-ups can you do?"

"Push-ups?"

"Get down on the floor. Give me twenty."

To my surprise, Frank took off his coat and got down on the Persian carpet. I could see from his grin that he was more amused than affronted, and although he struggled, he finally made twenty push-ups. I could see that Hoover appreciated Frank's moxie. We turned back to the maps.

"Our trip was mostly along the coast," Hoover explained, indicating the Antarctic Peninsula. "Vinson is inland here, just a little over seven hundred miles from the pole. Logistically, that's *way* more difficult."

* * *

Frank Wells and his partner Dick Bass invited me to come along as guide on any of the seven expeditions. They planned to pack them all into 1983. At the time, Jennifer was pregnant with our first daughter, and after she convinced me to accept Frank and Dick's offer and return to mountaineering, we also decided I shouldn't go on all seven trips, but only on those that would best support Frank and Dick's goals while at the same time contributing to my goals of supporting my family and, as Jennifer had pointed out, fulfilling my own passion for explora-tion "so I could be true to myself."

We decided I should go on the first expedition, to Aconcagua, the highest peak in South America, because it would be a chance to get to know Frank and Dick, and it would take only about three weeks. And that I should also go on the last climb, to Vinson Massif, the highest mountain in Antarctica, because it would be the best adventure, and I could help Frank and Dick with logistics. Then there was Everest. Frank and Dick were in discussions with one of the networks about doing a television special just on that climb, with the idea of attempting to make the first live video transmis-sion from the summit. Jennifer suggested I should go on that trip if I could get the job directing the film, and if I would promise not to go too high on the mountain or do anything too dangerous.

"What if I don't go any higher than eight thousand meters?"

"That sounds reasonable."

I would later learn Jennifer didn't know the metric system, but by then Frank and Dick had accepted my proposal to go with

Yvon Chouinard gives ice-climbing tips to Dick Bass as Dick
scales a sérac at the base of Aconcagua. **Rick Ridgeway**

them to Aconcagua and Vinson, and I had got the position as
field producer and director of the television show of the Everest
expedition. Still, we both felt that I would be at home between
the trips long enough to keep a balance between my adventures
and my family. Then another project I had in development, to
film the first direct coast-to-coast crossing of Borneo, got a green
light, and balance quickly shifted to unbalance, as it would be
a trip nearly two months in length that I would have to squeeze
between Everest and Vinson. Then I had an idea. I needed two
weeks in Indonesia to arrange logistics for the Borneo crossing.
What if Jennifer and our baby daughter came to Kathmandu
and joined me after the Everest climb? We could then go to

Indonesia and be together while I did the planning. Jennifer was uncertain, but I told her that after we got home I would still have a full month before I left again for Borneo, and with the two weeks together in Asia, maybe we could still preserve the balance between my work life and family life.

* * *

Most days, as planning for the climbing expeditions progressed, Frank and I had at least one telephone conversation.

"I need to print stationery," he said on one of our calls. "But before I can do that, we need a name."

"For the expeditions?"

"For the whole project."

"Have any ideas?"

"What do you think about Seven Summits?" he asked.

"Maybe."

"Seven continents. Seven climbs. Seven summits."

"It *is* catchy, the way it rolls off your tongue."

"That's it then. We're calling ourselves Seven Summits," he concluded.

Neither of us had any notion Frank had just coined a phrase that would enter the lexicon of mountaineering, become the lodestar for hundreds of overachievers, and even become a category listing in the *Guinness Book of Records*.

As I helped him plan the trips, I asked Frank if I could invite two friends, Yvon Chouinard and Dan Emmett, to join the expedition to Aconcagua. Frank quickly agreed, saying he was looking forward to getting to know both of them. I had explained to Frank that Dan was one of the three friends who had been Harvard classmates and had obtained the permit to climb Everest and had accepted my climbing partner Chris Chandler's suggestion to invite me to join the expedition.

Dan operated a real estate company in Los Angeles that he would go on to build into the biggest residential brokerage in Southern California. He was a successful businessman who had figured out how to go on adventures with his buddies and still be a dutiful husband to his wife and father to his two children. I was sufficiently clear-eyed to know that Dan's success as a businessman and a family man was not always easy. I picked up on the occasional tense word or sigh from his wife, but I also picked up on how they were a team, figuring it out.

Over the decades, from my position as a family friend, I watched from the sidelines how Dan and his wife raised a family that eventually grew to four kids, and how those kids as adults had fulfilling careers while remaining loyal to their passions and steadfast to their husbands or wives and their own children, and I knew that that outcome was not just circumstance.

After the Everest climb, Dan helped me figure out how to buy my fisherman's shack on the beach when the only money I had was a small advance from my book about the K2 climb. After the owner of the shack accepted the offer Dan had drafted—including a down payment that precisely equaled my book advance—Dan had helped me develop an outdoor marketing consultancy so I could earn enough money to make payments on the balance that the owner, also at Dan's suggestion, agreed to carry. Dan had then given me advice on how best to succeed in my new job as a consultant.

"There's nothing mysterious about it. You show up first, you leave last, and you make yourself invaluable as fast as you can."

When I met Jennifer, and inevitably had to look inward to ask myself if I was ready to get married, Dan was there again as my mentor, this time not by offering specific advice but by being an example of how to do it.

* * *

On the Aconcagua climb, I was looking forward to spending more time with Dan and also getting to know Dick Bass. In January, at the height of the austral summer, we started the three-day walk to Base Camp. On the second day we stopped for lunch in the shadow of a singular rock emerging out of a sandy expanse.

"Y'all look like you're in a natural theater in the open," Dick said. "How about I lay a poem on ya?"

By then I knew Dick enough to know that, like Frank, he was also gregarious and hardworking. Like Frank, he was in his early fifties, but in other regards, the two were opposites. Dick was the conservative Republican, Frank the liberal Democrat. Dick was the inveterate optimist, Frank the vigilant strategist.

Dick was also a romanticist, a part of his personality that Frank—like all of us—relished. That included a passion for popular poetry, something that Dick had told us he got from his third-grade teacher, who inspired him to memorize poems.

"How about 'The Men That Don't Fit In'?"

"Let's hear it!"

Dick stood in front of us like a preacher and, arms gesticulating, recited from memory the poem by Robert Service.

> *There's a race of men that don't fit in,*
> *A race that can't stay still;*
> *So they break the hearts of kith and kin,*
> *And they roam the world at will.*
> *They range the field and they rove the flood,*
> *And they climb the mountain's crest;*
> *Theirs is the curse of the gypsy blood,*
> *And they don't know how to rest.*

The regular route on Aconcagua is what climbers call a walk-up, but even then, at nearly 23,000 feet, we went slowly, to acclimatize. At Base Camp, Yvon stressed that in addition to taking time to allow our bodies to adjust, we should also go as light as possible.

"But we can't leave the Budweiser," Dick said.

"Budweiser?"

"I got two six-packs, to drink on the summit. We're gonna have a little party, and film it. Budweiser said they may do a commercial on us. That's how we're gonna pay for this extravaganza."

We compromised by agreeing to take only one six-pack, which Dick volunteered to carry. Even then, on our first attempt at the summit, several of us—myself included—had bad headaches and were nauseous. Faced with a section of the climb just below the summit called the Canaleta, which looked like it would be best done with crampons and ice axes—both of which we had left in camp when Yvon insisted we didn't need to carry the weight—we returned to our upper camp.

"That's it for me," Dan said in a tone that reflected his preternatural optimism. We knew Dan's wife was expecting their third child, and that Dan had set himself a date when he would head down to be home in case of an early delivery. The next day he turned and waved cheerfully as he headed down-valley.

We spent the rest of the day resting and acclimatizing, then got up early to give it another shot. I was the last in line, with Frank just ahead of me. We were moving slowly but steadily as we neared the summit.

"Five more steps," I said.

Frank reached the top, and Dick grabbed him in a bear hug. Frank, breathing heavily, slumped next to a cross that marked the summit. After a few seconds he looked at Dick and then held his hands over his ears as if his head might explode.

"You mean I made it?"

"I'm telling you, Pancho," Dick said with his wide Texan grin, using the nickname he had bestowed on Frank, "this is the beginning of a streak. We're going to knock 'em *all* off!"

Frank and Dick had hired a cameraman to come with them to film all seven climbs. Dick told him to start the camera, and then he pulled a can of Budweiser from its six-pack ring.

"Frank, this Bud's for you!"

Dick popped the top. Nothing.

He reached for another can and popped the top. Nothing. All six cans were frozen.

"So much for the Bud idea," Dick said. "Pancho, we got any other sponsors?"

I'm interviewing Dick and Frank at Camp II on Everest, at 21,000
feet, as part of my dual role as producer and on-camera color
commentator for the ABC television show. **Peter Pilafian**

Frank shook his head, and now he, too, had a wide grin. Arm
in arm, he and Dick gazed at the view, knowing nothing around
them was as high as they were.

"*Aah-eah-eaahhh!*" Dick yelled, giving his trademark
Tarzan call.

* * *

Two months later I was in Everest Base Camp with Frank
and Dick. This time the climbers were nearly all from the Pacific
Northwest, and some worked for the guide service on Mount
Rainier. Even though Frank and Dick were paying for the expedition, they were sensitive about being seen as "buying their

way up the mountain," and had ceded decision making to the expedition leader, who was a head guide with the service. I wasn't there as a guide, but rather as the director of an ABC television film documenting the climb.

In the early 1980s, guided ascents of Everest were still a novelty, and the climbers themselves had to secure a route through the Khumbu Icefall, just as we had done seven years earlier on the American Bicentennial Everest Expedition. Frank and Dick had been passing the days in Base Camp, waiting until the route was fixed, but Dick was getting antsy.

"I'm gonna get some exercise," Dick announced. "Gonna go on a hike. Down to Namche. Visit with the trekkers, meet some folks."

"You can't do that," Frank replied. "That's going the wrong way. We're supposed to be gaining altitude, not losing it. You've got to have respect. This is *Everest!*"

"Frank, you're always courtin' trouble by anticipatin' it. That's 'cause you're a lawyer. Trained to look at all the negatives. This is a mountain, not a courtroom. I'm just gonna take the problems as they come. Since there's no problems at the time bein', I'm gonna head down-valley and get some leg stretchin', do some sight seein'."

After lunch Dick loaded his backpack and left. As we watched him disappear down-glacier, Frank said, "What bugs me most is that he's probably right. He *will* come back and just march up the mountain to the summit." Frank paused, then looked at me with a wide grin across his whisker-stubbled face. "Doncha just love it?" he added.

Dick returned a week later, and the ropes and ladders saw him through the icefall and the route established through the Western Cwm. Dick, carrying a forty-five-pound pack, marched up the mountain to Camp II at 21,300 feet. It was now time for the expedition leader to select teams, and Frank was disappointed when Dick was told he would be in the third attempt and Frank, who was slower and weaker, in the fourth push.

Frank told the expedition leader he thought Dick should be on the second team, but the leader responded that neither of them was strong enough, and it was his responsibility to the team and to the television network to put two strong teams back-to-back, so at least one of them would get to the top.

"I agree with my partner that we've earned a spot on the second team," Dick said. "But I'm perfectly happy on the third team because I'm confident I'm going to make it no matter where I fall in line."

"Goddammit, Dick," Frank replied, "if you weren't so unselfish, you'd be easier to deal with."

The rest of us smiled at what we were calling "The Frank and Dick Show." Over the next week, while Frank and Dick waited in the lower camps, the first two teams reached the summit, including a cameraman of emerging talent named David Breashears, who was also a super-strong climber. David carried a video camera and battery pack to the summit and attached it to a small microwave transmitter. While the Sherpa helped him to point the transmitter toward a relay dish positioned on a hilltop above Namche Bazaar, David turned on the camera and videoed the other climbers as they made their last footsteps to the summit. It was the first live coverage in history from the top of Everest.

Then it was Dick's turn. With the expedition doctor, a Nepalese climber, and three Sherpas, they left to make their summit bid. It was mid-May, and the weather looked stable. Dick felt strong when he reached the South Col camp at 26,200 feet. He crawled into his tent, and his mates started the stove to melt snow; they planned to leave in the early morning.

Their luck held: there were no clouds in the predawn starry sky. By first light they were high enough to see the giants of the Earth below them: Lhotse, Makalu, Kanchenjunga, Cho Oyu. There was no wind, no clouds. Everything promised a perfect summit day. They stopped to rest, and the doctor, last on the second rope, arrived and sat down.

Dick Bass getting ready for his summit bid. We ribbed Dick about all the stuff he carried in his pack, but he returned our teases with relish whenever anyone asked him to use or borrow something they had failed to pack. **Rick Ridgeway**

"How you feelin'?" the doctor asked.

"Tired, but all right."

Dick took in the view, and then noticed something out of place about thirty feet away. It was faded orange and red.

"What's that?"

It was the freeze-dried body of a German climber who had bivouacked and died while descending four years before. Dick tried to force from his mind these "negative thoughts." They were now above 27,000 feet. The snow deepened and their pace slowed. He had his oxygen set at a low flow to conserve precious gas for the summit, but he still felt good. They climbed for another hour, making a slow but steady pace to 28,000 feet.

"This is as far as I go," the doctor said.

"What are you talking about?" Dick replied incredulously.

"I'm worried if we try to push on, we might get stuck on the way down, in the dark."

"But we're so close."

Dick was unable to persuade the doctor to keep going. The Sherpas were also reluctant. For a moment he considered going on alone, then he recalled the body of the German climber.

"OK. Let's go down."

* * *

Neither Frank nor Dick reached the summit of Everest, but they didn't pause before leaving for the next climbs on the list: Denali, Elbrus, and Kilimanjaro. Meanwhile, as planned, I rendezvoused in Kathmandu with Jennifer and our infant daughter. Carissa was then eight months old, and it was a challenge for Jennifer schlepping the travel crib, folding stroller, and three expedition-sized duffel bags of diapers. With Carissa in our arms, we sat in the same chairs in the lobby bar of the Yak & Yeti where we had sat when we met each other only two years before. It seemed much longer than that. We ordered gin and tonics and toasted our marriage.

In Indonesia, I spent a week arranging permits and chartering small planes to make caches of gear in remote villages of the Dayak, the indigenous peoples of central Borneo. During mornings and evenings, I spent time with Jennifer and Carissa. Jennifer was still uncertain whether I was making the right decision: the Borneo trip, added to the three expeditions of the Seven Summits climbs I was joining, meant I would be gone nine months of the first full year of our marriage. At least compared to the climbs, Borneo would be less risky. There would be one section of whitewater on a little-known river that had never been descended, but I told Jennifer that if the rapids were severe, I promised we would portage around them.

"Other than that, there's not too much that could go wrong."

Jungle Fever

Hour by hour, as we motored our dugouts upriver, the canopy of the jungle that arched over the narrowing tributary grew closer and closer.

"There!" Slade called. "Those two branches, they've touched!"

The canopy continued to enshroud the river and close out the sky, and I recited to myself the passage from *Heart of Darkness* that I had put to memory years before:

> *Going up that river was like travelling back to the earliest beginnings of the world, when vegetation rioted on the earth and the big trees were kings. An empty stream, a great silence, an impenetrable forest . . . and this stillness . . . the stillness of an implacable force brooding over an inscrutable intention.*

There were four of us on the expedition team, plus two more on the film crew. Our goal was to make the first coast-to-coast crossing of Borneo along a route that bisected the third-largest island in the world at its widest point. The traverse, crossing and recrossing the equator, was 800 miles as the hornbill flew, but, accounting for the oxbows, the on-the-ground distance was twice that long.

Jim Slade sat in front of me in the dugout. Before the expedition, I had known Jim only by reputation as one of the world's

John "Largo" Long (left) and Jim Slade poling their dugout upriver
and into the heart of darkness. Rick Ridgeway Collection

foremost river guides, having made first descents including
the Zambezi below Victoria Falls. Behind me, Jim "The Bird"
Bridwell and John "Largo" Long sat next to each other. Unlike
Slade, Bridwell and Largo had no white-water experience,
a potential handicap on the final section of our traverse, when
we planned to descend the un-navigated Kayan River, reputed to
have major rapids. I had climbed with both of them, and knew
that, as exemplars of a small band of Yosemite climbers called
"the Hardmen," they were used to tough challenges: they had
made the first-ever one-day ascent of El Capitan, scaling the
3,000-foot monolith in fifteen hours.

   We had departed Pontianak on Borneo's west coast eight days
before, traveling up the Kapuas River in a fifty-foot traditionally

I'm taking my turn at the helm of our charter boat we christened the *Borneo Queen*, as we motor up the Kapuas River. **Rick Ridgeway Collection**

built boat we had chartered. After a week, we left the Kapuas, transferring to two canoes, one for us and the other for our two-man film crew, plus gear. Earlier, we had passed another canoe heading downstream, and its boatman stared at us in such bewilderment he lost balance and fell in the river. At the end of our second day on the tributary we pulled the canoes ashore in a Dayak village called Tanjung Lokang. The Dayak are tribal peoples of the interior of Borneo who were notorious as headhunters who kept their trophies in the rafters of their longhouses. They had abandoned headhunting long ago, along with their bark clothing, trading the latter for T-shirts and cotton shorts, but they still covered their bodies in tattoos that extended to the tops of their necks.

This was the end of our initial river travel, and the Dayaks greeted us welcomingly. From here we would hike overland for ten days, crossing a mountain range and descending into the next watershed, which drained the central part of Borneo. Our hike would be through uninhabited jungle, and because we needed to carry food for more than a week—as well as camera gear—we wanted to hire a few of the Dayak as porters.

There was an American missionary who lived with his family in Tanjung Lokang, and he helped us negotiate an agreement with the village chief. The chief said he wanted to come along, and the missionary volunteered his teenage son to accompany us as translator. The teenager was eager and did not need coaxing. We divided our gear into porter loads, and the villagers who were coming with us all seemed excited.

On the evening before our departure the chief threw a party, producing several bottles of local moonshine. Everyone except the missionary's son started drinking. Soon we were all feeling the effects, especially Bridwell, whose personal code was animated by two imperatives: to climb hard and to party hard. I had been around a lot of dirtbags, but Bridwell took it to another level. Though he was not quite forty years old, his skin was already like leather, the result of years in the sun and wind and decades of smoking unfiltered Camels. I had been on day climbs with him, but never an extended expedition. His reputation for toughness was confirmed while we were ascending the Kapuas in our fifty-foot riverboat. One day at lunch he bit into a bone and broke off a piece of his front tooth. I watched as he rummaged through the boat's toolbox, stood in front of a small mirror, and—with one hand raising his lip and the other holding a metal file—smoothed the jagged edges of his broken tooth.

Now, as we were all enjoying the chief's hospitality and were all, save for the missionary's son, increasingly intoxicated, Bridwell announced he wanted a tattoo.

"Just like my brothers!" he said, pointing to the Dayaks.

The missionary's son translated the request to the chief, who broke into a smile, then went to a chest from which he produced a bottle of ink and a short piece of bamboo with four sewing needles tied in a tight bundle protruding perpendicularly from the end.

The chief told Bridwell to take off his shirt and lie on his side on the matted floor.

"Tell the chief I want something special."

The missionary's son translated. I could see the teenager was enjoying the impromptu bacchanalia, and since his father had shown us such gracious hospitality, I was hoping we weren't introducing, like an unwanted virus, any challenge to the father's inculcation of God.

"How about a butterfly?" the boy said excitedly, translating the chief's suggestion.

"Perfect!" Bridwell answered, his speech now slurred.

The chief, sitting cross-legged next to Bridwell, dipped the needles into the inkwell and hammered them into Bridwell's upper arm. The only thing Bridwell said was to bring him more moonshine.

* * *

We traversed the Muller Mountains in ten days, reaching the Mahakam, the next major river that drained central Borneo. The Dayaks and the missionary's son returned to Tanjung Lokang, and we descended the Mahakam River, ascended the Boh River, and then once more trekked overland toward the headwaters of the Kayan, the final river that would take us to the east coast of the island.

I started to feel sick, like I was catching the flu. In the jungle, getting sick is always worrisome; you never know at the outset if it's serious. Whatever I had, it was getting worse, and I had to stop frequently and wait until my nausea passed. When I began to sweat more than usual, the others divided the contents of my pack. We had expected to reach a village before nightfall,

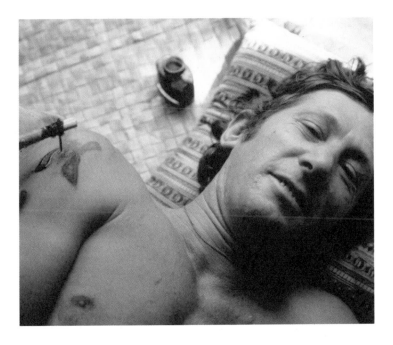

Jim "The Bird" Bridwell's tattoo predated by about three decades the resurgent popularity of body art. For decades Jim regarded the tattoo as a cool remembrance of his adventure in Borneo, even as his wife held a differing opinion. **Rick Ridgeway**

but I was getting increasingly dizzy and my pace slowed. At dusk, we reached a clearing that had recently been slashed and burned; the trunks of the big trees were scattered across an opening whose floor was still smoldering. I had to focus on my balance as we walked from one log to the next, feeling even more woozy in the furnace-hot air that wafted up from the coals below me.

I reached the other side, but with my slow pace it would be at least an hour before we reached the village.

"We know you can do it, Rick."

I went from being overheated to chilled. I put on my long-sleeved shirt and tried to focus on each step. It was like summit day on K2 without oxygen, and I told myself that if I could do that, I could do this. I conjured an image of my wife and daughter, and that worked. We entered the village an hour after dark.

The village was a single longhouse a hundred yards in length that sheltered thirty families. The chief took my arm and escorted me to his room, where I lay on a plaited mat and several women in sarongs took turns applying damp cloths to my forehead. I vomited throughout the night, unsure whether I was awake or asleep. In the morning my teammates learned that the village had an adjacent airstrip where a missionary plane landed once a week. That was the good news; the bad news was the missionary had been there just a couple of days before. Two hours later, however, I heard the drone of a single-engine plane, and soon Slade came into my room to tell me the missionary had been diverted by a squall and landed, intending to stay only until the rain cloud passed. The missionary had agreed to evacuate me.

Slade and the others supported me as I tried to walk to the Cessna. My shirt was soiled with vomit, and the missionary, who was also the pilot, told me to take it off. He rummaged in the back of the plane and found a spare T-shirt. I put it on. Across the front it said, "God Is My Co-Pilot."

* * *

I was too sick to sit in a seat, so they put me in the back of the plane. I was thankful for the cool aluminum floor against my skin. We took off and soon landed again, and the missionary said we were in another village and he would be back in an hour. I tried not to puke. We took off again and the missionary said we were heading to the coastal town of Tarakan, where he lived, and I could stay at his house.

His wife met us at the small airport, but I was too weak to walk. The missionary found someone to help, and they carried me to the car. I was curled into a fetal position, unable to straighten out. At their house, the missionary and his wife struggled to get me to the downstairs laundry room, where there was a mattress on the floor. The missionary's wife brought me water, but I was unable to keep it down. They told me it was Sunday, and the only clinic with a good doctor was closed.

"I'm flying to Samarinda tomorrow morning," the missionary said. "There's a German doctor there who is very good. I'll take you to his clinic."

They said they were going to the Sunday market with their two children, and they would be back in two hours. I lay on the mattress, and suddenly I was convulsed with nausea and stomach cramps. I crawled to the toilet and vomited while at the same time evacuating my bowels. The room was swirling. I crawled back to the mattress, thinking that I might die before I could get to a doctor. I survived the avalanche; I had lived while Jonathan had died, but now I might die too, leaving my wife and daughter behind just as Jonathan had left his.

I made it to the mattress that thankfully was on the floor. I closed my eyes, and suddenly, as though transported by magic, I was in Europe—in Vienna, in the early nineteenth century. I was in an ornate ballroom, dressed in knee britches, a silk shirt with ruffled collar, and a waistcoat, and on my head wore a powdered white wig. I was in a line of men dressed the same, and across from us was a line of women wearing embroidered dresses that widened like ornate cones from their improbably narrow waists. A full orchestra played a waltz, and together the men danced to the women, and we each selected our partners. I chose a beautiful woman and, holding her waist, twirled across the palace floor with her. Then I realized I had the ability to zoom my vision. I focused on her dress just below her exposed bosom, and my vision magnified until I could see the warp and weft of the threads of her gown, and then the threads themselves, each with thin hairs texturing its surface. Then I zoomed out until I could see the woman, but now her beautiful face had metamorphosed into a monstrous gargoyle with nostrils that exhaled red steam. In a panic I opened my eyes, and the hallucination stopped.

I regained my breath and closed my eyes, but another hallucination started. I tried to stay awake but must have fallen asleep, as I have no memory of what happened next—not until later the next day.

* * *

The call of the muezzin entered my consciousness, the tinny Arabic song like an echo from another land in another time in another life.

"My clinic is next to a mosque," the German doctor said. "There's a dozen of them in the city now, and they're all competing. This one just got a new loudspeaker."

"I didn't know if I was dreaming."

"How are you feeling?"

"The nausea's gone."

"Dextrose I.V. with Compazine. You were very dehydrated when you arrived, with a temperature of a hundred and five."

"Do you know what I have?"

"I've sent blood and stool samples to the lab. Probably typhoid. There's a new strain here in Kalimantan that's immune to immunizations. And it's virulent."

With each drip of the I.V., I sensed an incremental increase in strength. Still, my muscles burned as though they were on fire; the German doctor said that was from the lactic acid concentrated in my muscles from the dehydration. Two days later I was able to stand, but could only take two steps before the burning was so intense that I had to sit back down. Four days later I could walk across the clinic. The missionary pilot picked me up and took me back to Tarakan, to another missionary family who had volunteered to house me while I continued my recovery.

Two weeks later the missionary and his family drove me to a dock looking across the delta where the Kayan River emptied into the ocean. It still took some effort to walk the distance to the end of the dock. I was thin, and so was my hair: much of it had fallen out, and I looked like a cancer patient. At the end of the dock, I could see a motorized longboat approaching. It tied off at the dock, and my teammates got out and we hugged each other. They had made it, and so had I.

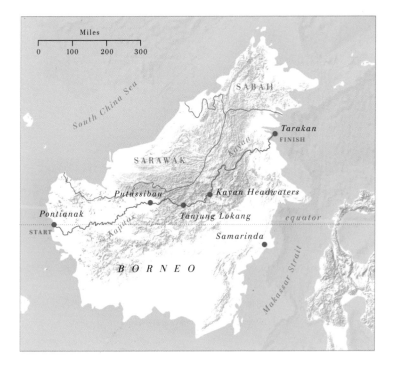

Our route from west to east across the world's third-largest island, more or less on the equator.

Difficulties Are Just Things to Overcome

We knew from the beginning that Vinson Massif, at least from a logistics perspective, was going to be the hardest of the seven summits. No privately organized expedition had been to the interior of Antarctica. Frank Wells was in charge of logistics, and through a contact at the National Science Foundation—which manages the US Antarctic bases—he inquired about chartering one of their ski-equipped C-130 aircraft but was turned down. It was a setback, but Frank was undaunted.

He continued to call every lead he could find, and soon learned about a DC-3 owned by some airplane enthusiasts who had retrofitted it with turbo-prop engines, including a third one in the nose, as well as skis, so it could fly supplies in the High Arctic. Frank arranged to charter the plane, known as the Tri-Turbo, but the obstacles didn't stop. The plane's owners said the aircraft had to be insured, and Frank found a group of underwriters at Lloyds, but they said the plane had to have an experienced pilot. Frank signed Clay Lacy, one of the greatest pilots in the history of aviation, but Clay dropped out for health reasons. The owners of the plane introduced Frank to a British pilot named Giles Kershaw, who had 5,000 hours of flying time in Antarctica alone. Giles agreed to fly the plane.

The next challenge was how to refuel the plane. The Tri-Turbo didn't have fuel capacity for the round trip, and none of the bases

The Tri-Turbo tied down to ice anchors at the base of Mount Vinson, the highest peak in Antarctica. **Chris Bonington** in Antarctica had extra fuel. The challenge seemed insurmountable. After spending sixty-eight days above 18,000 feet to climb K2, I thought I knew something about tenacity, but Frank simply refused to take any setback as anything other than a challenge that had to have a solution. He made a deal with the Chileans to parachute a dozen fuel drums onto the glacier next to their base on the Antarctic Peninsula. Giles said it would be easy to land there and pump the fuel from the drums into the Tri-Turbo.

"I've been reading about Shackleton," Frank told me, "and I found a quote I like. 'Difficulties are just things to overcome.'"

Another difficulty was money. The Seven Summits Odyssey, as Dick Bass called it, was stretching Frank and Dick's pocketbooks. They worked a deal to share expenses with Yuichiro Miura—known as The Man Who Skied Down Everest—who wanted to ski down the rest of the Seven Summits. British climber Chris Bonington was added to beef up the team's climbing strength.

Giles and some of the crew took off to fly the Tri-Turbo to Chile, while the rest of us flew commercial. In Punta Arenas, our jumping-off point on the Strait of Magellan, Giles gathered us in the fuselage for a safety briefing.

"This is the life raft," he said. "Pull this tab and it inflates. It has a canopy, a few survival rations, but there is a problem. It holds eight and there are eleven of us. If we should go down, stay calm and follow me out the door."

Frank was grinning, but also shaking his head. I could tell he didn't know if Giles was joking or serious. The raft did look small, so I assumed that if we went down we were probably fucked no matter what, but I also knew—as did all of us, including Frank—that we couldn't be in better hands having Giles as pilot.

Frank leaned into my ear and said, "In my business, everyone *pretends* to be characters."

But I could tell Frank was exhausted. By the time we were airborne and passing Cape Horn he was slumped in his seat. A few

Giles Kershaw grew up on a tea plantation in India where he roamed the jungles in his childhood. Attending boarding school in England was like a prison sentence, but he found freedom again in the great ice sheets of Antarctica. **Rick Ridgeway**

hours later a brief opening in the clouds allowed Giles to land on the glacier next to the Chilean base, where we could see our fuel drums on the snow. After refueling the Tri-Turbo, we pitched our tents and slept a few hours, then took off for the interior. The weather cleared, and ahead was a range of three glacier-covered mountains rising near the base of the Antarctic Peninsula.

"The Eternity Mountains," Giles said. "That one is Mount Charity. The other two are Hope and Faith."

We were silent. The sky was cloudless. We reached the great ice cap of the interior, and we were now farther south than any privately funded expedition had ever reached. There was flat ice as far as we could see, and we could see several hundred miles.

"Whenever I fly this route," Giles said, "I think of Lincoln Ellsworth, when he flew across Antarctica following this same route. Faith, Hope, Charity, he was the first to see them. He had some bad weather and had to land three times to wait for it to clear. You see, he had no idea what mountains might be ahead. Even if he could have climbed to thirty thousand feet, he wouldn't have known for sure whether there was a mountain in front of him higher than Everest. Think about that. I mean, really think about that. It was just fifty years ago, but there were still parts of the Earth that were completely unknown."

* * *

Giles circled the landing zone he had selected near the base of Vinson. He gently eased the Tri-Turbo to test the surface, and the plane's skis hit hard against the wind-sculpted sastrugi. He powered the engines and climbed up and circled for another approach. No one said anything as Giles eased the plane down again and the skis again hit hard as they clipped the sastrugi. The Tri-Turbo slowed and stopped, and we cheered.

Everything was going according to Frank's meticulous planning. Over the next four days we established Base Camp at 9,300 feet, then Camp I at 11,500 feet. Frank and Dick were doing a good job hauling their share of food and equipment, but Chris Bonington noticed they weren't sharing all the camp duties.

"You two have come a long way toward developing your climbing skills," Chris said to Frank and Dick, "but to be seasoned mountaineers, there remains one thing. You must learn to cook."

Frank moaned. Chris was apparently unaware of Frank's aversion to cooking, and I smiled as I waited to see how the exchange unfolded.

"Now I don't mind cooking," Dick said, "but Pancho here has told me that because we're paying for this extravaganza, we shouldn't have to cook if we don't feel like it."

"Wait a minute," Frank retorted. "I never said any such thing. We've decided to be equals with the other climbers whether we're paying for it or not."

"But on Denali I was going to offer to cook and you said, 'No, don't tell anyone that or we'll be cookin' from here on.'"

"But I never said I don't have to cook because I'm paying for the trip."

"Not in those exact words, but that's what you meant."

"But it's the crassness of putting it that way."

"Now that's the trouble with you Democrats. Never call a spade a spade. Listen, I'm happy to cook, but if you don't want to, well I'm paying for half of this odyssey and I don't want to be a second-class partner."

While the rest of us smiled at the latest episode of The Frank and Dick Show, our cameraman quietly assembled the stove and started cooking.

The weather held, and we were soon in position for a summit attempt. Leaving high camp in the morning hours, we decided to hold a comfortable pace right to the top—with twenty-four hours of daylight, we didn't have to worry about stopping for dusk. An hour out of high camp Chris said, "This may be the loveliest day of my climbing career."

An hour and a half later our heads were lowered into a brutally cold gale. Frank's nose was soon in the first stages of frostbite, and conditions were continuing to deteriorate. We all agreed we needed to descend to make sure Frank didn't suffer permanent damage.

"But we need to make sure someone gets to the top," Frank countered. "I think Rick and Chris should go on. The rest of us can try later."

"This is your and Dick's expedition," I objected.

"No, it's all of ours. You guys get to the top, we all succeed."

"But it's your Seven Summits. You and Dick need to get to the top."

"We'll have another shot. Now get going."

The others departed, and Chris and I kept climbing. We braced into the worst blasts, with gusts of sixty knots and temperatures of thirty below. My goggles were so iced I had to rely on Chris's fuzzy figure to guide me. At one point, about six hours after his initial judgment on the weather, Chris stopped and yelled above the wind, "These have got to be the worst conditions I've ever climbed in!"

I was sapped of energy. It had been less than three months since I'd had typhoid fever and, dizzy from the altitude, I had to turn back while Chris went on alone to reach the summit.

* * *

That made the expedition a technical success, but it wasn't enough. "We'll just keep trying," Frank said. But on our next bid three days later, we were again turned back by foul weather. We still had food and supplies, and Frank and Dick wanted to hang on. "I've got this thing," Dick said, "that the proverbial third time is usually the one that works the charm."

Frank wanted Dick and me to make the next try because Dick was stronger than he was, and I was feeling better, so the pairing increased the chances of at least one of them making it. There was no wind, but the temperature was forty below, and when we stopped to rest, Dick and I discovered our water bottles were frozen solid. I tried to eat a candy bar, but it was like biting down on steel. As we "rested" we walked around in small circles to keep our toes warm, swinging our arms to centrifuge blood into our fingers.

"Talk of your cold! through the parka's fold it stabbed like a driven nail," Dick said.

"Dan McGrew?" I asked.

"No, Sam McGee," Dick answered, referring to another of his favorite Robert Service poems. "I always enjoyed readin' it, but *livin'* it is something else!"

"I'm getting more worn out from the rest than the climbing," I answered. "Let's keep moving."

As we continued upward, we stamped our feet with each step to force blood into our toes. We constantly switched our ice axes, one hand to the other, as the steel conducted cold through

Frank Wells on our first attempt to reach the summit of Vinson. My wife, Jennifer, who was photo editor at Patagonia, Inc., in 1983, published this shot in one of the early Patagonia catalogs, and in the years that followed Frank would show it to friends as though he had won an Oscar. **Rick Ridgeway**

our double-layer mittens. My goggles fogged and I made the mistake of trying to clear them—they instantly froze, and I had no choice but to go without. We were unroped, as there was no way in such cold to stop and make the belays that would have justified using a rope. Finally, we climbed out of shadow and into sunlight that gave us at least a psychological boost. Dick was behind me, following my footsteps. The slope steepened and I could only hope Dick was focused.

We reached the top of the steep slope and continued up a ridge. Dick stayed about forty feet behind me. Ahead I could see the tip of the ski pole Chris had left on the summit. It was thirty feet away.

I'm on the summit of Vinson, trying to stay warm. Note the frozen eyelashes. Our expedition was only the third time the highest mountain in Antarctica had been climbed. **Rick Ridgeway Collection**

"Dick!"

"Yeah?"

"We've got thirty feet to go before you're standing on the highest point on the coldest continent."

"Are you pullin' my leg?"

I reached the summit and in less than a minute Dick joined me. We bear-hugged, and I wasn't sure if it was for joy or just trying to stay warm. I decided it was for joy because I had tears in my eyes.

"Dick, I got a tear in my eye and now my eyelashes are frozen."

"If our eyes we'd close, then the lashes froze till sometimes we couldn't see."

"Dan McGrew?" I asked.

"Still Sam McGee."

"Let me take your picture."

Dick posed on the summit holding a Snowbird banner. With my eyelashes frozen, I had trouble seeing through the viewfinder. I pulled them apart, but then realized I was out of film. I found a plastic film container in my pack, but the lid was frozen. I hit it with my ice ax and the container shattered into a dozen pieces. I reloaded the camera, advancing the film carefully so it wouldn't shatter in the cold. I got the shot and then handed the camera to Dick, to get a shot of me. He made the mistake of taking off his glove, and instantly his finger welded to the camera and he had to peel it off, leaving literal fingerprints on the camera.

"And the careless feel of a bit of steel burns like a red-hot spit."

"Sam McGee?"

"No, Blasphemous Bill."

Dick took my photo, then we shouldered our packs and started the descent.

* * *

Back at high camp we found Frank, Yuichiro, and the others preparing to leave on their summit attempt. Twelve hours later we were reunited: everyone had made it to the top. It was a joyous group that descended toward the Tri-Turbo waiting at the base of Vinson. The air was crystalline, and we could gaze beyond the range to the great icecap that curved downward to the edges of the horizon; we could *see* that the Earth was round.

"I've got an idea," Frank said to Dick as we continued. "We'll title the book *The Eighth Summit*."

"What's the eighth?"

"That's the secret I've gained after attempting the other seven. That the world is so big and so varied that there's no way to see it all. But you'll never get bored trying."

Frank and Dick went straight to Australia to hike up Kosciuszko. When they were back in the States, the Seven Summits Odyssey year was over, and Dick hosted a reunion at Snowbird for the climbers who had been on the seven expeditions. You couldn't tell from the smiles on Frank and Dick's faces that they had narrowly missed the highest of the Seven Summits.

Word was out that others were trying for the Seven Summits record, including Reinhold Messner, considered the best high-altitude climber in the world. All the contenders had climbed Everest, and all were trying to get to Vinson, the reverse of Frank and Dick's predicament. In a way it represented the difference between them: Messner and the others had spent most of their lives becoming consummate climbers, while Frank and Dick had concentrated instead on business. When it came to a logistical challenge like getting to the interior of Antarctica, the businessmen had an edge.

But Dick wasn't going to give up. At Snowbird, he announced he was going back to Everest later that year.

* * *

Frank would have loved to go back with Dick, but his wife reminded him that they'd had a deal that after the Seven Summits year was over, Frank would put his mountaineering chapter behind him.

I also needed to put 1983 behind me. It had been the first full year of my marriage, and I'd been gone nine out of the twelve months. The next year I accepted mostly jobs that were near home. I traveled back and forth to the Channel Islands, which I could see from my front window. The islands had recently become a national park, and Nicholas deVore and I were doing a story for *National Geographic Traveler*.

For me, it was ideal, as I got to spend time with our toddler, Carissa, who was starting to talk. Jennifer and I had also begun to talk about giving Carissa a little brother or sister. We had torn down the fisherman's shack and were living in a rental three doors away while a real house was under construction. Living on the beach was still more my idea than Jennifer's, and she eventually confided that when she looked at the ocean through our front window, instead of admiring the Channel Islands she remembered the tidal wave.

In April, I made a deal with Frank and Dick to write the book about their Seven Summits Odyssey. For the rest of the year I drove to Los Angeles every few weeks to spend a day or two with Frank, going over the manuscript. Dick would sometimes fly in from Dallas, and once the three of us rendezvoused at Snowbird.

Dick was busy running the ski resort, and also planning a return to Everest. He had arranged to pay a team of Nepalese police officers, who had a permit to attempt the mountain, to add him to their roster, along with David Breashears, who would be Dick's guide. There was a Dutch team who would be on the mountain at the same time, however, and since the Nepal government was supposed to limit Everest permits to one team at a time, the Dutch protested that the Nepalese police had used their influence illegally to get their permit. Dick was concerned, but confident they would work it out.

I was enjoying my time with Frank and Dick, and they both became increasingly close friends, especially Frank. Since I was staying at his house so frequently, I was privy to his challenge of deciding what he was going to do with the rest of his life. Some state Democrats had leaned on him to run for the US Senate, but political life didn't appeal to him, or to his wife. He was a businessman, but when you've been the president of a Hollywood movie studio, you don't find your next job scanning the classifieds in the *Los Angeles Times*.

One day Frank got a call from a Hollywood investor named Stanley Gold, who was close to Roy Disney, the nephew of Walt. For several years the Walt Disney Company had been struggling, and recently it had been the target of an unfriendly takeover that had threatened to break up and sell off the parts of the Magic Kingdom. Gold wanted to know if Frank might be interested in becoming the president and CEO.

Over the next few days Frank shared his thoughts with me as he considered the offer. It was a dream job, but Frank hesitated because Disney was so complex that the dream could become a nightmare if he tried to turn around the company with just himself at the top.

"I know another guy who would be a perfect partner with me," Frank told Gold. "Michael Eisner, who runs Paramount. What if the two of us ran Disney as a team?"

Frank Wells and Michael Eisner took over The Walt Disney Company as president and CEO, respectively, and they would go on to make corporate history, turning Disney into one of the most valuable entertainment companies in the world. For me, it was an enduring lesson of what you can do when you share the spotlight. Looking back, I can see times when I forgot that, and I can see how things always started to go better when I remembered it again.

* * *

Dick and David made their way through the icefall, and Dick was feeling strong as they climbed up the Western Cwm to Camp II. That evening on the radio, the Nepalese Ministry of Tourism, which oversaw Everest climbing permits, told them they had withdrawn the permit for the Nepalese police expedition. Dick had no choice but to once again turn back.

Before leaving Kathmandu, he found out the permit for the coming year had been awarded to a Norwegian team. Dick then flew to Oslo, and after several weeks of negotiation he had talked the Norwegians into adding David and himself to the team.

"Rick-O," Dick told me, using the nickname he had given me, "I got to get up this thing, so you have a good ending to your book."

By then Dick had turned fifty-five, and if he did manage to get to the top, he would be not only the first to climb the Seven Summits, but also the oldest to climb Everest. The following year Dick and David went back, and once again, despite blisters on Dick's feet, they made good time through the icefall and the lower camps. At the South Col they met some of the Norwegian team coming down from the summit.

"It's a long way up there," they warned Dick, "and there's no time to set up belays, so we climbed unroped."

David realized that if he and Dick hoped to get to the top and back before dark, he couldn't spend the time belaying Dick, and further, if he didn't set up belays, it made no sense to tie themselves together with a rope.

"Dick, wearing a rope will mean we both get killed if you slip."

Dick understood the logic and reluctantly agreed. They decided to have a rest day at the South Col, to give Dick's blisters another day to heal. The following day they left at 2:00 am, accompanied by a Sherpa. They climbed steadily, and when it started to get light they stopped to rest. The sky was clear and there was no wind.

"How you doing?" David asked.

"I'm gonna make it."

They reached the spot where two years before Dick had turned back when his companions refused to go higher. At 28,500 feet the snow hardened, and Dick's crampons barely pricked the surface. The slope steepened and fell away on both sides. Dick was very aware he had no rope. Above the Hillary Step the slope began to ease. He could see David and the Sherpa. They had stopped. Above them there was only deep blue sky.

Is that it? Dick thought. *How far is it?*

He couldn't tell; his perception was off. He needed strength. He started playing in his mind the theme song from *The Bridge on the River Kwai*. He stood straighter and started to march in step to the music in his head. A minute later he reached his companions.

"You made it, Dick," David said as they hugged. "You're the oldest ever on the summit of Everest, and the first on the Seven Summits!"

* * *

My phone rang. It was 3:00 a.m.

"Hello?"

"I just got news from Kathmandu."

It was Frank Wells. My mind cleared. There were only two reasons why Frank would call at that hour. Either Dick had made it, or Dick was dead. Frank's voice was two octaves above normal. My foreboding crystalized to fear.

"It's . . . it's Dick . . . Dick's . . ."

Frank was now stammering, his voice breaking. My gut clenched.

"Dick . . . he's . . . he's . . . made it! He's climbed Everest. We've got the Seven Summits!"

Dick Bass on the summit of Everest. Once down to Base Camp he called me on the satellite phone. "It goes to show ya," he said, "that the second half"—by which he meant life after fifty—"can be and should be the best half." **David Breashears**

Chapter Nine

The Boy Scout Compass

Sixteen days after Dick Bass stood on the summit of Everest he arrived in Los Angeles, and Jennifer and I drove down from Ventura to have dinner with him at Frank's house. Jennifer was into her eighth month of pregnancy with a baby soon to be our second daughter, and while the drive was uncomfortable, she was looking forward to seeing Dick, who reminded her of the loquacious Texans she had grown up with in her early childhood home in Dripping Springs, before the family moved to Oregon.

Dick was gaunt, his lips cracked and bleeding and his voice hoarse, but he didn't disappoint Jennifer, regaling us with a detailed monologue of his Everest ascent that continued uninterrupted for nearly an hour.

"Dick, you're going to lose your voice," Frank said.

"Pancho, I'm just livin' up to my nickname: Large-Mouth Bass."

"Your dinner's getting cold."

"I got to get these stories out while they're still fresh, especially for Rick-O here," Dick countered. "He's now got the perfect ending for our book."

I was nearing completion of the manuscript for *Seven Summits*, and while Dick was right about having a good ending, the eventual ending of the book turned out even better because it described another celebratory dinner we had two months later, this time on Hidden Peak, at the top of the tram

Tom Brokaw, on his first snow and ice climb, skirts a crevasse
on the Kautz Glacier, Mount Rainier. **Rick Ridgeway**

157

at Dick's Snowbird ski resort. Nearly everyone who had been part of Seven Summits was there, as well as many friends of Frank's and Dick's—more than 500 people, not counting the seventy-member Utah Philharmonic Orchestra, which played "Climb Every Mountain."

Even though it was staged on an 11,000-foot mountain, Dick had insisted the event be black-tie. In turn, Jennifer had insisted I purchase a new tuxedo for a sum that represented the reconciliation I was still making between the economies of my pre- and post-marriage life. I had recently sold for $500 the Fiat station wagon I had brought into the marriage. I had purchased it twelve years earlier for $1,750 and, using dirtbag math, I had calculated it had been a good investment, until I had to use the cash to pay $550 for the tuxedo. I couldn't help being green-eyed at Yvon because he had *rented* his tux. For the next twenty years, maintaining his dirtbag integrity, Yvon continued to refuse to buy a tux, and instead borrowed mine, joking that he and I had an excuse to only attend every other black-tie event that we were both invited to.

* * *

Writing *Seven Summits* had kept me close to home for over a year, countervailing at least in part the nine months I was gone during the first full year of my marriage. When I had the manuscript complete, I sent it to Frank and Dick for final review. Frank returned it with a few notes in the margins, but Dick made edits to nearly every paragraph.

"It's no longer my voice or my writing style!" I complained to Jennifer.

"It's not your story," she replied. "It's Frank and Dick's story."

"But I'm writing the story, even if it is their story, so it needs to be *my* voice."

"Stop it!" she said with a force that made me not only shut up but reflect on my habit of voicing my frustrations to her to a point she became frustrated with my frustrations.

By then our second daughter had been born, and after getting both kids to sleep I stayed up and wrote in my journal, noting
that while I would never say or do anything abusive to Jennifer,
voicing my frustrations, complaining all the time that I'm falling
short of my self-imposed goals, and then acting out my frustrations by becoming frenetic and tense was itself a kind of abuse.

We had been married for over four years, and even though
I didn't talk with my friends too much about their marriages,
I knew from watching those who were older and who already
had long marriages—friends like Frank Wells and Dan Emmett—
that you had to keep assessing yourself and your behavior and
your decisions.

One of those decisions had arisen a few months before the
Seven Summits gala when Yvon and I had been invited to join
an expedition to Bhutan to attempt a remote mountain called
Gangkhar Puensum. At nearly 25,000 feet elevation, it was not
only the highest peak in the country but the highest unclimbed
mountain in the world. It would be an expedition with similari-
ties to the one in China five years earlier, when that country first
opened its doors to mountaineers, and we had attempted to climb
Minya Konka. Bhutan was opening its country to climbers for
the first time, and a group of Americans had won the coveted
permit. As with Minya Konka, the approach to the mountain
would be through country little known to the outside world. And
like Minya Konka, Gangkhar Puensum was in the eastern end of
the Himalaya, where the mountains are hit hardest each season
as the monsoon moves inland off the Bay of Bengal, loading
slopes with heavy, wet snow.

Returning to a high mountain prone to avalanche gave me
pause, as it did for Jennifer, even though she relied on me to
assess the risk. It was a complex decision. *National Geographic*
was interested in a story for the magazine, and in me as the
writer. The expedition was scheduled for the fall of 1985. That
would be nearly two years since my last major climb, the trip
to Vinson, and returning to mountaineering, and especially to

a mountain in such a little-explored area, was appealing. Still, I had to respect my responsibility to my family. I talked to Yvon, and he, too, was cautious about the danger, but also attracted to the adventure.

"If we stay on the ridge and off of any slope that even had a whiff of avalanche potential . . ." I speculated.

"Yeah, we could probably manage the risk," he replied, completing my sentence.

I remembered that, on the way out from Minya Konka, when we reached the pass that offered the last view of the mountain, Yvon had derided the mountains as too big. Now he was turning his back on that determination, and so was I, and I knew it was because the attraction of going to a place few outsiders had ever seen was outweighing the risk of returning to a big mountain.

Vowing to be careful, we agreed to join the expedition. Yvon and I met with the expedition's leader, Phil Trimble, to discuss the team. Phil had been the leader of our 1976 expedition to Everest, and he understood the importance of having a core group of very strong climbers for a big Himalayan peak. There were still a couple of open positions, and Yvon suggested adding his close friend and longtime climbing partner Doug Tompkins, and I recommended my K2 climbing partner John Roskelley. Phil agreed, and Doug and John both accepted the invitation.

I had never met Doug Tompkins, but for some time Yvon had been saying that he wanted to get the three of us together on an adventure. When Yvon first mentioned the idea, I recalled the summer of 1967, when I did my first rock climb. That was when my mother, concerned about me trying to teach myself how to climb, had paid to send me to Outward Bound in Oregon. When the course finished, I drove my Chevy panel truck back to Southern California, stopping in San Francisco to visit a climbing shop called The North Face, part of a company by the same name that made tents and sleeping bags. It had been founded and was still owned by a climber named Doug Tompkins. The shop was a hangout for a group of climbers that included Yvon

Chouinard. Yvon and Doug were both older than me, and they were both in my pantheon of climbing gods. The day I visited the store neither of them was there, but I used my money, keeping just enough for gas to get home, to buy four Chouinard carabiners that remained part of my climbing rack for the next twenty years.

* * *

Yvon made Patagonia's warehouse available for packing food and gear for the Gangkhar Puensum expedition. We shipped the boxes, each the weight of one porter load, to Calcutta for transshipment to Thimphu, the capital of Bhutan.

At the same time, I was polishing the manuscript for *Seven Summits*, incorporating all of Dick Bass's edits and discovering that the new tone of the book was a better fit with the story. When I told that to Jennifer, she smiled, but didn't say anything.

That summer I had also been in touch with the newscaster Tom Brokaw about Yvon and myself guiding him up Mount Rainier. I had met Tom seven years earlier on the way home from K2. Upon landing in New York, the expedition leader Jim Whittaker received a message from NBC inviting him and the summit climbers to appear on the *Today* show. Jim had to get back to his home in Seattle, and the others wanted to get back to their own wives and families. I was the only one who could make it.

At the NBC studios in Rockefeller Plaza, the escort who met me at reception looked surprised. That was understandable. I had on an aloha shirt—the only thing I had when we got back to civilization that wasn't shredded—and a pair of billowy Pakistani pants I had bought in the Rawalpindi Bazaar. I wore flip-flops because of blisters on my feet. I hadn't had a haircut in five months. The skin on my face was peeling, and the cracks on my lips hadn't yet healed, so blood ran down my chin when I smiled. The studio escort reached out to shake hands but recoiled when she saw my fingers, black from frostbite.

In the green room I was introduced to Jane Pauley and Tom Brokaw. Jane raised her eyebrows and Tom grinned. I had been told that Brokaw would be the one to interview me.

"I can guarantee you," he said, "there's never been anybody to come on the *Today* show looking even close to the way you do."

The interview went well, and Tom was pleased. Back in the green room we shook hands, and he was careful not to squeeze my fingers. He offered to stay in touch. I spent most of the next year writing my book about the K2 climb, and when *The Last Step* came out Tom invited me back on the show to talk about it. After the interview we again shook hands, and this time he didn't have to be careful; other than the end of one finger that was slightly rounded, there was no lasting damage from the frostbite.

"I've always been fascinated with climbing," Tom said. "I'd like to try it someday."

"Come out to Wyoming," I replied. "My buddy Yvon Chouinard and I will take you up the Grand Teton."

The next summer Yvon and I picked Tom up at the Jackson Hole Airport. After a practice climb called Baxter's Pinnacle, Yvon told Tom he was a natural, and proposed that instead of doing the regular route on the Grand we should try something more challenging: the Direct Exum.

"The regular route is for doctors and lawyers who want to be guided so they can say they've been on the summit of the Grand," Yvon said. "There's nothing on the Direct Exum harder than what you did on Baxter's. Just more of it!"

Two days later we departed in the predawn from the high camp on the saddle between the Middle and the Grand Teton. There were no clouds and no wind, and on the summit we could see from the fields of Idaho to the mountains of the Wind River Range.

"You guys have no idea how much this means to me," Tom said.

"You did great," Yvon replied. "You're now an official Do Boy."

"What's a Do Boy?"

"It's a phrase my friend Doug Tompkins came up with. I think he got it in Japan or someplace . . . I'm not sure . . . but it's our

Another mountain conquered

NBC Today Show host Tom Brokaw, center, enjoys a beer and a moment's rest with his climbing partners Rick Ridgeway, left, and Yvon Chouinard, right, after a successful ascent of the Grand Teton. In town last week on a western vacation, Brokaw fulfilled the plans he and Ridgeway (one of four Americans to reach the summit of K2 in 1979) formulated during a Today show interview. No slouch, Brokaw first climbed Baxter's Pinnacle on Monday with his famous guides as a warmup and then followed them up the direct Exum route on the Grand, a difficult climb in anybody's book. About the sport itself, he said, "I would recommend that before going out everybody should take a complete climbing course," and jokingly added that his partners "Dragged me all the way up and all the way down." Chouinard indicated that Brokaw definitely has what it takes, saying, "We wouldn't have taken him up if he wasn't a natural." Brokaw left Jackson last Friday after descending the peak but Ridgeway remained in the area to climb with Chouinard, an old surfing buddy from California. Brokaw's visit to the valley came during a four-week vacation from his morning show, when NBC will be testing potential replacements for the TV host who will move on next spring to co-anchor the network's nightly newscasts with Roger Mudd.

The local paper ran a story after Yvon Chouinard and I took Tom Brokaw up the Grand Teton. It was my birthday, and back at Yvon's cabin we had a celebration with dozens of climbers showing up. One of them looked at Tom and said, "What do you do?" Tom looked at me and said, "I knew I was going to like these guys." Courtesy of *Jackson Hole News & Guide*

little tribe of friends who go around having adventures. The Do Boys. We do things. None of this lying around on our asses."

* * *

Now it was time to introduce Tom to snow and ice climbing. Yvon and I were looking forward to doing another climb with Tom, and we realized it would also be a good chance to get in shape for the Bhutan climb, so Yvon had invited Doug Tompkins to join us. Tom had asked if a friend of his named Rick Graetz could come along as well. Tom had told us that Rick was an avid outdoorsman and a good skier and mountaineer, and we said we were looking forward to meeting him.

Yvon and I arrived at the Seattle airport and then walked to the gate where Doug's flight was scheduled to arrive. Tom was already checked in to a downtown hotel, and Rick Graetz was arriving the next morning. When Doug appeared, Yvon introduced us. Doug looked to be about five foot seven—a couple of inches taller than me. He was lean and fit, with short-cropped salt-and-pepper hair, and he grinned when we shook hands, a shake that was neither firm nor flaccid. He was dressed in pressed chinos and an oxford shirt tucked in and held by a leather belt simple in design but beautifully burnished. His eyes moved quickly, and he had a bounce in his gait.

We rented a car and drove to the hotel and convened in Tom's room. Yvon introduced Doug, and soon we went to work organizing gear. Tom held up his ice ax and crampons. "Remember, guys, I have no idea how any of this stuff works."

"Don't worry," Yvon said. "We'll take some time on the way up and give you a lesson."

"I've been around you enough to know I should be worried," Tom replied. "You guys are sandbaggers."

"When you're around Yvon," Doug said, grinning, "there's two things you have to watch for. One is when he says, 'The weather looks solid, so let's leave our tent behind.'"

"And the other?" Tom asked.

"When he says, 'We got this climb in the bag, so let's eat all our food.'"

The next day we drove back to the airport to pick up Rick Graetz. Rick's flight was late, so we decided to have lunch at the airport.

"I've got some food in my rucksack," Doug said. "Let's eat outside."

Since I didn't know Doug beyond a few stories Yvon had told me, I assumed we would be eating protein bars and trail mix on a bench in front of baggage claim. Outside, however, Doug pointed to a grove of Douglas fir on an island in the middle of an adjacent highway.

"Hey boys, over there."

Without waiting for anyone else's opinion, Doug ran across the road, scaled a fence, and crossed the highway to the island. We followed him, and on a grassy opening between trees he spread a large cloth napkin and pulled from his rucksack two French baguettes, a large block of aged Manchego, and a wide-mouthed water bottle filled with roasted red peppers marinated in extra-virgin olive oil and rosemary.

"Got the bread this morning at a little bakery just down the street from my place."

I knew Doug lived in downtown San Francisco. Yvon had told me that Doug grew up on the East Coast but dropped out of private high school to become a ski racer and climbing bum. Even though he never got past tenth grade, Doug was a natural entrepreneur, having started The North Face in the early 1960s and later selling it to invest in his wife Susie's clothing company, which they renamed Esprit.

I recalled that a year after I had stopped at the North Face store on Columbus Street in San Francisco, hoping to meet Doug and maybe even Yvon, I heard they had driven their van to the southern tip of South America and climbed a mysterious, ice-encrusted tower of granite named Fitz Roy, in a place called Patagonia, a name that suggested the outer edge of the known world, and a feat that made them even more godlike. Now I was eating lunch with both of them—along with the most famous television anchorman in the country—in the middle of a highway with cars whizzing by on both sides.

* * *

That evening we camped on a rocky moraine overlooking the Nisqually Glacier. After setting up the tents, Yvon—who is an excellent cook, and on our trips prepares most of the meals—was struggling to assemble a new stove.

Yvon Chouinard gives Tom Brokaw some on-the-job training:
how to do a standing glissade. **Rick Ridgeway**

"Look at how complicated this thing is," he complained.
"Must have been designed by some asshole with an advanced
degree in engineering."

Doug picked up the instructions and started reading.

"I think I found the problem," Doug said.

"What?" Yvon asked, holding stove parts in each hand.

"It says right here, 'Not to be operated by immature persons.'"

I was enjoying the repartee, and I could see Tom was too.

"I knew I was with the right guys," he said with a smile.

Yvon smiled as well, and, consulting the instructions, he and
Doug got the stove assembled. Even though I was just getting
to know Doug, I had heard enough stories that I knew he and

Yvon had an iconoclastic sense of humor. On their 10,000-mile road trip to climb Fitz Roy they brought surfboards and skis, and stopped often to surf, and once they were far enough south they climbed up and skied down a snow-covered volcano. On the mud-splashed back window of the van they wrote "Puercos Deportivos," translated literally as "Hogs of Sports" but more loosely as "Fun Hogs." It defined their approach to sport, and their belief that "doing" was more important than "winning." On the summit of Fitz Roy, they erected a small flag that read "Viva Los Fun Hogs," and for decades the banner was on the wall above the receptionist's desk at Patagonia headquarters.

In the years ahead, as I joined them on more Do Boy adventures, I would come to realize how that banner represented my own shift in how I thought about the sports. When I was fourteen and saw that issue of *National Geographic* with the article about the first American ascent of Everest, and the photo of Jim Whittaker on the summit holding his ice ax with the American flag tied to it, the flag was consistent with what I understood as a kid to be the idea of committing everything you had to the summit, to the victory. Just like the country had done with winning World War II. As I became a climber and got to know other climbers, however, I realized most of them were rebels against the mainstream culture, and flying a flag that said "Viva Los Fun Hogs" on the summit in place of the American flag was a perfect expression of both the rebellion and the commitment to a sport that at its core had no tangible economic value. The great French alpinist Lionel Terray had succinctly captured that idea when he titled his autobiography *Conquistadors of the Useless*.

* * *

The next morning, we descended the moraine to the glacier, and Yvon showed Tom how to strap crampons to his boots.

"Now just walk around for a few minutes and get used to them," Yvon said.

With the box checked for Tom's first lesson, we crossed the Nisqually Glacier and continued in an upward traverse toward the Kautz Glacier. At our lunch stop, Yvon took a few minutes for Tom's second lesson: how to use his ice ax to self-arrest. He had Tom slide down the slope, turn, and dig his pick into the snow until he stopped.

"OK," Yvon said. "You got that one down."

We continued the upward traverse. We had gained about 4,000 vertical feet and we had another thousand to go before reaching a place on the map called Camp Hazard—at 10,800 feet. The slope steepened as we ascended a section on the glacier called the Turtle Snowfield. Doug was in the lead and disappeared over the crest. Yvon was just below him, then me, then Rick, then Tom. Yvon stopped to rest, and in a few steps, I reached him.

"Maybe we should rope up Tom," I suggested.

"No, we taught him how to self-arrest. Anyway, it looks like it eases off right above us."

Yvon left and I waited. Rick was almost to my position.

"You going to wait for Tom?" Rick asked when he reached me.

"He looks like he's doing OK," I replied. "But I'll wait and make sure."

Rick continued, and soon Tom reached me.

"Last but not least," I said, trying to sound encouraging.

"This is why I'm called the anchorman."

"Catch your breath, and then I'll follow you."

He smiled, and after a few breaths kept going, and then after a few minutes hooked his crampon on his leg and fell and started sliding toward me. I moved quickly and planted my ax and positioned my boot behind it and stopped him, even though he had already turned on his belly and was starting to position his ice ax to arrest his fall.

"Way to set up a self-arrest," I said.

"If the insurance guys at NBC saw this, they'd shit," Tom replied.

In late afternoon we reached Camp Hazard and set up our tents, and were on our way again by 7:00 am the next day. We climbed first on bare rock and then back on snow, stopping to strap on crampons and, to Tom's relief, rope up. We traversed toward a slope that we had no choice but to cross. It was below a dangerous chute, and even in the cool of morning, occasional rocks clattered down. Séracs from the adjacent glacier balanced above us like the Sword of Damocles.

"We want to get across this as fast as we can," Yvon said.

"This is what we call objective danger," I explained to Tom. "When the only way to manage the risk is to expose yourself to it as briefly as possible."

Doug untied from our rope and dashed across the slope beneath the chute. Tom was absorbing this as Yvon started coiling the rope.

"Aren't we staying roped up?" Tom asked.

"The rope slows us down too much," Yvon answered. Without saying anything more, he stood and put his pack on.

"Shouldn't we wait for Graetz?" Tom asked, pointing down the slope to Rick.

"Better to wait for him on the other side, where it's safer," Yvon said. Then he got a mischievous grin, which I knew meant he had come up with a clever line.

"Tom, it's just like catching a cab in New York. Nice guys finish last."

Yvon turned and scampered quickly across the slope, and Tom followed, focused on not catching a crampon on his pants. I followed, then Rick. We were now on the Kautz Glacier, and we began ascending a slope sculpted with sun cups that formed a repetitive pattern in the morning light. The spikes of our crampons sunk securely into the firm snow, squeaking with each step. The slope steepened, and Yvon stopped while Doug kept going.

"It's steep enough here that you need to plant the pick of your ice ax, like this," Yvon said, demonstrating the move. "Then place your crampons like this, alternating between your front points and turning your boot to use your bottom points."

"It's called the French technique," I added. "Something that Yvon brought back from the Alps and introduced to American climbing."

"Shouldn't we rope up?" Tom asked.

"Oh yeah," Yvon said, "that's probably a good idea."

"Another accelerated lesson from the Chouinard-Ridgeway School of Mountaineering," Tom said.

Meanwhile Doug, climbing without a rope, was several hundred vertical feet above us. He was always moving fast, and always with apparent confidence—something I guessed was probably an ingredient of his success. We reached a step in the slope, split end to end by a deep crevasse. We walked parallel to the edge until we reached the narrowest point, then jumped across. When it was Tom's turn he paused.

"I bet some people who have never climbed on snow and ice might look down into something like this and freak out," he observed.

He then jumped across, making the leap with aplomb. An hour later, clouds began to swirl above us, and it started to hail. Doug waited for us, and we all stayed together as we ascended into the whiteout. The slope continued to ease and then it flattened.

"This must be the top of the glacier," Doug said.

"But which way is the summit?" Yvon asked.

We knew the top of Rainier was a broad rim encircling a caldera, so even though the spot where we were was flat, it wasn't the summit. We took out our map and guessed our most likely position, but even then it was difficult to know with precision the direction to the summit. It wasn't so much that we had to get to the exact highest point, but that we had to find the standard route to the top, as that was the best way to get down safely.

"My best guess is that way," I said, pointing with my ice ax into the whiteout. Visibility had dropped so much I could only see a few feet past the others huddled around the map.

Yvon Chouinard (left) teaches Tom Brokaw how to change his ice ax from one hand to the other while simultaneously placing his crampons securely on the snow. Climbers today will look at this shot and say, "What? No rope nor hard hat!" Back then we studiously minimized gear against an estimate of the risk. Hashtag Old School. Rick Ridgeway

"Would a compass help?" Tom asked.

"You have a compass?" Yvon replied.

"My Boy Scout compass," Tom said. "Always be prepared."

Tom found the compass and handed it to me, and I aligned it atop the topo map.

"That way," I said, pointing into the opaqueness. We reached the summit and found the standard route. By midafternoon we were in the main hut, and on our way home the next day.

* * *

Twenty-nine years later, Tom was diagnosed with cancer, and after a difficult surgery he began an arduous recovery. The Do Boys cheered him on. I put together a photo album of our many adventures, including our ascent of Mount Rainier, and mailed it to him. A few weeks later, Jennifer was going to New York, and she arranged to have lunch with Tom and his wife, Meredith. The two, by then, had been married for fifty-three years. Our wives had been close friends for decades, and together we were an extended family. At lunch Tom told Jennifer that he had received my photo album and, with tears in his eyes, told her how much it meant to him.

Back home in California she told me that Tom had given her a gift to give to me. "He told me to tell you it's been in the top drawer of his dresser for a long time," she said.

She handed me a small box. I opened it, and inside was the Boy Scout compass.

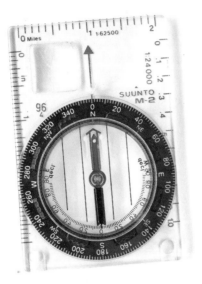

The Boy Scout compass that
Tom gave to me.

The Edge
of the Map

Phil Trimble, the leader of our Gangkhar Puensum expedition, left the States early to travel to Bumthang, the region in central Bhutan where the mountain was located, to scout the best trail to Base Camp. The rest of us planned to rendezvous in Calcutta and fly from there to Thimphu, where we would spend two days organizing gear and supplies, then drive to Bumthang to join Phil.

While waiting for everyone to arrive, John Roskelley and I decided to explore Calcutta. It was good to see John again. Since we had climbed K2, he had gone on to become one of the world's top mountaineers, making the first ascent of a granite tusk in the Karakoram called Uli Biaho Tower. He also climbed Makalu, the fifth-highest mountain in the world, where, near the top, as his teammates wore out, John kept going, reaching the summit by himself.

After K2, John and I had stayed in touch, climbing together occasionally in his home state of Washington, and once in Wyoming with Yvon. John and I had also gone on an overnight hike in the Ojai backcountry with our two kids, as part of an assignment to write a story on family camping for a backpacking magazine. John brought his son Jess, who was three years old, and I brought my daughter Carissa, who was the same age. It was January, but the forecast was for clear skies. We planned to hike for several miles along the Sespe River, and since this

Yvon Chouinard and Doug Tompkins on the summit of an unclimbed and unnamed peak. The original objective, Gangkhar Puensum, rises in the background. **Rick Ridgeway** was in the years before kid carriers became popular, I modified a Kelty frame pack to hold my daughter.

"Repeat after me," I told Carissa before we started hiking. "I will not pee in the pack when I am riding in the pack."

That night my plastic water bottle froze solid, inside the tent. The kids slept well, however, and in the morning they were enthusiastic to keep hiking.

"You two behaved just like real mountaineers," John told the kids. "Spending the night in your sleeping bags passing gas."

In Calcutta, John and I started the day with a stroll in the park across from our colonial-era hotel. In the middle of the park there was an area about a hundred feet around demarked with a knee-high, wire-mesh fence that encircled a warren of holes with hundreds of rats crawling in and out. Around the perimeter dozens of park strollers were tossing bits of food into the arena and watching the rats, some missing legs, fight for each morsel.

"Most parks," John observed, "people feed the pigeons."

Visiting the train station, we had to step over hundreds of people lying on the bare concrete to cool themselves against the heat. Outside we watched a caravan of chanting Hare Krishnas beating tambourines. Included among them were two long-haired Westerners in marigold-orange robes, each staring at the sky with a blissfulness that was strangely disconcerting. At every corner beggars, many of them missing limbs, accosted us.

John and I shared a room in the hotel. In bed that evening, before going to sleep, I watched the fan circle slowly in the center of the high ceiling.

"We have to be careful. This climb is going to be dangerous."

"We'll question every decision," John replied.

"I miss my kids."

"So do I."

In the middle of the night John cried out in his sleep.

"You OK?"

"I had a nightmare. I was backing up in my truck and you were on the ground and I ran over you."

"Try to get some sleep. We have to get up early to catch our flight."

* * *

In Thimphu we checked in to our hotel and read a message from Phil Trimble that he had made it to Bumthang and was leaving to scout the local trails. We were looking forward to our two full days in Thimphu. In the mid-1980s the city had about 20,000 inhabitants and only a couple of thousand tourists a year, and we felt like we had the storybook capital to ourselves. On our first day, locals gathered in the town center for a game of pickup basketball. On our second day, the handsome twenty-nine-year-old king showed up to play, and whenever someone passed him the ball both teams stood at attention while he shot. The king's team won.

"It took me nineteen expeditions to the Himalaya," John said, "to finally find Shangri-la."

I knew that on most of those expeditions John had been with small teams of close friends that included some of the best alpine climbers in the world. On the few expeditions with larger teams with more disparate members—including our expedition to K2—there had been feuding among the climbers. With eight climbers on our Bhutan team, it wasn't large but it was disparate. John and Doug, for example, were in many ways opposites. John had grown up in Spokane, working in construction and mining, and enjoyed hunting. Doug traveled between Esprit's design studios in Milan, Tokyo, New York, and San Francisco, and enjoyed fencing. They both had a sense of humor, however, and it was my hope that would be sufficient common ground for them to enjoy each other's company.

I still only knew Doug from the three days we had been together climbing Rainier, and from a party Jennifer and I had attended at Doug's home in San Francisco. The party was an annual event with friends who came in from around the world. When we arrived, Jennifer and I entered through an arched gate and walked a path through a grove of redwoods to a small house ·

built with Japanese-like minimalism. It wouldn't have been that special except it was in downtown San Francisco, and I could see between the redwoods the pyramidal Transamerica building rising a dozen blocks away.

Inside the house there were paintings by Fernando Botero and Otto Dix, a large Francis Bacon triptych, and a Balthus of a young nude with her leg provocatively propped on a chair that made Jennifer's eyebrow rise. (In years ahead, Doug would sell his art collection to support his wildland conservation work, and I would next see this painting, called *Alice in the mirror*, in the Georges Pompidou Center in Paris.) Doug had invited Jennifer and me to spend the night, and in the guest room he pointed to an Edward Hopper above the headboard and said, "If you sit up in bed, don't lean against the painting because it's wired to police headquarters and the cops will show up."

I had been around Doug enough to suspect that he, too, lived by Yvon's maxim that you don't have to be as concerned about breaking rules if you write the rule book. That was confirmed even before we left for Bhutan. The expedition was sponsored by Rolex, and the company had given each of us an Oyster Perpetual wristwatch with our name engraved on the back. Neither Yvon nor Doug wore a watch, and as soon as they got their Rolexes they donated them to an auction to raise funds for an environmental group.

"You don't need a watch to know what time it is," Doug told me. "There's clocks everywhere. Watches are just about status and money. That's why I don't hire people who wear watches."

"Anything else you look for? When you're hiring?"

"How they walk. If they come down heel first they're usually clumsy and don't have a lot of energy. People who walk on the balls of their feet, they tend to have more energy."

* * *

It took two days in a minibus to get to Bumthang. When we arrived, there was no sign of Phil, who we assumed was still scouting the route to Base Camp. Since there were no maps of the area, the government in Thimphu had sent a couple of people to the district a few months before to determine the route to Base Camp, but Phil had thought it was still a good idea to confirm their findings.

"It's pretty cool that as we near the end of the twentieth century," I had said when Phil had originally proposed he do a reconnaissance, "there are still places you can get lost because there aren't any maps."

By 1985, Landsat satellites had photographed most of the planet's surface, but there were still a few places with little on-the-ground cartography: the region on the south side of the Kunlun Mountains in Central Asia; a small pocket of the Upper Orinoco in the Amazon Basin; a tiny triangle of jungle on the west end of Irian Jaya, in the Indonesian archipelago.

And the Bhutanese side of the Himalayan crest. I was used to thinking of my friends and me as adventurers, but now we really were explorers, which I assumed should make the guys at the Explorer's Club happy, even if Doug and Yvon didn't wear their watches.

The yaks and yak drivers we had arranged to ferry our gear were already at the roadhead, waiting impatiently. We were at the confluence of two rivers, and it looked like a trail that followed the larger tributary was most likely the way Phil had gone. Not wanting to frustrate the yak herders, we decided to take a chance and start hiking.

The trail took us through a pristine forest of Himalayan blue pine, and even though between us we had been on more than thirty expeditions to the Himalaya, this was the first time any of us had seen a forest with no visible sign of logging. In late afternoon we stopped and set up camp. We had our fly rods, and soon Yvon caught a three-pound brown trout. I was fishing with Doug.

"You getting along with everybody?" I asked.

"Yeah, getting along fine. I may not be friends with them, you know, long-term."

While Yvon Chouinard caught a three-pound brown trout, this was the best I could manage. **William Thompson**

"How's that?"

"Well, like John."

"John? He's a really good guy. We were in a tent together on K2 for a long time. He's really dependable, and he's got a good sense of humor, which helps when you're stuck in a tent."

"No, no, he's a good guy, I know. It's just that he's a little, you know, like this," Doug said, flattening his hand and using it to scribe an imaginary vertical line. "Kind of on a straight path, maybe not too flexible."

"How can you tell?"

"Listen to the way he conjugates verbs."

"Verbs?"

"Yeah, he uses mostly preterit and command tenses. Hardly any subjunctive or conditional conjugations."

* * *

We were just sitting down to a trout dinner when a local arrived with a note from Phil. He had taken the other fork and was in the adjacent valley, to the east. The next morning, we reversed ourselves and caught up with him at a small army outpost where the body language of the half dozen soldiers suggested that they thought they had been assigned to the lowest rung of hell.

"We're still in the wrong valley," Phil said. "We need to be in the drainage you guys were starting up."

Talking to the locals, Phil had found out that when the government guys from Thimphu had come to the area to do their scout, they had pointed up the valley that we were now in and asked the locals if it was the way to Gangkhar Puensum. The locals had said yes, and then Phil realized the locals called all the mountains in the area Gangkhar Puensum. To make matters worse, Phil said that since we only had a few weeks on our climbing permit, there wasn't time to go back down with all the yaks and then go up the right valley.

"Then we're screwed?" Yvon asked.

"Not necessarily," Phil replied. "We have two alternatives we could do in this valley. First, it might be possible to climb the east peak of Gangkhar Puensum, which we can get to from here. Not as high, but still a major summit. Or second, I got a glimpse of the other peaks at the head of the valley, and there are some great-looking mountains maybe twenty-one or twenty-two thousand feet high."

I could see some of the team looked disappointed. Yvon and Doug, however, seemed to take the news with a shrug. I suspected they might have felt a measure of relief.

"I prefer smaller peaks, anyway," Yvon said, confirming my suspicion.

I wasn't sure where John stood, but then he looked at us and nodded in agreement. Phil then wrote a letter to the government officials explaining that they had sent us up the wrong valley, so we were going to climb the mountains where we were. He gave it to a young Bhutanese to run back to the army outpost, where there was a telegraph wire. I could see a grin starting to grow on John's face. I wasn't sure about his verb conjugations, but I knew he had an ability to lighten things up.

"When I was young," he said, "I made every summit I tried. Then I started to miss a few. Now I can't even find them."

* * *

The next day, the herders gathered their yaks to freight our gear to the head of the valley. These yaks were big and burly, different from the ones in Nepal, which had been diminished by inbreeding with cattle. They also had a deep-throated cough that in the cold morning air condensed into puffs of steam. We asked through our interpreter if they were sick.

"Oh no. That is yak talk."

"What do they say?"

"They speak of love."

We started up the valley, hiking ahead of the yaks. The trail meandered through a forest of tall bamboo and broad-leaf evergreens. It was raining, and we hiked with umbrellas, adding to the sense of walking through a beautiful park. I was feeling good, realizing that my relief we couldn't attempt Gangkhar Puensum was outweighing my disappointment that we couldn't attempt it. There was still a possibility we could try the east summit—and that could also be hazardous—but it seemed more likely we would be climbing smaller peaks, choosing only ones with safe routes. With the weight of the original climb lifted, I was enjoying more fully the experience of just being in such a pristine and wild place with this eclectic group of adventurers, especially Doug, whom I was hiking behind that morning.

Doug Tompkins on day two of our approach
hike to Base Camp. **William Thompson**

"What did your father do?" I asked him.

"He was an antique dealer, in New England. But only museum-quality American pieces from 1700 to 1850. When I was a kid, he bought me a book on antiques that showed four different examples of a particular class of furniture, from poor to excellent, explaining why they were rated that way. That book and then my father's tutoring is how I trained my eye to judge quality. Now I apply it to everything I do."

"What else did you learn from him?"

"He told me once, 'It's not how much you sell something for, but how much you pay for it.' So you see, he taught me about margins. At the same time, he was scrupulously fair. One time I tailed along to a church in the middle of nowhere that was selling some furniture. My dad immediately spotted this rectory table that he wanted. He asked the priest how much they were asking, and the guy said two thousand dollars. My father then told the priest he wanted to buy it, but for four thousand. When we were back in the car, I asked him why he did that. He explained that he would sell the table for eight thousand. Then he looked at me and said, 'It only works when it's fair to both sides.'"

* * *

The trail ascended through a forest of pine and fir, and, as we gained altitude, oak and rhododendron, and then juniper. Above tree line we made camp next to a seasonal hut used by the herders. There was a garden, resplendent with large turnips, and our Bhutanese cook added a few to our yak-meat stew. The next morning, we ascended to a morainal cirque where we could just see under a bank of clouds the snout of a nearby glacier. That meant we were at the head of the valley, and we set up Base Camp.

The next day the clouds parted briefly, revealing glaciated mountains on three sides, including the east summit of Gangkhar Puensum, where we could see only one possible route, and it was festooned with hanging glaciers and double cornices that looked exceedingly dangerous; to get to it we would have to climb a lower rampart that looked just as risky. Rolex might be disappointed that we wouldn't be climbing Gangkhar Puensum, or even its satellite summit, but there was palpable relief knowing we were down to one option: safer routes on lower peaks.

The clouds closed again, and we spent the day reading, writing in our journals, and sitting in our community tent sharing stories. The next morning the sky was clear, and Yvon joined me as I started the stove to heat water.

"We haven't seen one jet contrail since we've been in Bhutan," he said when I handed him his cup of tea.

The others joined us. We were all in good moods; after breakfast we planned to move camp to a higher elevation, and from there we could scout and then attempt to climb some of the lower peaks. There was no rush to get moving, as the weather was stable, and we didn't have far to go. Then a Bhutanese runner arrived with a telegram from the capital. He gave it to Phil, who read it to himself.

"Fuck!"

"What's it say?"

"It says we have permission only to climb Gangkhar Puensum, and if we can't climb the east summit, we can't climb anything."

"First, we got Rolex pressuring us to go over the wall," Yvon said, referring to the lower rampart of the east summit of Gangkhar Puensum. "And now the government telling us the only thing we have a permit for is to go over the wall."

"So, what do you think we should do?" I asked.

"Just what we were going to do," Yvon replied. "Finish our reccy, and then if things look good, instead of climbing we'll just do a little exploring."

You can't break rules if you write your own rule book.

We stood around our campfire, fingers encircling our cups of tea, in agreement our goal now was simply to do a little "exploring." After a slow breakfast, we moved camp to a high meadow colored with blue gentian, purple aster, and white edelweiss. The sky remained without clouds, and a small stream of clear water purled between cushion plants.

"Camp Shangri-la," Yvon said.

We pitched our tents, and the tent stakes drove easily into the cushioned meadow, yet they held firmly as I tautened the guy-lines; I stood and paused and considered the satisfaction of a perfectly placed tent stake. John unloaded his pack and inflated his sleeping pad. I was relieved that he seemed in a buoyant mood; the day before he had been in a funk and had told me he was thinking of giving up climbing.

"You leave your family," he had said, "and you wonder if you're going to end up buried under snow on some peak in north-central Bhutan that no one has ever heard of."

Yvon Chouinard uses a fuel bottle as rolling pin and a snow
shovel as breadboard to make chapatis. **Rick Ridgeway**

I had wondered if he was just glum from the gloomy weather,
or from the team with its disparate members, or the challenge of
finding the mountain, or, if we ended up attempting Gangkhar
Puensum East, the challenge of finding a safe way up.

Now I was relieved he seemed to have regained the levity
more typical of his demeanor. I knew him well enough to have
a suspicion about what had caused his funk. It was related to an
issue he'd had seven years before on K2, after we had arrived at
the base of the ridge we would climb, and everyone had taken
equipment from the boxes and started shuttling loads to the first
camp. There was no plan or strategy in selecting what equipment should go first, and John had voiced his frustration that

we lacked a good plan and, for that matter, what he considered good leadership.

I suspected John had been having a similar frustration on this trip. I watched Yvon and Doug pitch their tent. Neither of them needed a defined plan, and both of them bristled at anything associated with top-down authority, such as the telegram from the Bhutanese government. If the fishing was good, you fished, and if the climbing was good—and the route safe—you climbed.

And me? I recognized my predilection not only to understand these different sides of my friends, but to appreciate their disparate attributes. But was this actually a strength? Doug had told me he wasn't going to be long-term friends with John, but I knew I was going to be long-term friends with Doug *and* John. While it was easy to assume this was something I should feel good about, it made me wonder if it was at the cost of having a firm position or stand on issues like the one of whether you liked or disliked top-down management.

I looked again at John, Yvon, and Doug. They were all so certain in their opinions that it was a default response for them nearly always to take sides on any issue. Once again, where did this leave me? Looking at John, I thought again back to K2, when my climbing partner Chris Chandler began an affair with Cherie, whose husband was also on the climb, and my hesitation to take sides.

"You have a tendency to avoid conflict," Jennifer would tell me a few years later. "That's probably because your parents argued and divorced when you were a kid."

Whether or not that was the reason I delayed taking sides in the conflict that divided the K2 team, once I was on the A-Team and Chris was on the B-team, it led to a falling out between us that I was never able to repair.

I recalled that day in Kathmandu having breakfast with PK, the Sherpa leader from our Everest expedition in 1976, when he told me Chris and Cherie were attempting a potentially dangerous satellite summit of Kanchenjunga. I had written the letter to Chris, and I learned later PK had delivered it, but I never got a reply. I did get occasional updates from mutual friends on how Chris and Cherie were doing. I heard that while they never made the circumnavigation in the sailboat they had built, they had sailed it around the Pacific Northwest. They also had continued to climb, and they returned to Kanchenjunga, this time to attempt a winter ascent. Again, it was just the two of them, with a few Sherpas in support. When Chris and Cherie reached their high camp, Chris collapsed from an onset of cerebral edema. Cherie tried to carry him down, but Chris died, and Cherie suffered severe frostbite, requiring amputation of all twenty of her toes and fingers.

When I got the news, I thought about the time Chris and I had made a new route on a high peak in the Peruvian Andes. The cheapest way to get to Peru was out of Miami, and we decided to drive Chris's aging Chevy sedan cross-country. Coming down from Seattle to pick me up in California, he read Ken Kesey's *Sometimes a Great Notion* cover to cover, propping the book on the steering wheel. In Joshua Tree, we stopped for two days so he could teach me how to climb cracks. In New Orleans, we stayed up all night joining a conga line of dancers weaving out of one bar and into another. The car broke down, and after removing the license plates and burning the registration we abandoned the vehicle on the side of the highway and, with three huge duffels of gear, started hitchhiking. Outside of Mobile, a state trooper pulled over and slowly got out, adjusting his Ray-Bans.

"Where you boys goin'?"

"Miami. And then South America!"

"That so? Looks to me like nobody wants to give you a ride, which is understandable."

Uh-oh, I thought, knowing that Chris, like he always did, had a stash of marijuana in his duffel.

"I'm sure somebody will give us a ride," Chris said, trying to sound positive.

"Well, *I'm* going to give you a ride . . . from here to the other side of Mobile, where I never want to see your long-haired asses again."

I remembered how the cop had to call another squad car because all our duffels wouldn't fit in his trunk. In Peru, while putting up the new route on the major peak, Chris and I had done all the lead climbing. I thought back to Everest, when Chris had made the summit, without me. I had asked him what it was like, standing on the highest point on the planet, and he said it was a trip. Literally a trip—on the way to the top he had taken a full dose of LSD. Back then, Chris lived his life like a speedboat at full throttle. By K2, however, the boat had started to slow, and his own wake was tossing him in ways he tried to resist. I knew that in a transactional way I had traded my friendship with Chris for the summit of K2. Over the years, I would never be able to conclude for sure if the benefit was worth the cost.

After I heard Chris was dead, I wrote to Cherie, telling her I hoped as a nurse she could find her way forward, working without fingers in an occupation that required fingers. Once again, I never heard back.

* * *

With the tents up, we made dinner. The sun dropped below the ridge and we put on our parkas and pulled on our watch caps. In this alpine zone there was no wood for a fire, but nevertheless we stood around our small stoves as though they offered heat, and while we ate we decided it would be useful, for our own reference, to name the surrounding peaks, still illuminated in the light of day's end. We christened the one we would try to climb the next day, naming it Explorer Peak. If that climb went OK, we might have a go at Rolex Peak, or Mount Oyster Perpetual.

The next morning, we left camp after first light and in an hour reached the toe of the glacier. It was smooth and steep, and Yvon swung his ax into the ice and the pick resounded with a high-pitched *Thaaangg.*

"Styrofoam!" he said with a grin.

I knew that meant the ice was perfect: not so hard to make ax and crampon placements difficult, but not so soft that the placements might pull out. We sat and strapped on crampons. There were four of us: Doug and Yvon would be one rope team, and Phil and I would be on the second rope. The others had gone off to explore the cirque, and perhaps try another climb. With his crampons secured, Yvon shouldered his pack. His rope was still in it. He started to climb the steep ice slope, and Doug followed, a few feet off to the side, to stay out of Yvon's fall line.

"Aren't we going to rope up?" Phil asked.

"I'll free solo with those guys," I said, "and trail our rope. Then belay you up."

I knew Yvon had judged the ice to be so perfect that, even though it was steep, there was no need to rope up. I knew Phil wasn't nearly as experienced climbing ice, and I knew I also wanted to experience the gratifying tension when you climb without rope or belay, when you have no choice but to climb with irreducible focus.

Following Doug, I climbed off to the side of both of them in the possibility—even as it seemed an impossibility—that one of the Do Boys might make a mistake. But I wasn't thinking of that because I wasn't thinking of anything. I was in the zone where movement absorbs thought.

When the length of rope I trailed reached its end, I belayed Phil as he climbed. Once on the glacier proper, all of us roped up, as there could be hidden crevasses; it was a risk that required management. When we reached the ridge of the cirque, we opened our parkas to cool our bodies and sat on our packs and ate candy bars. Looking above, the ridge was sharper than it had looked from the base. We continued, skirting cornices, balancing on knife-edges, ascending carefully up snow-covered rock. On the summit there was only room for two at a time. Doug and Yvon took the first turn, waving to me as I took a photo of them. They descended and waited while Phil and I took our turn, arms out for balance as we stood on the diminutive pinnacle.

* * *

We spent one more day "exploring." John and Doug climbed Rolex Peak. The rest of us climbed to the eastern ridge of the cirque, reaching the glaciated crest by midday. We could see eastward along Bhutan's border with China, toward India's isolated Arunachal Pradesh, and northward into Tibet, a panorama dominated by Kula Kangri, a massive unclimbed 25,000-foot mountain that was part of a border dispute. It added to our sense of adventure that we were gazing across territory so remote no one was sure who owned it.

One of my teammates took the time to sight the compass directions of the peaks and to get altitude readings from all the high points. He drafted maps of our cirque, scribing the ridgelines, noting the summits, and using his altimeter to calculate rough elevations.

"Maybe you should draw dragons in the margins," I said.

"Dragons?"

"You know, in the Middle Ages, when cartographers got to the edge of the map where the rest of the world was unknown, they used to write, 'Here Be Dragons.'"

"Kind of appropriate, since we're in the Land of the Thunder Dragon," Yvon added, referring to the traditional name for Bhutan.

Back in camp, the yaks and yak herders had arrived. The expedition was over, and despite not being able to find our mountain, things had worked out. As we packed our gear, Yvon said there was one thing that was bothering him.

"The maps," he said.

"The maps?"

"I don't think we should publish them."

"Why not?"

"The same reason I stopped reporting the new climbs I do in the Tetons. So the next guys who come along have to figure it out. So they'll have the same sense of discovery."

"That makes sense. But what should we do with the maps?"

"Burn 'em."

"Burn 'em?"

"Yeah, torch the mothers. It'll be the perfect ending to our trip."

Yvon Chouinard, the iconoclast. It took a moment for all of us to think it through, but soon we were into the idea. My teammate pulled out the maps he had so carefully drawn, and with his BIC lighter set them on fire. We stood around, cheering him on.

"Let there be dragons," Yvon said.

You know you're off the edge of the map if you burn the map. **Rick Ridgeway**

Elixir of Youth

"Check this out," Yvon said, handing me a copy of *Earthwatch* magazine. It was an article about the fjord region of southern Chile. In the opening photo, three rock spires covered in rime ice rose above a dense green forest bordering a deep, blue fjord. The caption said, "From the fjords of N.W. Tierra del Fuego."

"We could get those collapsible kayaks you can check as baggage," Yvon said. "Paddle in there and climb those things."

There was a reason we called ourselves the *Do* Boys. I signed up, and so did Doug Tompkins and Jim Donini, another of the Yosemite "Hardmen." That was the easy part. More difficult was finding information about the enigmatic spires. The photographer, when we tracked him down, told us he had taken the shot on a rare clear day from the ferry out of Puerto Natales, just north of the Strait of Magellan. Research through back issues of *The American Alpine Journal* turned up one climber who had been in the area.

"That place has the worst weather in the world," the climber told us. "I was there two weeks and only caught one glimpse of the peaks. The one in your photo is like a small Fitz Roy called Cerro de La Paz. If you're really going in by kayak, watch out for the williwaws. Miniature tornadoes that'll flip you. And the current, I've seen it up to twelve knots in the narrows, so fast it makes standing waves."

Jim Donini (left) and Doug Tompkins celebrate the only sunny day on the entire sea kayak and climbing adventure in the southern fjords of Chile. **Rick Ridgeway**

At the latitudes between fifty and sixty degrees south—what sailors call the Furious Fifties—the wind circles the Southern Ocean uninterrupted until it slams into the Patagonian Andes. Then it compresses up, down, and around the fjords and peaks in gusts that hit so hard they feel like hammer blows.

We couldn't find any good maps, but the climber who had been in the area suggested we stop by the cartography office of the Instituto Geográfico Militar in Santiago. Although the office archivist was friendly, we were initially disappointed he didn't have any good maps. Then he pulled out a folder of eight-by-ten aerial photographs taken on a rare day with no clouds. They were remarkably sharp and detailed.

"These have incredible resolution. Who took them?"

"The navy."

"The Chilean Navy?"

"No, I think the British. In World War II. When they were searching for the *Graf Spee*."

I knew the story of the *Graf Spee*. In 1939, the German pocket battleship had been sinking Allied ships throughout the South Atlantic, and the British were searching the region for the marauder. They eventually cornered it in the Río de la Plata, where the battleship's captain scuttled the boat in front of Montevideo. I had been there a few years earlier and had seen the conning tower rising out of the harbor, the water opalescent from oil still seeping out of the hull.

Studying our "maps," we could see the first obstacle was a ten-mile-wide bay that would require paddling against the prevailing westerlies, exposed to williwaws. After that, it would take another sixty upwind miles to get to the outer archipelago and the three spires of Cerro de La Paz.

We convinced ourselves it would be smarter to charter a fishing boat in Puerto Natales and have it drop us off near the peak. After climbing, we could assemble our kayaks and paddle back to Puerto Natales, following a route that would require a portage between two fjords, but would shorten the return.

All of us had spent enough time in Patagonia to know that the plan was not without risk. We would have to stay on our toes to keep out of harm's way, but staying on our toes was one of the satisfactions on an adventure like this one. It had been three years since our last Do Boy trip when we tried to climb Gangkhar Puensum in Bhutan, and we felt good about the way that trip had ended. I knew neither Yvon nor Doug had ever really wanted to make a serious attempt on the peak because it was going to be so dangerous that managing the risk was best done by not even setting foot on the peak. They had gone on the trip because it was a chance to explore a region no Westerner had seen, and, if I was honest with myself, I had felt the same, and so had John.

Since Bhutan, I had been on several trips: fly fishing in Patagonia with Yvon, ski mountaineering in the Yellowstone backcountry with Tom Brokaw. I also had spent more time with my family, including a Christmas vacation with Dick Bass at his Snowbird ski resort, where he regaled the kids with poems and stories. It was the same for Doug and Yvon. None of the trips, including Bhutan, had challenged us in a way that required significant withdrawals from our stores of energy and enthusiasm. In that sense we were like batteries that worked best with an occasional discharge in order to be fully recharged. It wasn't just a physical recharge, either. When you pursue adventure sports for decades, you learn to use your mind to make your body do what you want it to do, even as over those decades your body starts to talk back more loudly. Maybe we needed a good Do Boy trip *especially* because we were approaching that stage of our lives where we needed confirmation that our minds still had veto power over our bodies.

"I've got maybe ten good years left," Yvon told me. He had just turned fifty, and tendinitis in his wrists and elbows had plagued him of late, as well as a chronically sore neck from his Fun Hog road trip with Doug from California to Argentina, when Yvon had dove headfirst into a murky stream in Colombia, hitting a rock and cracking a vertebra in his neck.

* * *

We negotiated with three recalcitrant abalone divers to take us to the outer archipelago. They were young and their boat was old, but its high-cut bow sliced nicely into the growing waves as we crossed the wide bay against a headwind that strengthened to forty knots, with stronger gusts. We took shelter in the small cabin that smelled of aging shellfish, and heated water for tea on a cast-iron woodstove.

"Hey, Fig!" Doug yelled to Yvon above the noise of the diesel and the pounding of the waves. "Feels like we're onto something."

"Fig" was Doug's nickname for Yvon, something he had picked up on that road trip to Argentina to climb Fitz Roy. The granite tusk had only been ascended twice, and never by the route they had selected. For week after week, it rained or snowed, and high winds made it difficult even to walk. The climb took two months. At one point, Yvon's ice ax skewered his knee, and to recover he had to lie for fourteen days in a wet down sleeping bag in a snow cave. He marked his thirtieth birthday flat on his back in the cave lit only by opaque light through the cracks between snow blocks. Now, exactly twenty years later, the original Fun Hogs were back in their original playground.

We anchored in a remote canal that bifurcated two of the outer islands. The four of us who had chartered the boat—including the two of us who at that point in their careers each had a net worth in the tens of millions of dollars—slept in the boat's austere forepeak between wood ribs greased with abalone juice, while the young crew, who in today's lexicon would be called "artisanal fishermen," slept soundly on padded berths in the galley next to the woodstove.

In the morning as we motored up the narrows the clouds allowed for a few blinking glimpses of the sun, but never a sighting of any mountains. The abalone divers dropped us off on a forlorn toehold of flat land along an otherwise sheer-sided fjord.

"The mountain is there," they said in Spanish, pointing into the speeding clouds. The dive boat weighed anchor and disappeared into a squall that marched down the fjord with such force it blew a wall of spindrift a hundred feet high.

"Well, boys," Yvon said. "We've cut the cord."

I looked around. There was no indication, other than us and our gear, of the presence of human beings. The nearest habitation was sixty harsh, wind-raked miles away. Yet this is what we had come for.

Since we couldn't see the peaks, we still didn't know for sure if we were in the right place. Then a hole appeared in the clouds and moved toward us.

"It might open," I said with more hope than expectation.

We stood as the hole approached the spot where we hoped our mountain might be. We waited, then glimpsed a wall of vertical rock. In another beat, the clouds opened to reveal the spire, covered in fresh rime ice, directly above our camp.

"It *is* a miniature Fitz Roy!"

In an instant, the peak disappeared. But now that we knew where it was, we made plans to carry a load of gear to its base. Of the several species of southern beech in the forests of Patagonia, the thickest and gnarliest is *Nothofagus antarctica*, the stuff we pushed through, high-stepped over, and crawled under for two miles. At our latitude of over fifty degrees south, the tree line was only a little more than 2,000 vertical feet above the coastline, and soon we entered the alpine zone. With no trees for protection, we felt the full force of the Patagonian wind. When it shoved from behind, we loped along as though on motorized roller skates. When we turned into it, we had to lower our heads and lean forward, each step like a leg press of 200 pounds.

"This wind . . ." Yvon yelled as loud as he could, turning his head, ". . . is the kind . . . you bite into . . . and chew."

* * *

Mussels foraged off shoreline rocks were our mainstay, and with each day of bad weather, our midden of empty shells grew higher. **Rick Ridgeway**

Back in camp we watched the rain sheet off our kitchen tarp. Three days passed, four, five. Between williwaws we jogged back and forth on the short cobblestone shoreline. At low tide we gathered mussels and steamed them by the potful. Between meals we lay under our makeshift tarp, trading books. Doug's titles were all about conservation and the environment—he had become a student of Deep Ecology, a way of looking at humans as only a thread in the fabric of nature, a species with no moral right to dominate other species. Of all the Do Boys, Doug was taking the deepest dive into what he now referred to as the environmental crisis, and that was the most frequent topic in our daily conversations around our small fire of smoldering wood.

Six days, seven, eight. Our mussel shell midden grew. Twice, our altimeter showed a 300-foot drop, the biggest diurnal barometric change any of us had seen. The only visible change in the weather, however, was that between the lows the winds, which we estimated by the speed of the clouds scudding past the peaks, seemed to drop from over fifty miles per hour to under forty miles per hour.

More than any of us, Jim Donini was getting antsy. He was at the wrong end of a string of bad-luck climbs, where weather had forced him down just short of topping out, and he was determined that this trip would end what was now six summitless expeditions in a row. But Doug had to be home in another ten days. Since we judged it smart to allow a week for the kayak paddle back, we knew it was time, bad weather or not, to make a move.

Under a sky that looked like a spreading gray bruise, we hiked to our cache and sorted gear. We scuttled up a glacier and over a bergschrund to the beginning of the roped pitches. Though we were on the lee side of the spire, the wind blew in madcap vortices that drove the icy rain up and under every overhang. Short breaks in the clouds revealed glimpses of fresh rime ice on the spire above. Even at the base, the wind forced us to yell at point-blank range. I figured there was no way and said as much.

Doug agreed. Yvon said nothing. Jim just shouted, "I've come here . . . to climb! I'm going up . . . at least a pitch . . . or two."

He started uncoiling our two ropes. I looked up again and yelled, "I don't see a future . . . up there!"

Yvon remained silent.

"Anyone going with me?" Jim yelled.

"I'll go!" Yvon yelled back.

As Jim led off, he tied both ropes to his waist in the European style of climbing. The wind bellied the double rope in an airborne arc from his waist to Yvon's belay. I watched him place a chock, and could tell it was less for protection and more to reduce the pull of the rope. Ice water sheeted down the rock, then blew back up on the gusts, soaking them both. Doug and I stood at the base, stamping our feet and waving our arms for warmth while Yvon and Jim completed two more pitches. It was 5:00 p.m.; it would be dark by 9:00 p.m. They were maybe one-third of the way up. They had no bivouac gear, and Doug and I assumed they were going for it.

"Let's climb around the other side!" Doug yelled. "Maybe there's another route that's easier."

It would have to be easier, because Jim and Yvon had our rope. By the time we wound our way around and up a few hundred feet, it was after 7:00 p.m. The climbing was steep and loose, and, now on the windward side, we could move only one foot or hand at a time for fear a gust might blow us off the rock. We gave up and descended.

It was near dark when we got back to the col. There was no sign of Yvon and Jim.

"Maybe they rappelled down the other side!" Doug yelled.

"I hope so!" I yelled back.

"Let's go back to camp. They're probably there."

The wind had increased, and we had to lean head down and push hard to make every step; in the hardest gusts we had to hunker and cover our heads as the wind was now picking up rocks and blowing them through the air. In the beech thickets, our boots made sucking sounds with each step through the bog, and sharp-edged leaves cut our hands.

"They're probably brewing tea right now," I said.

It was a little after midnight when we got back to camp. No candlelight or flashlight.

"They're asleep," Doug said. Then he yelled, "Hey, Fig! Wake up."

There was no answer. Our two tents were empty. We slumped under the plastic tarp, picked at some food, then crawled into our sleeping bags. From his tent I heard Doug say out loud, "You'll be OK, Fig."

I lay in my bag thinking of the climb on Minya Konka eight years before, how I had escaped the avalanche with only bruises and a torn bicep, and Yvon with a concussion and a few broken ribs. My bicep had healed, but with a deformed hollow that I now outlined with my fingers as though it were a talisman.

I jerked awake to a nightmare of Yvon and Jim lying lifeless at the base of the spire. When I opened my eyes I saw the yellow tent fabric lit by the amber glow of first light. I heard a cooking pot clank.

"Doug?"

"No. It's me."

"Yvon!"

From the other tent I heard Doug's voice. "Hey, Fig!"

I opened the tent door. Yvon was starting the stove. Jim was sitting next to him. Their pants were shredded, their hair wet and pasted against their heads.

"There were some tough pitches," Jim related when the soup was ready. "Five-nine, five-ten. Freezing rain. We topped out at nine p.m. The rappels were miserable."

"We had to keep moving," Yvon said. "Bivouacking would have been suicide."

When they had completed the rappels, they began the trudge back to camp. It was dark and the wind too strong to stand, so they crawled and slid on their butts.

"Oh man, I'm wiped," Yvon said.

He crawled into his tent and after a few minutes I heard the slow, steady breathing of deep sleep. He and Jim woke mid-morning, and one look at them was sufficient to know we would be taking a rest day. Jim nursed a mass of water blisters on his hands and arms that were presumably a reaction to the stress he had endured. Yvon stared mindlessly at the water dripping off the tarp as he massaged his wrists and elbows.

"I was surprised you followed Jim," I said.

"I just went up thinking I would clean his pitch. Then we did another, then another. I guess by the fifth pitch, I knew we were going for it."

Paddling into the uninhabited Fjord of the Mountains. **Rick Ridgeway**

"How's the tendinitis?"

"If it doesn't get any worse, I can paddle. If I get into it slowly."

The aerial photographs had shown a possible shortcut to get back to Puerto Natales. We were camped at the beginning of a long, dead-end fjord, but halfway up it there was a side bay that led to what appeared to be a short overland portage to an opposite side bay that led to the big bay on which Puerto Natales was located—on the opposite shore.

The immediate challenge was the five-mile upwind paddle in the fjord in which we were camped. For safety, we planned to stay close to the cliffs; if a williwaw flipped any of us, at least we could crawl onto the rocks. With icebergs from tidewater glaciers floating by, we knew we could only survive being in the water for a few minutes.

We paddled into the fjord, trying to stay close together. But Doug and Jim, in a double kayak, made better headway than Yvon and I, both in singles. Soon the first williwaw roared down on us, one gust so strong it pinned me against a cliff where the surge bashed my fabric-skinned boat against the rocks. Twenty minutes later, another one hit and we fought to stay upright.

"We've got to stay on our toes," Yvon said from the shelter of a tiny cove. "This is serious."

We waited for the williwaw to subside. Yvon pushed off first, then disappeared around a corner. I followed, and as the full channel came into view, I could see another williwaw had nailed Yvon. He was capsized, straddling his upside-down boat and working to paddle it back to the cove. He had just made it to shore when another blast hit. As we dragged our boats across the low-tide stones, I saw a pinched look on his face.

"We have to be careful," was all he said.

We hiked up the coast and found Doug and Jim huddled, like we were, in a tiny bight. Everyone agreed we had to camp and wait for the williwaws to cease. The next morning, the wind eased, and we paddled to our portage. It took two days to back-pack everything to the opposite fjord. Carrying the boats was the worst; even collapsed, they made awkward loads that snagged every beech branch. It was raining more than usual. In one section, the undergrowth was so dense we had to crawl on top of it, occasionally breaking through to the forest floor ten feet below. The only silver lining was that, other than the possibility of spraining an ankle or breaking a leg, we were out of danger.

With the portage complete, we reassembled the kayaks and with the wind at our backs flew like banshees down the fjord. Finally, we could see the last gauntlet: the ten-mile-wide bay. As expected, a phalanx of williwaws marched across the open water. But we had a plan: we would hug the coast and paddle upwind until we gained a windward advantage. Then we would camp, and the following day cross the open water, seizing the grab loops on each other's boats to raft together, *Kon-Tiki* style, and letting williwaws blow us home.

We reached the shoreline of the bay and started paddling upwind. It was getting dark. The shoreline cliff had no breaks. There was nowhere to stop, much less camp. Then a small inlet came into view. I could just make out Doug and Jim's boat ahead. It was blowing forty knots. I hoped Yvon was behind me but dared not turn to look.

My arm and stomach muscles were burning but I couldn't let up. Not for a single second or a single stroke. I made the lee of the inlet, then turned to see Yvon grimly stroking a few yards behind. The boats made a grating sound as we pulled them ashore in the tiny cove. Months later, Yvon would confess that in that final stretch he doubted he could make it. He knew going backward would take him into the bay, into the night, and into certain death. In that twenty minutes of frantic paddling, he had looked as closely into the abyss as at any time since we had ridden the avalanche down that remote mountain in eastern Tibet.

* * *

The next morning the wind eased, we rafted our boats, and by late afternoon we were back in Puerto Natales. No crowd came to greet us, just a few kids curious to see our boats. We lined up for a portrait, showing one of the youngsters how to push the button on the camera.

"Good trip," Doug said.

"We pulled it off," Yvon replied.

"How are your wrists?" I asked.

"Holding up. In fact, I feel great."

Yvon looked across the bay at the fishing boats in the way he does when he's thinking. He made a slight smile and turned back to me.

"You know," he said. "This trip was just what I needed."

The Do Boys on the beach in Puerto Natales at the end
of our adventure. Jim Donini, me, Doug Tompkins, and
Yvon Chouinard (l to r). Rick Ridgeway Collection

The Larsen
Ice Shelf

The polar explorer Will Steger had an idea to dog mush
across Antarctica at its widest point. He invited five companions—each from a different country and each bringing
complementary skills and strengths—to complete a journey
that, beginning to end, would require 220 days to cover
3,750 miles.

The International Trans-Antarctica Expedition was going
to be expensive, and Will made deals with a French television
channel and with ABC. I got the job directing both film crews.
Compared to the expedition members, my involvement was
going to be relatively easy: our four-person film crew would
join the team at a few key points, hitching a ride on a small
plane the expedition had chartered to bring fresh supplies, and
on each visit we would stay with the expedition team for one
to two weeks.

The Russian member of the team, a veteran polar explorer
named Victor Boyarsky, had talked his government—which
back then was still the Soviet Union—into donating a plane to
fly the team to Antarctica. The Russian Ilyushin IL-76 landed
in Minneapolis, the nearest airport to Will's home base and
logistics headquarters in Ely, Minnesota. We loaded on board
several tons of food and supplies, as well as thirty-six polar
huskies—a few of which were the last descendants of Admiral

The Trans-Antarctica team crossing an enormous crevasse halfway up the
Weyerhaeuser Glacier, which connects the Larsen Ice Shelf to the interior
ice cap. **Damien Morisot/Courtesy of Will Steger Collection**

Byrd's dogs bred for his Antarctic explorations in the 1930s— and we took off.

I found the boxes containing the expedition's sleeping bags, and made a nest of down feathers that allowed me one of the best sleeps on a flight I have ever enjoyed. At dawn, out the window I could see the high peaks of the Cordillera Blanca, bringing memories of my ascent of the highest peak, Huascarán, when I was twenty-two years old. It was my first climb of a high-altitude, glaciated mountain. How wondrous if somehow I had been able to look up from the summit and know that all these years later I would be flying over the peak nestled in a mound of down feathers listening to the huskies in adjacent pens howling in anticipation of their breakfast.

* * *

A week later the expedition members, supplies, sleds, three dozen huskies, and the film crew were assembled at a starting point called Seal Nunataks, a series of peaks emerging from the Larsen Ice Shelf near the tip of the Antarctic Peninsula. That was the beginning point of the continental traverse that was going to take more than seven months, and because the team wanted to cross the interior through the South Pole at the height of the austral summer, we were starting at the height of the austral winter. The film crew and I expected to ski with them for a little over a week.

We worked to load the three twelve-foot wooden sleds. Each team member wore a Gore-Tex suit with a small flag of their country sewn on the chest pocket. It was sunny and the temperature was only ten degrees below zero, allowing us to work without the large mittens we would need on a normal day. Will had the most polar experience, having been the first to make an unsupported dog-sled expedition to the North Pole, as well as a south-to-north traverse of Greenland, but Victor Boyarsky and Jean-Louis Étienne were seasoned polar explorers as well. The others—a Chinese, a Japanese, and an Irishman—had between them decades of experience in the Arctic and Antarctic working for the polar-survey departments of their respective countries' governments, and they had complementary skills: Geoff the Irishman and Keizo the Japanese were experienced dog handlers, and Dahe the Chinese was a glaciologist.

"I would have preferred if everyone was single," Will had said. "But Dahe and Victor are married, and they were appointed by their governments to go on the trip."

I felt sorry for Dahe and Victor for being away from their families for so long, and even though I had known them for only a few weeks, they both seemed resolved to the long separation. For me, I felt blessed that I had this opportunity to be with the team for a couple of weeks, to get the flavor of an Antarctic dog-mushing expedition, but then to return to my wife and family. Our third child, Connor, had been born the year before, and was now a little over a year old.

I also felt privileged to be on one of the last dog-mushing teams that would be allowed on the frozen continent; due to fear of distemper passing to seals, the signatory countries of the Antarctic Treaty voted to forbid dogs on the continent once our Trans-Antarctica Expedition was finished.

With the sleds loaded, the dogs' harnesses were fastened to the line. They had been sequestered for over a week in the cargo hold of the Ilyushin, and now they howled in anticipation of the one thing they had been bred to do: pull, and pull hard. I was crouched in front of the lead sled, my eye looking through the viewfinder, when the first team lurched against their traces so hard that the stake anchoring their sled ripped from the ice. When I realized what was happening, I leapt to the side, but not before two of the lead dogs mowed me down, knocking my camera into my forehead. The other two teams then took off in pursuit. I packed my camera as fast as I could and skied furiously to catch up to the charging huskies, blood running from my forehead down my face and dripping off my chin.

On that first day we traveled for only two hours before we set up camp because the goal of the day was not the number of miles traveled but the list of chores rehearsed: loading and unloading the sleds efficiently, setting up camp quickly, feeding ourselves and the dogs. We had only six hours of light each day, but we had everything completed before dark. We were still on the broad flank of the Seal Nunataks at a high enough elevation to see down the Larsen and the adjacent mountain ridge of the peninsula to peaks that were 200 miles away. The shadows were long and, in the far distance, low hills rising from the Larsen were sharp against the sky, as though outlined with a fine-point pen. The low light revealed textures on the floor of the shelf, small cups and ridges sculpted by wind. More than I anticipated, the Larsen, an ice sheet over underlying ocean, looked similar to the vast continental ice cap of the Antarctic interior.

The French camera crew and I jammed into our tent and I volunteered to cook our dinner: freeze-dried pork with black bean soup and rehydrated onions that I sautéed and added to the sauce I then served over pasta. The French were complimentary of the dinner, and so far my effort to integrate myself with them was paying off. We cleaned the dishes, and one of them poured from a stainless-steel flask a small portion of the French apple brandy Calvados into each of our cups, and then they each lit a cigar. Knowing this was an opportunity to advance my efforts at integration, I accepted a cigar and lit it. Soon the inside of our tent was worse than any smog day I could remember growing up in the L.A. Basin in the 1950s, and, saying I had to pee, I stepped outside. It had dropped to about thirty below zero, however, so after a couple of minutes I decided a little smoke in the lungs was better than a little frostbite on the toes.

As I crawled back into the tent I said, *"On se gèle les couilles!"*

"Riiick, you know the French argot! *Très bien!*"

I admitted I was only parroting what one of them had said earlier when he had come into the tent.

"What's that mean, anyway?" I asked.
"It means it's cold enough to freeze your balls."

* * *

The next morning it was still dark as we crawled from our tents, but by the light of the stars I could see the dogs or, more accurately, the small mounds of windblown snow that indicated where each of the animals had curled up and remained motionless so the snow could drift over them and provide insulation. As soon as they sensed we were getting up, however, they emerged from their frozen cocoons and began howling in anticipation of their breakfasts of canned dog food appropriately called Science Diet. The amount of food—human and nonhuman—consumed in a day had been carefully calculated. This was my third expedition to the Antarctic, a place that, once you are away from the coast, is nearly devoid of life. That absence of life had revealed by contrast how my own life depended on the life support I had with me, and that in turn had made me viscerally aware of the formula by which all wild animals begin and end each day: that calories in must equal calories out.

In the days ahead the ice honed my awareness. We seldom rode on the sleds but rather hooked a short section of rope over one of the two handles at the back of each sled to hold us if we fell into a crevasse. We then skied alongside, keeping pace with the dogs. Even by the second day we were in a routine such that my thoughts became lost in the metronomic glide of one ski and then the other until there were no thoughts. I have a memory of being startled from this meditation by the brilliance between my skis of yellow dog urine against white snow. Each day the sun appeared for a few hours and scribed a line just above the horizon before disappearing, and one evening after we set up camp and fed the dogs we stood silently, our hands wrapped around our hot-cocoa mugs, in awe of the eternally slanting sunlight refracting through cirrostratus in an aurora of such spectacle we thought we could hear a vast tinkling of celestial ice.

Unloading our gear, food, and dogs on King George Island near the tip of the Antarctic Peninsula. Residents of nearby Chilean and Soviet bases gathered to watch our landing in the giant Soviet Ilyushin IL-76, which nearly ended in disaster when the pilot landed short of the runway. The impact was so violent, the wings bent downward, nearly hitting the snow and creating so many hairline cracks that the plane was unable to make it back to Russia and had to be mothballed. **Per Breiehagen**

Geographers had divided the Larsen Ice Shelf into four sections, prosaically labeled Larsen A, B, C, and D, and our starting point, Seal Nunataks—a series of volcanoes that in more temperate latitudes would have been islands—was on the border between Larsen A and B. After a week, when we expected to reach Larsen C, the Twin Otter would pick up those of us on the film crew and take us back to Punta Arenas while the six expedition members continued south; we would join them again several weeks later.

On the day the plane was scheduled to arrive, a storm brewed up. We tried to drive the dogs into the spindrift, but as the wind increased it became too difficult, so we set up camp to wait it out. Another day passed. I was used to this life, but in five days I was turning forty, and I hoped to mark the milestone at home with my wife and kids.

The main activities while stormbound in small tents are sleeping, eating, and telling stories. Since my tentmates were French, and I didn't speak French well enough to easily follow conversations, I spent the hours reading books and writing in my journal until my fingers numbed. I also read previous entries in my journal, reliving events from earlier in the year that included a description of a trip to the Tetons to visit Yvon. My family had been with me, and toward the end of our stay Jonathan's daughter, Asia, had joined us. She was now nine years old. After Jonathan's death, Yvon and I had stayed in touch with Asia's mother, and we had seen Asia now and again. On this visit we had taken her hiking and fishing, and, seated on Yvon's lap, we'd let her steer his old Toyota down the dirt road leading to the Chouinards' cabin. I noted that I hadn't talked to Asia about her father, or how he had died, but that someday, as she got older, I knew that would happen.

Late on the second day of the storm I heard from a neighboring tent Will Steger's voice making a radio call to the expedition's base in Punta Arenas. When he finished, he yelled through the tent wall, "There's a high-pressure cell moving in, and the plane should be here in the morning!"

My French tentmates gave a cheer and passed the flask of Calvados. I went outside to pee. It was dark but there was no wind. The clouds had cleared, and it was cold. Back in the tent, I crawled into my sleeping bag and waited until it warmed up. I was content, and with contentment my thoughts turned from where I had been and where I was going to be to where I was. The winter starlight alone was sufficient to illuminate the walls of the tent, and soon I could hear the rhythmic breathing of my companions as they slept. Then in the polar night there was a crack within the ice. It wasn't strong enough to shake the tent or wake my companions. It also wasn't alarming: much of my time in tents has been camped on glaciers, so I was used to the sound of cracking ice. But this crack was different. It didn't reverberate the way cracks do on glaciers; it was quick and shallow, and it reminded me that I was sleeping on ice that was not a frozen stream over rock, but a frozen sheet over an ocean.

* * *

Three months later I returned to Punta Arenas and rendezvoused with my three French filmmaking friends. The next day we were scheduled to fly south in a vintage DC-6 to join the team, which was by then approaching the Ellsworth Mountains, the range that included Vinson Massif, the peak I had climbed in 1983 as part of the Seven Summits expeditions. To reduce costs, the Trans-Antarctica Expedition shared the charter with Reinhold Messner, the most accomplished mountaineer of the day, who, with an Austrian companion, intended to ski unsupported from the landing zone near the Ellsworth Mountains called Patriot Hills to the South Pole. I had corresponded with Messner when he wrote to me after reading my book *The Last Step*, about our ascent of K2 in 1978, but I had never spent much time with him in person. Now, because of mechanical issues, the DC-6 was late arriving in Punta Arenas, and Messner and I had a chance to get to know each other.

By the time the DC-6 arrived the weather in Patriot Hills had deteriorated, so we continued to wait. Two days, three, four. Each day we went to the airport, ready to go in case the weather improved. We sat in the airport restaurant and bar telling stories. There was a small film crew traveling with Reinhold to film his departure from Patriot Hills; they would return, just as we would, after a day of filming Will and his team. There was also a separate German film crew recording Messner's departure from Punta Arenas, but they didn't have authorization from him, and I could see Reinhold's patience with them was growing thin.

Finally, we received a radio call from Patriot Hills that the weather was improving. We loaded into the DC-6 and took off. Forty-five minutes later I could see through my window an opening in the clouds that revealed huge graybeards from the southern sea crashing against the tip of a rocky shore. It was Cape Horn, and as we flew past we began our crossing of the Drake Passage.

That morning I had sent a fax to my wife, wishing her and our kids well and assuring them I would be safe. I was sitting in the front row of passenger seats. Reinhold was behind me, and when I turned, I could see he was looking intently at the back of my seat. He was not staring but rather he was focusing, most likely on the challenge of his ski traverse to the pole. The others were mostly napping or reading.

A half hour later, I felt the plane bank. Out the window I could see we were changing course. For a moment I assumed we were at a waypoint and altering compass direction accordingly. But then the plane continued to bank, and I could tell we had turned around. I stood and looked at the others; everyone seemed oblivious to the change except the French soundman, a tall and broad-shouldered climber from Chamonix who went by the nickname "Le Grand," who looked up from his book, and Reinhold, who had raised his eyebrows questioningly. With my index finger I drew a circle in the air, and Reinhold nodded in understanding. We stood and walked forward to the cockpit. The pilot and copilot were talking into their headphone mics, but I could see from the compass we were heading north instead of south.

After landing, the pilot told us the headwinds had been too strong to allow us to continue. We returned to our hotel, and the next morning we went back to the airport. The weather report over the Drake was still bad. One day passed, then two. I was sitting at the bar with Reinhold, drinking a beer. The unauthorized camera crew was at the other end of the bar. That morning Reinhold had told them to return to Germany. They had demurred, not saying anything, and now one of them raised his camera and set it on the bar and pointed it toward Reinhold and turned it on—we could hear the whir of the film passing through the gate.

"*Das ist genug!*" Reinhold yelled, slamming his beer on the bar as he pushed off from his stool like a launching rocket, flew to the other end of the bar, grabbed the cameraman, and pushed him hard against the wall. He would have pummeled him if we hadn't talked him into backing off. Messner spoke to the film crew in German, and we didn't need a translator to know that the message was some version of "Get the fuck out of here."

The next day we were again sitting in the airport bar. There was no sign of the unauthorized film crew. We learned the delay was now because of mechanical issues with the plane, and we wondered if the real reason we had turned around on the previous attempt wasn't because of strong headwinds but because of something else. While we didn't discuss it further, our silences suggested the scenarios that were worming into our psyches. I was at a table next to the bar, picking at my lunch, seated with Le Grand, the soundman. Of the French crew, he was my favorite. He had trained himself to be a sound recordist, and nearly all his jobs involved films about outdoor sports that often required him to get into extreme positions; in his day job he was a climbing guide, a member of the Chamonix Guides, which was to say that if climbing guides were compared to soldiers, he was in the Delta Force.

"Do you have any deadlines for other jobs?" Le Grand asked.

"No, but I'm on a fixed salary with ABC. I don't get anything for all these extra days. How about you?"

"No jobs, but my wife is going to have a baby soon. A little girl."

I wasn't sure what to say. I pushed at the food on my plate.

"How long have you been married?"

"We never married. We have been together for eight years."

I didn't answer. He looked out the window, then turned back.

"For over six years, we were like this," he said, bringing his hands together, and then he opened them apart. "She had a daughter, ten years old. The little girl became sick. I think in English you call it meningitis."

He pointed his fingers to his head.

"She died in two days."

He looked out the window again. I could see he was starting to cry.

"We were in the hospital for two days. We talked for two days, about important things."

"Matters of consequence," I said.

"Matters of consequence?"

"It's a phrase I picked up, from *The Little Prince*. You know, *Le Petit Prince*? Saint-Exupéry."

"Yes, of course—we talked about matters of consequence. After the girl died, we decided to stay together. It took a while, and we talked about it a lot, but then we decided to have a baby."

* * *

The next day we were told the weather in Patriot Hills was improving and the forecast for the weather over the Drake Passage looked promising. We loaded our backpacks into the DC-6, sat in our seats, and fastened our belts. The engines turned and fired and settled into a fast idle that even inside the fuselage was loud. Then the engines slowed and stopped. We looked at each other, and in a moment one of the crew came aft and said a generator light had come on. We returned to the restaurant, and then were told the repair might take hours.

I was sitting with Reinhold and his ski partner. We were quiet, each in our own thoughts. I was staring at the pages of my journal where the day before I had recorded my conversation with Le Grand. I turned to where I had taped a photo of our three kids lying on the floor, giggling, and looking at the camera. They were looking at me, as I took the photo. On the inside cover there was a dried flower also taped to the page. It was a wild iris I had found inside a book I had given to my wife during our courtship while we were staying at Yvon's log house in Jackson, sleeping together in the bed Yvon had been given that was found in the abandoned cabin of his poet laureate, Robinson Jeffers. I ran my finger over the flower, feeling its form under the transparent tape. I closed my journal and looked at Reinhold.

"I'm not going," I said.

"You are what?"

"I'm not going to fly on that plane. It's too dangerous."

Reinhold didn't say anything. I could see his jaw working. He breathed deeply, and then he said, "You are making the right decision."

We were again quiet, each looking in a different direction.

"You have no idea all the things I have been through," Reinhold said. "All the things . . . and I am still here, still alive. And now?"

He turned and looked at me, and our eyes held.

"And now I am going to die in this fucking airplane."

* * *

The next day I caught a commercial flight home. Out the window I could see the mountains of central Chile, the places where I had had some of my adventures. But over those years I had never done anything close to turning my back so definitively on one of my commitments.

I found solace in reminding myself the commitment I was leaving was subordinate to the commitment to which I was returning, and I pledged never to doubt my decision to weigh the risk of loyalty to one commitment against the possibility of never coming home from the other. I recalled how at the airport gate, when I was departing on the expedition to cross Borneo, I had said goodbye to Jennifer and she had started to cry and I held her and she said she wasn't going to wash my dirty clothes, in case something happened to me.

"That way I'll be able to smell you. Even your underwear."

"Even my underwear?"

She started to laugh, between her tears. Jennifer owned an inveterate wariness, a skepticism against things always turning out OK. Where most of us get on the airplane thinking about where we are going and what we are going to do once we're there, she would think about the plane crashing.

"I visualize disasters," she had told me. "Very realistically."

I knew this was rooted in the horror of surviving the tidal wave that broke apart their boat when she and her first husband were sailing off the coast of New Guinea, the nightmare of losing her husband and her unborn baby. That had not prevented her from boarding a plane or driving a car or going on a vacation. The only thing she never did again for the rest of her life was get in the water and swim.

In the first weeks that followed our engagement, when she moved into my beach shack just south of Montecito, I began to realize she lived more fully in the moment than anyone I had ever known. It was how she went about her daily rounds—how after she got out of bed she held the warm washcloth to her face for a full minute, how she tasted her food when she ate, listened to someone when they told a story, held a baby, or talked to a young girl or boy. It was so different from the way I went through my days, focused on my goals and along the way developing a habit of believing that things would get better once I had completed the next expedition or finished the next book or made the next movie.

"You are always waiting for Godot," she had told me, offering no other comment or explanation. It wouldn't be the only time she would tell me something that she would leave to me to figure out.

We had been married for about five years when she told me she needed to talk to me. "You are not affirming me," she said.

What did that mean? The next day I brought her blue irises. She loved freshly cut flowers, and blue irises were her favorite. She gave me a nod and a slight smile. I brought her coffee in bed each morning, a gesture that I continued for the rest of her life. Over time, I realized that while gestures were important, this was not the affirmation she had in mind. It was rather to understand her deeply, to understand her attributes and to make sure she knew that I knew, because she knew that was the only way two people can love each other profoundly.

* * *

Now out the window of the plane we were passing the mountains of Peru, mountains I had climbed in what seemed like a previous life. I looked at the photo of the kids taped to the inside of my journal.

Don't worry, I said to myself. *I'll be home in time for Halloween.*

JOURNAL
1989

PROPERTY OF RICK RIDGEWAY

IF FOUND PLEASE CALL COLLECT:

805- 648- 6598

CALIFORNIA, USA

FLOWER I FOUND IN MATTHIESSEN'S "AT
PLAY IN THE FIELDS OF THE LORD"
GIVEN TO JENNIFER AND DATED AUGUST, 1981,
JACKSON, WYOMING

FLOWER I FOUND IN MATTHIESSEN'S "AT
PLAY IN THE FIELDS OF THE LORD"
GIVEN TO JENNIFER AND DATED AUGUST, 1981,
JACKSON, WYOMING

The inside cover of my journal for 1989. On the next page I had taped the
photo of our three kids, but this page had taped to it a wild iris that I'd
found pressed between pages of a book I had given to Jennifer.

Talking to Beluga

It was a clear day with a cell of high pressure stabilized across the High Arctic. Out the window of the plane, the sun reflected off the inlets of Great Slave Lake, the Slave River flowing in from the south, and the Mackenzie flowing out to the west. There was as much water as land, and the land was mostly rock, scoured over the eons by the ebb and flow of glaciers. From horizon to horizon, there were no signs of the handiworks of humans.

Across the aisle, Doug Tompkins, the Do Boy-in-Chief, was also looking out the window, and I guessed he was likewise appreciating the largely untrammeled expanse. Behind him was another good friend, Doug Peacock, who had a map out and was tracking our position. Yvon had met Peacock a few years before, and he had become part of our Do Boy posse.

"If we had living national treasures, like the Japanese," Yvon had said, "I would nominate Peacock."

Doug Peacock was a double-tour Green Beret medic in the Vietnam War, who had returned to his Midwest home with what today would be called post-traumatic stress disorder. He loaded his backpack and camping gear in his truck and drove west. He was armed, and he had enough self-awareness to recognize that he was potentially dangerous. He wandered through the Rocky Mountain states, and when he ran out of money, he stopped at a pay phone to call home. An operator came on and told him to

Doug Peacock on Somerset Island in the High Arctic, vigilant for beluga whales ... and polar bears. **Rick Ridgeway**

deposit two dollars and ten cents. He put the coins he had on him in the phone, and when the operator said, "Please deposit twenty-five more cents," Doug asked the operator to wait while he returned to his truck to rummage through his pack for extra change. He found a quarter. Back in the phone booth, however, the line had gone dead. He redialed the operator, who told him the phone did not return change.

He walked to his pickup and got his 12-gauge and loaded it with double-aught. The first double blast tore the phone off the wall of the booth. A few more salvos and the phone booth folded. He walked back to the truck, got his gas can, doused the remains of the phone booth, and tossed a match into the mix. Back on the road, he looked in the rearview mirror and saw black smoke rising.

With his backpack full of supplies, he wandered the back-country of Yellowstone. Doug was alone on a trail in the most remote corner of the park when he came face-to-face with an alpha male grizzly. The bear reared on its legs. Doug drew his .44 Magnum Ruger and aimed it between the bear's eyes. Then, looking into its face, he slowly lowered his pistol. Doug Peacock's days of witnessing death were over, even if it might mean his own. The bear lowered to all fours and turned and left.

Doug spent the next several seasons living alone in the remote Yellowstone backcountry with bears, at a place he called the Grizzly Hilton that he alone knew about. The bears were his redemption. He watched them, and he recorded notes about them. He bought a used 16mm camera and filmed them. He lived with them, and they accepted him, even if one day the dominant male came into his camp and ripped apart his dirty clothes and anything else that held his smell. Little by little, Doug Peacock became more of an expert on the behavior of wild grizzlies than the grizzly experts.

With redemption came re-engagement. He began migrating south and overwintering in Arizona, where he became friends with the writer Edward Abbey. Doug's redemption was not entirely complete, however, and Ed picked up quickly that Doug himself was like a wild bear; to an extent, he even looked and moved like one. Like a bear, Doug became increasingly fierce about protecting his habitat, and for Doug that was everything that was still wild in the West. Ed the writer imagined Doug and a band of like-minded enviro activists, armed and dangerous, hell-bent on protecting their habitat. The result was *The Monkey Wrench Gang*, and the central character, Hayduke, was not just inspired by Doug Peacock. Hayduke *is* Doug Peacock.

* * *

The trip to the High Arctic was kind of out there—even for a Do Boy adventure. Cunningham Inlet, on Somerset Island, just north of the Arctic Circle, was one of only a few places in the High Arctic with high concentrations of beluga whales. Doug Tompkins and I had our collapsible kayaks with us, in hopes of kayaking with the whales. On this trip, however, the Do Boys were only hangers-on; the core of our group had come to *talk* to the whales.

The trip organizer, Jim Nollman, was a musician who had made a name for himself with a children's recording of him singing with 300 turkeys. For his next book, *The Man Who Talks to Whales*, he played music to orcas in Puget Sound with instruments designed to play under water. He was confident the orcas were singing back. Now Peacock and I were doing an article for *Outside* on Nollman, and a Chicago record producer had also come along. The producer told us he had never slept in a tent or in a sleeping bag.

The trip promised an amusing display of our species' tendency to organize into quirky subcultures, but it was the promise of viewing species other than *Homo sapiens* that was for me the greater attraction. Little by little, year by year, the central appeal of my adventures was shifting from the sports done in wild places to the wild places themselves, and, increasingly, to the wildlife in those wild places. Or maybe not shifting as much as amplifying: I still loved the sports, but that passion was becoming eclipsed by the gratification of simply being in wild places among wild animals. Part of it was solace, but the other part was that my time in wilderness was affording me a greater awareness of how, in the web of life, I was an animal among animals.

* * *

The Twin Otter left us on a gravel bar close to where Cunningham Inlet opened to the Northwest Passage. We had an Inuit man with us named Simon; he wasn't so much a guide as a liaison, required by the government. Simon had a rifle, to protect us against polar bears, and he also had his eight-year-old son, an addition we welcomed. We hoped to learn more about the Inuit and their culture by having a father and son along, and we hoped the boy would learn a little about outsiders, even if our particular group was a little quirky.

The quirkiness included the fact that Peacock himself was armed, not with a gun but with an eight-foot spear with a steel tip modeled after an Anasazi point he had found in the Desert Southwest.

"The rifle's an unfair advantage over the bears," he had told us when he produced the spearhead from his luggage and then searched Resolute, during our stopover, for a suitable shaft. He explained further that while the spear point was inspired by the Anasazi, his strategy for its use was modeled after the Maasai and their alleged ability to thwart a charging lion by jamming the butt of a spear into the ground at the precise moment of the lion's leap so that the beast impaled itself.

With our camp set up, Simon asked Peacock if he could check out the spear. The Inuit hefted it, ran his thumb along the point, handed it back to Peacock, then picked up his rifle and patted it with a gesture indicating, "Thanks, but I think I'll stick with this."

Even in summer the inlet still had sea ice that moved in and out with the diurnal ebb and flow of the tide. After breakfast the next morning Doug Tompkins and I assembled our kayaks and paddled out. There were no belugas, but the day before, as the Twin Otter circled the area before landing, we had seen out the

Jim Nollman and his floating drum. "Of all nonhuman species," Jim would later tell a reporter, "belugas may possess the dearest rudiments of true language." **Rick Ridgeway**

window a small hut at the back end of the inlet: the outpost of a wildlife biologist named Tom Smith, who was studying belugas. Tompkins and I paddled a couple of miles up the inlet and pulled our boats ashore on a gravel beach. We started walking toward the hut, but before we got there, Smith met us halfway. He was lean, weathered, and full-bearded: Ahab of the Arctic.

"Kayaking in the bay, you will scare the whales and jeopardize my project," he said by way of introduction.

"We don't want to do that," I offered with a conciliatory tone. "We can just stick to the mouth of the inlet."

That seemed to ease the tension, and while he didn't invite us inside, he did tell us more about his study.

"These Cunningham belugas winter in Greenland, where the Inuit hunt them. I've been studying this population for ten years, and it's declining."

He explained that his study centered on attaching transmitters to the whales' fins using what he called "a surgical procedure." I assumed it meant capturing the animals and drilling a hole through their fins.

"These animals are skittish."

No shit, I thought to myself. *Hunted on one end and drilled on the other.*

Tompkins and I paddled back to our camp. Jim Nollman had unpacked and assembled his equipment, which included an array of waterproof drums attached to inflatable floats. Wearing a dry suit, he waded into the water up to chest level, and started playing the drums. No belugas. He tried one rhythm and then another, but the only animals around were a flock of Arctic terns squawking overhead, and it was my guess their cries had less to do with the drums than the probability that we had set up camp near their nests.

While Jim continued to beat on the drums, Doug Peacock said he was going on a walk to explore the island and asked if anyone wanted to come along. No one else other than me expressed interest, so I left, following Peacock carrying his eight-foot spear. Within minutes I was questioning my decision to join Peacock, especially after Simon, with his rifle, had declined to come along. A half hour later we paused to scan our surroundings.

"This island all looks the same," I said.

"What do you mean?"

"You know, open tundra. Seen one part of it, seen it all."

"You wanna go back?"

"That's what I was thinking."

* * *

Two days later a pod of belugas entered the inlet. Jim rushed to the water, drums in hand, waded in, and started playing. The whales didn't seem to pay him any mind. They were pure white with rounded heads, and they seemed like creatures perfectly adapted to this far end of the planet, evolved, like their terrestrial counterpart the polar bear, to blend into a world of black and white.

The whales continued past our camp, toward the end of the inlet where, presumably, Tom Smith would count and observe them. Over the days, our Chicago music producer had somehow, against all apparent odds, befriended the biologist. That day, as he did most days, he walked the two to three miles from our camp to Smith's hut to visit. The sun continued its circle above the horizon, and the rest of us went to sleep. I was in a slumber when I heard someone yelling. I looked out my tent door and saw the Chicago producer running toward us.

"Polar bears!"

"Polar bears?"

"They're chasing me. They'll be here any minute."

I dressed quickly and crawled out of my tent. Others had overheard the commotion, and they were also emerging. Everyone but Peacock, who always set up his tent a distance from camp, for the solitude. Sure enough, there were three white dots heading at us, but they were still a half mile away. Through our spotting scope, I saw a large female adult and two cubs ambling directly toward us at what appeared to be a normal but intentional gait. I could see the muscles on the female quiver with each step.

"Doug. Peacock!" I yelled. "Wake up!"

Simon's son ran to his tent to wake his father. In a minute Simon emerged, fully dressed. The bear and cubs were now about 300 yards out. Simon loaded a round into the chamber of his rifle. The producer told us he had been walking back to our camp when he turned and saw the bears behind him. He started running, and every time he turned, they were still there.

Peacock was standing next to his tent, glassing the bears. Then, without explanation, he started walking toward them.

"He doesn't have his spear," Tompkins said.

"That's our boy," I replied.

Peacock walked a hundred yards and then crouched behind a low rise in the otherwise open tundra. By now we could see that the bears weren't coming directly at us, but were on a line that would pass above our camp. Peacock had already seen this, and he had put himself in position to get a better view.

In a few minutes, the sow and cubs crossed above Peacock and then past our camp, seemingly paying us no mind. Peacock walked back, and together we followed the bears. At one point we got too close, and the sow suddenly turned and stood on her rear legs. We got the message, and stopped. She lowered, turned back to her cubs, and then descended to the mouth of the inlet that, with the flood tide, was choked with sea ice. We watched through binoculars as the mother bear ventured out onto the ice, and the cubs followed.

"There's another bear," Peacock said.

"Where?"

"I don't see it. I just know it's there."

"How?"

"The way the female's acting. There's another bear around."

"How is she acting?" I asked.

"I don't know how to explain it."

Simon looked through his binoculars and watched for a full minute, glassing the surrounding ice.

"There's no other bear," Simon said.

"Yes, there is," Peacock countered.

I could see by his body language that Simon was dismissing this crazy white man who had never been to the Arctic and never seen a polar bear and who carried a spear as though that were any kind of protection. We were silent, watching the mother and her two cubs grow distant.

"There it is," Peacock said. I looked through my binoculars and watched another female with another cub appear from behind a pressure ridge in the sea ice.

* * *

The sky grayed and it snowed in brief flurries and we spent the next couple of days sipping tea and telling stories. We told Simon how Tom Smith had been attaching satellite transmitters to the whales, and how he had then determined they spent winters in Greenland. Simon told us he was opposed to the idea of placing transmitters on whales, and he was thinking of organizing an Inuit protest.

"Why do you not like it?" I asked, anticipating he would give me an answer that had something to do with respect for the whales.

"If we kill a whale and it has one of those tags, we won't eat it."

"Why not?"

"Because it will be sick."

"That doesn't make any sense," Doug Tompkins said. "The tags no doubt cause pain, but they don't cause sickness."

"We don't like the idea of putting the tags on the whales and doing all these studies."

"But the studies are showing the whales are declining," I said, despite my own conflicted view about drilling holes in their dorsal fins to get that information.

"Since the whales are declining," Tompkins said, "would you and your friends be willing to stop hunting them?"

"No."

"Why not?"

"It's our right to hunt them."

"If all the whales disappeared," Tompkins continued, like a prosecutor probing a witness, "all the whales except two, a male and a female, would you hunt them? The very last two whales alive?"

"Yes, I would."

* * *

Just as Peacock had become more of an expert about the behavior of wild grizzlies than the experts, Jim had managed something similar with orcas. His assumption that belugas were equally, if not more, intelligent than orcas would, in the years ahead, be confirmed by continued studies of belugas, including the case of a beluga observed in Norway wearing a Russian-made harness with camera mounts. Cetacean experts speculated with confidence that the whale had been trained as a spy; the local media nicknamed the suspected agent the "White Russian."

On our last day in camp, I woke feeling a draft blow into my tent and down the top of my sleeping bag; even in a half-slumber, I noted the drifting air was warm. Outside, I felt a gentle wind coming up from the south. Low-altitude cumulus patterned the sky as I sat on a folding chair in front of our mess tent, drinking fresh-brewed coffee.

"The belugas are back."

I looked up and saw the pod entering Cunningham Inlet. Jim donned his dry suit and grabbed his drums. I got into my kayak and paddled out. It was the same kayak I had bought for the trip to the Magellanic fjords in Chile to climb the rock spire a few years before. Later, I would take the kayak on a Do Boy trip in the Russian Far East. I loved the kayak like a friend because, like friends, that kayak and I were connected through shared experiences. On this trip the relationship was expanding not because it was my vehicle to go on another adventure, but because it was my means to get close to these animals.

Doug Tompkins and I had now kayaked close to the whales enough times they were beginning to overcome their initial temerity. Across the water came the sound of Jim's drums. I neared the pod, and they did not shy away. One of the white whales came alongside me and turned its head; for a brief moment our eyes held, two species looking at each other.

Pausing on my walk with Doug Peacock across the open tundra of the interior of Somerset Island, where the only shadows are yours and your companion's (unless a polar bear shows up!). **Doug Peacock**

Chapter Fourteen

Jungle Mirror

Most of the mountains in the Amazon's Guiana Shield—the broad uplift of quartzite spanning Colombia, Venezuela, Brazil, and Guiana—are *tepuis*, with vertical sides and flat tops. In the late seventies, a year after the Bicentennial Everest Expedition, I had climbed one of them with Mike Hoover, who had directed the television show on the Everest expedition and had told me one of the most important parts of getting into filmmaking was having good ideas.

That was when I had told him I had a three-drawer file cabinet labeled, bottom to top: Ideas, Good Ideas, and Great Ideas. The labels were meant to be a joke, but inside the Great Ideas drawer was the folder with notes on the idea of climbing one of the *tepuis* called Autana. It not only looked like a challenging climb—the peak was shaped like a giant cut-off tree trunk—but it also had a large cave just below the summit that went straight through the mountain one side to the other, like the eye of a needle. Further, the local Indians believed the cave was the lair of a dinosaur-like creature that descended at night to raid villages and eat humans. I wrote a proposal, Mike sent it to ABC, and a few months later we were on our way to climb Autana. There was no dinosaur in the cave, but we reached the summit, the film was successful, and I added filmmaking to the things I did for a living.

The Yanomami who joined us to help carry the gear were unaccustomed to the cooling breeze caused by the speed of our motorized dugout, and one of them curled up in my lap for warmth. Monica Dalmasso

I loved the jungle, and that attraction was one of the reasons I'd made the crossing of Borneo. While doing research for my proposal to climb Autana, I had learned of a rock spire called Aratitiyope that was in an area said to be uninhabited by even the most isolated tribes. On a geology map from the 1930s, the area was blank except for the words "region of suspected granitic outcrops." Under the Roraima Shield, deep beneath the quartzite, was an ancient batholith, a dome of granite. Was it possible the quartzite had eroded, exposing the granite, which perhaps had eroded into a rock spire?

Eventually I found an article in a French climbing magazine about a team who had climbed the peak in the previous few years. It was indeed granite, and it rose more than 2,000 feet above the jungle. The nearest village of Yanomami people was fifty miles away, and that village had been visited by anthropologists only in the last decade.

ESPN agreed to my proposal to put together a small team of climbers and a camera crew to attempt Aratitiyope. I called two elite rock climbers, Paul Piana and Todd Skinner, who were also working cowboys from Wyoming. They immediately signed up to be the lead climbers and main characters in my film. In Caracas we chartered an old DC-3 to fly us to a remote mission on the Upper Orinoco River, where we arranged for dugouts with outboards to take us upriver. We figured this would take about a week; from there we would go overland, hiking for another week. To help carry the gear, we hired porters from the more westernized Ye'kuana, along with the Yanomami. We would have preferred to take all Yanomami but we had been warned in Caracas by "old jungle hands" that the Yanomami did not understand the concept of work for hire, and since we were going into an uninhabited region, the hunting was sure to be excellent; if the Yanomami sighted game, they might drop their loads and disappear for days.

We hired fourteen Ye'kuana and five Yanomami, including one named Alberto who had lived in the mission for several years

On our flight in an aging DC-3 to a remote mission where we started our journey, we had the pilot fly an extra hour inland so we could do an aerial reconnaissance of Aratitiyope. Our route followed the thin arête in the center that rises left-to-right from the base. Kike Arnal and spoke Spanish; he would be our translator. We left the mission, heading upriver. I shared a boat with two Yanomami, and one of them, looking for a place to nap, curled in my lap. At first, I withdrew, but then realized that my reaction was acculturated, so I relaxed and draped my arm over his shoulder. He was naked save for a thin red loincloth. He smelled like sweet oil and his skin was cool against my legs.

That afternoon we camped on a sandbar, swinging our hammocks between trees and tying a rain tarp over our sleeping area. I usually travel with fishing line coiled on a compact hand reel I bought in a hardware store in southern Patagonia, and at river's edge I attached a silver minnow lure, twirled the line like a lariat, and cast it into a slow-moving pool. On my first cast, I landed a piranha.

"That's a critter you don't see in Wyoming," Paul said. He was wearing his cowboy hat and a cowboy shirt with pearl buttons.

"They're good to eat," I replied. "We can have them for dinner."

"Let me try and catch one."

I handed the reel to him and he twirled the line like someone who had spent a lot of time lassoing cattle. In a minute he landed another piranha, and before I could say anything he reached his fingers into the fish's mouth to remove the lure. Instantly the piranha clamped down on his thumb. He didn't jerk or yell or scream. Instead, he calmly used his other hand to pry open the fish's mouth. There was a sharp tooth in the front, and it went in one side of his thumb and out the other, right through the nail. Remaining calm, he slowly pried his thumb off the tooth, then raised it like he was giving a sign of approval.

"That," he said, "is gonna make one goddamn good story."

* * *

By the time we finished pulling our canoes to shore at the last Yanomami outpost, every villager was gathered to meet us. It didn't appear to be an obvious welcome: all the adult men, naked except for small red loincloths, held bows and arrows, and some had machetes. Alberto explained to one of the men, who we assumed was the chief, that we were going to Aratitiyope, and that we needed another porter and were hoping to hire someone from the village. That seemed to put them at ease.

The chief and Alberto discussed the matter, then Alberto turned to me and indicated one of the villagers.

"That guy will go with us."

"Great. Tell him we'll wait while he goes to his hut and gets his stuff."

Alberto translated my message to the headman, who replied to Alberto, who turned to me.

"He doesn't need to go to his hut. He has everything he needs."

I looked at the man. He held his bow and several arrows and he had a machete. Like the others, he had a small red loincloth that covered only his privates. He would be gone from his village for about a month.

"OK," I said. "I guess we're ready."

The tributary we followed began to narrow, and we lay in the boats watching the jungle slowly squeeze out the open sky until finally the canopy touched and then closed over the water. We were now in an area without any human habitation. Our progress slowed as a Yanomami man in the bow of the lead boat cut through deadfall across the stream with his machete. When we encountered a tree across the river too large to cut, we pulled the boats up on the shore and started overland through untracked jungle.

On the second day, I was following a Yanomami when suddenly the native dropped his pack and, with bow and arrows, dashed into the jungle.

There goes the first one, I thought. I dropped my own pack to follow him, not out of concern he might have abandoned his porter responsibility, but out of curiosity over what had caught his attention.

From the rear he appeared completely naked. He was moving fast, and I struggled to keep up. Through an opening in the understory below the trees, I again caught sight of him. He was now moving slowly and stealthily. He had nocked an arrow. Then I heard them: a troop of monkeys, perhaps a hundred yards distant. Standing in a shaft of light, the Yanomami made a monkey call, then hunched over and began a monkey pantomime. From my position fifty feet away, I stood silently and watched.

The monkeys, seeming curious, moved in to get a closer look, and at the critical moment the Yanomami straightened, pulled his bowstring, and released his arrow. *Whoosh!* The monkeys went wild; the shot missed. The Yanomami turned and looked directly at me—my first indication that he knew I was there—and he smiled and started laughing.

* * *

A few days later we arrived at the base of the spire. When we started the first pitches up the near-vertical granite, the Yanomami laughed again. Some of the climbing was hard, but well within the skills of Paul and Todd. Still, we were slower than we had estimated, and a week later we found ourselves low on food. On our last bivouac before reaching the summit, we sat quietly on a ledge with only the sound of the sickle wings of nightjars slicing the air. The moon was full, illuminating towering clouds rising over a jungle unoccupied by human beings. Perhaps humans had even bypassed this area when they first moved through the Amazon on their way from the Bering Strait to the Strait of Magellan.

The next day we reached the summit. Paul and Todd launched their cowboy hats like Frisbees into the air. We were early enough that we were back in Base Camp by dark. We were hungry, very hungry. I sat on a log next to Paul, and one of the Yanomami set a basket on the ground between us, indicating that we should eat. By this time it was dark, but I could see that the

All they had—all they needed—were their bows and arrows. Though a few had machetes to chop vegetation. **Rick Ridgeway Collection** basket was full of plum-sized fruits. Paul and I started eating them, then more, and more. I turned on my headlamp to see how many were left. We both looked into the basket. The fruits were crawling with maggot-like worms.

"Turn off the light," Paul said with a cowboy drawl.

I turned it off, and we ate the rest of the fruit.

* * *

Back home, when I thought about the climb, I often thought about the Yanomami and the monkey dance, and once when I reconstructed the vision fully it gave me a chill. There was something about it that I couldn't shake. Finally, I figured it out. In that shaft of light in the jungle, maybe for the first time in my life, I had seen a human acting as pure *Homo sapien*, an animal among other animals. I had seen who I used to be.

"Other cultures are not failed attempts at being you," said philosopher Wade Davis in reference to "The Other." "They are unique manifestations of the human spirit." **Kike Arnal**

Do Boy Meets
Do Girl

In January 1991, Doug Tompkins took off from San Francisco in his Cessna 206 to fly to Patagonia. He had piloted a small plane from California to South America several times, starting in 1961 when, only weeks after getting his pilot's license, he loaded his wife, Susie, and their two young daughters into his then even smaller Cessna 182 and flew to Chile.

A few years after that first trip, Doug sold The North Face, the company he had founded, and invested the money into Esprit, the company he and Susie had founded. Now, twenty years after that, he was again flying south, this time after a divorce that had been both nasty and public. Susie had raised enough money from investors to buy out Doug's half of the company. Now he had money, and with it a resolution to advance his increasing passion for wilderness conservation. He had started a foundation that made cash grants to small environmental groups, but for Doug, it wasn't sufficiently fulfilling.

About the same time, Doug had partnered with Yvon to purchase and protect a small forest of monkey puzzle trees, the ancient *Araucaria araucana*, in southern Chile. The land had been comparatively inexpensive, and the result brought palpable gratification: you could walk through the forest and feel like you were walking through a cathedral you had saved from a wrecking ball. What if he bought other lands in the Patagonian region

A section of the coastline in southern Chile that Doug purchased shortly after returning from the initial scouting trip in 1991. Today, this is one small part of the 994,000-acre Pumalín Douglas R. Tompkins National Park. **Antonio Vizcaíno** of Chile and Argentina, the one place in the world that always seemed to pull him back?

Now he found himself once again flying south in his small plane, this time to scout estancias in Argentina and Chile, some so large they encompassed entire watersheds. He timed his investigation to overlap with a weeklong training, or "philosophy session," as Yvon put it, for Patagonia executives that the company had organized on an estancia near Fitz Roy.

* * *

The goal of the session was to train upper-level executives to take more of the responsibilities of running the company from Yvon and Kris McDivitt, who, since 1979, had been Patagonia's CEO. Patagonia had started in 1973 when it split from Yvon's other company, Chouinard Equipment, which made climbing hardware, and for the first few years it was run by a group of managers. When Yvon knew it was time to appoint a CEO, he turned to Kris. She had started as an assistant shipper for Chouinard Equipment when she was still in high school and worked her way up. She had also worked her way into Yvon's confidence, and this was built on a foundation of mutual trust and loyalty that made Yvon comfortable giving her responsibility beyond what her experience would have justified in any traditional business.

"Kris was a quick study," Yvon said.

"Yvon was the entrepreneur, and I was the one trying to do it better and faster," Kris replied.

"She could fathom my mercurial creativity."

"Yvon was the visionary, and I was the engine."

Kris was also able to run the company during Yvon's frequent and sometimes long absences on climbing, fishing, surfing, and skiing adventures. Yvon liked to tell friends his MBA stood for Management by Being Absent, but the trips added value: he was testing products and coming up with new ideas, and both he and Kris understood how important that was. With the two at the helm, the company had grown past $100 million in annual sales.

Kris McDivitt (right) meets with a designer during her
tenure as Patagonia's first CEO. **Rick Ridgeway**

When Yvon and Kris finished their retreat, they returned
with the other executives to the nearest town, El Calafate, where,
by prearrangement, Doug met up with them. Doug wanted Yvon
to join him on his survey of estancias, and he had invited me to
come along as well. I flew to Argentina and rendezvoused with
everyone in Calafate.

The Patagonia team said they needed a day to download notes,
so Doug decided to fly his Cessna to Río Gallegos, the provincial
capital, to look up titles and maps of some of the estancias he
wanted to investigate. He invited me to come along, saying we
would be back in time to join Yvon and his team for dinner.

I had never flown with Doug but knew he had a reputation
as a pilot who was both skilled and bold. It was less than an hour
to Río Gallegos, and soon I could see ahead of us a small city
on the Strait of Magellan that I assumed had to be it. In a few

more minutes, however, the town was out my side window, and we appeared to be flying past it.

"I thought we were going to Río Gallegos?"

"We are."

"Isn't that Río Gallegos?" I asked, indicating the town we appeared to be passing.

"Yeah."

He didn't say anything more, and I feigned a kind of "OK" shrug. Then he said, "We're low on gas."

I could see we were following a highway. Soon we got to a stop sign and turned right, following another road that led to the town, which was now out our front window. I then realized that we were following the road in case we ran out of gas and had to make an emergency landing.

"Not much traffic today," I said.

"I think it's the weekend."

We started our approach to the airport. As we descended, the plane bucked violently in the strong Patagonian wind.

"See that rope under the wing?"

I had already noted two ropes, each about three feet long, attached to the tie-down rings.

"Yeah?"

"After we land, I'll keep taxiing and you open your door and work your way out on the strut and grab the rope and then hang on it with your body weight so I can turn. Otherwise we might flip."

"OK."

We landed and then taxied, staying headed into the wind until we got near the hangers.

"OK, get out!" Doug said.

I opened the door, stepped onto the footpads on the wing strut, and, holding the strut in both hands, hit the tarmac with my legs whirling like the Road Runner in the cartoons with Wile E. Coyote. I worked my way to the rope, grabbed it, then hung my body weight on it, feet wrapped around a knot on the end. Doug then turned the plane with the weighted wing into the wind. Two airport attendants ran to us, and together we tied the wings and tail to the anchor loops in the tarmac.

The main street of Río Gallegos was lined with native beech trees all bent in the same easterly direction: living testaments to the wind. Even though it was the weekend, Doug had arranged to have the government office stay open, and we spent several hours studying maps and deed documents.

"I want to take a look at this place," he said, indicating it on the map. "It's an estancia called Rincón, bordering the east face of San Lorenzo. You know that peak?"

"I've heard of it."

"A five-star mountain. We'll fly up that way with Yvon and check it out. You'll think you're back in the Himalaya. And the whole place along the base of it, it's for sale. Imagine that! Any place else in the world, it'd be a national park."

* * *

That night at dinner, Doug took an empty seat next to Kris. "Hey kiddo, how you doing?" he said, patting her on the back.

Kris had met Doug only a few times and her impressions had not been positive, especially after Yvon had asked Doug a couple of years before to give the keynote address at a Patagonia sales meeting. In his speech Doug said the company should encourage intra-office sex because it kept the juices flowing among employees. I was in the audience sitting between Jennifer and Malinda. I could see my wife's one eyebrow raised in her inimitable expression of dubiousness, and I could hear Malinda, as could everyone in the auditorium, say, "Over my dead body."

After dinner, Doug asked Kris to come back to the lodge where he and I were staying so he could show her photographs of the estancias he wanted to investigate. Kris said it was getting late, and she needed to get up early for their flight to the United States.

"Hey, you can do me a favor," Doug said. "I've got a duffel of books I've been reading. With Rick and Yvon coming along, it's too much weight in the plane. You mind taking it back for me?"

* * *

The next morning the wind was blowing, but it was clear on the leeward side of the Andes as Doug, Yvon, and I flew north. Doug decided to make a close pass by Fitz Roy, and the small plane bucked so violently in the turbulence that I had to brace my body so I didn't pull any muscles in my back or neck.

"We already climbed that thing," Yvon said, indicating Fitz Roy. "We don't need to look at it anymore."

We continued north. Through the cockpit window San Lorenzo rose in singular dominance. At a little over 12,000 feet, it is the second-highest peak in Patagonia, but because it is so far south it's encrusted in perennial ice, making it—despite its relatively low altitude—the most Himalaya-like mountain in the Southern Cone of South America. As we approached the peak, we had a better view of the steep east face.

"Over six thousand vertical feet," Doug said. "And the face has never been climbed."

We flew over the grassland valleys at the base of the mountain.

"Estancia Rincón," Doug said. "A five-star place, and it may be for sale."

We circled a ranch house and could see someone step out the door, wave to us, and get into the pickup parked in front. We landed on the estancia's grass strip, and the pickup pulled alongside our plane.

"René Negro," the driver said, shaking our hands. "*Bienvenidos a Estancia Rincón.*"

Inside the ranch house, we sat around the pot-bellied stove passing a gourd of maté. René was handsomely dressed in a long-sleeved cotton shirt, neck cravat, and beret. For his part, Doug wore his trademark pressed chinos, carefully tucked-in oxford shirt, and Argentinian espadrilles with no socks. Yvon and I both wore Patagonia plaid shirts and bombachas, the company's take on the wide-legged pants with button cinches on the bottom cuffs worn by Argentine gauchos. Yvon had sworn to the sales team that they "would go like hotcakes," but sales had stalled. This may have been due to the fact Yvon and I had been the fit models, and when men with longer legs than ours—at least 90 percent of the adult male population—wore them, they looked like they were dressed for a flood.

After a tour of the 37,500-acre ranch, René dropped us off at the beginning of a cattle trail that went up a valley defined by a lateral moraine coming off the east flank of San Lorenzo. In addition to scouting the ranch as a potential protected area, we could also scout the peak for a potential future climb.

"We'll be back in three days," Doug told René.

We shouldered our packs—or, in Yvon's case, he positioned a tumpline on his forehead that held the pack's weight. As with bombachas, the company also made and sold the straps, and as with bombachas, not too many people were buying them. That hadn't dissuaded Yvon from continuing to evangelize the benefits of the tumpline, a technique used by the majority of remote peoples around the world to carry loads.

"The weight goes from your forehead straight down your back to your feet," he said to anyone who asked.

Yvon claimed the tumpline had cured decades of neck pain from his injury during the Fun Hog trip to climb Fitz Roy when he dove headfirst into a muddy river and hit his head on a submerged rock. I had tried it on previous trips but given up because it was hard to look up, and as a birder, that had become too frustrating. Still, I appreciated Yvon's dedication to the tumpline because it reflected his habit of always looking for ways to improve a product, especially when a product, like a pack that had shoulder straps and a waist belt, was taken for granted by everyone as just the way a thing was made.

As we continued up the valley, we lost sight of Doug. He usually hiked faster than everyone, and Yvon and I were used to just letting him go. After a couple hours we saw him ahead, stopped next to the small river running down the valley, having lunch. We set down our packs and joined him. When we stood to go, Doug picked up a cow skull lying next to the trail and held it in front of his face so that he was suddenly transformed into a chimera that triggered in me a kind of vague connection to a time when we ourselves were just another animal living among animals.

"Just a second. I have to get a photo."

Over the years I have occasionally looked back at that shot. To me, it is an insight into what made Doug such a skilled designer: I am convinced he had a sense, when he picked up that skull, of the effect that holding it in front of his face would have. Years later, walking through a retrospective of Picasso's work, I would see a bull's head made of found metal scrap and realize that Pablo Picasso and Doug Tompkins had been channeling the same primordial link to the same ancestral memory.

* * *

In late afternoon we arrived at a *puesto*, a small hut built to shelter gauchos guarding sheep and cattle in their summer pasture. The structure was ramshackle, but we cleaned the floor, started our small gas stove, made tea, and sat outside enjoying the sunset. Under the shadow of San Lorenzo, the place was stunningly beautiful, even if much of the ground was overgrazed and in various stages of erosion.

"Like just about every estancia in Patagonia," Yvon said.

The sheep industry in Argentina was in crisis. The price of wool was low, and land productivity was decreasing as ranchers, trying to make ends meet, overgrazed the land, further decreasing its productivity. We suspected it was this cycle that was causing René Negro to give up and sell.

"You pull these sheep off," Doug said, "and I bet these grasslands would recover. Just imagine what this place would look like."

As evening approached, we erected Doug's North Face tent, which was big enough for the three of us. Doug owned the

Doug Tompkins channeling his inner Picasso. **Rick Ridgeway**

tent not out of loyalty but because the company, at least with tents, had adhered to the quality he had established, and to the design he had cocreated when he partnered with the genius architect Buckminster Fuller to develop what today is known as the dome tent.

In the morning we hiked to the head of the valley, scrambling high on scree to get a better vantage of the east face of San Lorenzo looming over 6,000 feet above us.

"The route goes up that central icefield," Doug said. "Looks like there may be a bergschrund at the top where you could bivouac."

"I doubt you could get that high in one day," Yvon judged.

"You don't want to bivy in the middle of the face," I added. "Too much objective danger—look at that sérac near the top."

"It looks stable," Doug said. "Probably been like that for a while."

"Stable until it's not stable," I countered.

We all agreed it was a potential Do Boy project, even though I knew for me the adjective *potential* had a different definition than it did for Doug. Two days later we loaded into the 206 and flew north, landing at the small town of Los Antiguos. Yvon and I took our backpacks out of the plane and said goodbye to Doug, who was continuing north to look at more estancias while Yvon and I were going to do some fly fishing in the region.

"I'll call you guys when I get back," Doug said.

"Let me know what you find," Yvon answered.

Doug started the plane and took off, and Yvon and I put on our packs and walked to the road and stuck out our thumbs.

"Kind of going from one extreme to the other," I said. "Our own private plane to hitchhiking."

"Living on the extremes is where you want to be," Yvon answered. "You just got to be careful about spending too much time in the middle."

* * *

A month later I was back in California when Doug called me. After flying his Cessna back from Chile, he had returned to San Francisco.

"I found another estancia up north from where I let you guys off," he said. "On the Chilean side, south of Puerto Montt, in a fjord called Reñihué. Looks like the wildest parts of the British Columbia coastline. Five-star place."

Doug told me he was already in conversations with René Negro about possibly buying Estancia Rincón, and he was going to talk to the owners of the estancia in the back of the Reñihué Fjord. Then he changed the subject.

"Hey, I was calling to ask you about something. You know Kris? The woman who was with us in Calafate, who's running Yvon's company?"

"Yeah?"

"She's a good friend of yours, right?"

"She's the only person other than me that's been in the delivery room for the birth of all three of our children. If Jennifer and I were Catholic, she'd be the kids' godmother."

"I thought you knew her well. She's not married anymore?"

"One of those things. She and her husband just grew in different directions."

Later that day Kris called.

"I'm going up to San Francisco tomorrow," she said. "I've got a duffel of books that Doug Tompkins unloaded on me. I don't know why I volunteered to take them. Anyway, I know you've climbed with him quite a bit, right?"

"We've been on few trips together."

"That's what I thought. Tell me about him. You think he's a good guy?"

The east face of San Lorenzo, the unfinished project of the Do Boys. Rick Ridgeway

Chapter Sixteen

The Road
Less Taken

A year after the trip to Patagonia, when Yvon and I met up with Doug Tompkins, the Do Boys rendezvoused in Khabarovsk, a city in the Russian Far East on the bank of the Amur River facing the border with China. Our plan was to sea kayak for 200 miles along the nearby coastline of the Sikhote-Alin Mountains, home to the endangered Siberian tiger.

Yvon had gotten the idea from the wildlife biologist Maurice Hornocker, who had a research station on the coast. Several of the Do Boys signed up: Yvon, Doug Tompkins, Doug Peacock, Tom Brokaw, Jib Ellison, and me. While Doug Tompkins was still investigating the idea of purchasing the two estancias he had found in Chile and Argentina, he was also interested in learning more about the threats to native forests in Siberia, thinking he might also get involved in supporting efforts to protect boreal ecosystems. Doug Peacock was looking forward to seeing the only place on the planet where tigers shared habitat with brown bears. Tom Brokaw was also interested in conservation topics, as well as a respite from his life in New York. Yvon and I wanted to explore a coastline that, as far as we could tell, no one had ever kayaked.

Like Yvon and Doug Tompkins, Jib was an experienced kayaker, and also an experienced white-water rafting guide. He had a degree in philosophy from Reed College, and during a senior

The Do Boys pose behind the helicopter that will take us to the headwaters of the Bikin River in the Russian Far East. Doug Tompkins, Tom Brokaw, Dmitry Pikunov, Jib Ellison, Doug Peacock, and Yvon Chouinard (l to r). **Rick Ridgeway**

259

seminar on nuclear deterrence he came up with the idea that rafting could promote détente between the United States and the Soviet Union by bringing together Russians and Americans who, once they were literally in the same boat, would become ambassadors for peace. His Project RAFT—Russians and Americans for Teamwork—had since become a reality, with expeditions on the Katun River in the Altai Mountains of Siberia and the Obihingo River in the Pamir Mountains of Tajikistan; I had been fortunate to be with him on both trips, and we had become good friends.

* * *

In the coastal town of Terney, we met up with Maurice at his research station, called Tiger Camp. We also met a few of his colleagues who were based in the camp, including a Russian tiger biologist named Dmitry Pikunov, who went by Dima, and an American named Dale Miquelle, a postdoc studying big cats.

"We've collared some of the tigers in the area," Dale told us. "A few weeks ago, I was watching one of them on our monitor that was staying put, indicating it likely had made a kill. I went to investigate and found the carcass of a deer, but also prints of both a tiger *and* a bear. I was bent over the carcass when suddenly the bear burst out of the woods, charging straight at me. I jumped back and fell headfirst down an embankment. That startled the bear, and probably saved my life. We went back later and confirmed that the tiger had taken the deer and the bear had driven off the tiger. It's the first confirmation of who is more dominant."

I could see the delight on Doug Peacock's face, both because it confirmed what he already suspected about his beloved bear's order in the hierarchy of the wild Earth, and because visiting these remote mountains, where we would be in close company with top predators, was for him the raison d'être for our adventure.

Maurice's team had arranged a meeting in Terney with the local authorities to discuss our plans to sea kayak the coast. In a small office near the harbor, the officials—who claimed to be from the Department of Tourism, even though there was no tourism on the coast—told us that we would have to have two guides, one truck following us on land and a motorboat to accompany us on the water, and pay a fee of a little more than $2,000.

"Fucking extortion," Peacock said as he paced the room like a bear in a cage.

Peacock went outside to vent while we tried to negotiate with the officials. Tom had experience talking with Russians, but it was mostly at a high level, including a one-on-one with Gorbachev. Jib, on the other hand, had a history of dealing with the apparatchik. Meanwhile, Tompkins, who had neither interest in nor patience for the negotiations, had been outside talking to Dima, the Russian biologist we had met at Tiger Camp.

"Boys, Dima's got a plan," Tompkins reported. "There's a Russian helicopter scheduled to land this morning to pick up some milk containers—it's literally the weekly milk run."

Dima had told Tompkins he could make a deal with the heli pilots to take us to the headwaters of a river called the Bikin, and instead of kayaking the coast we could kayak the river—there were no big rapids, so our sea kayaks should work. Dima told Tompkins the area was a vast wilderness and was the largest remaining stronghold for tigers, and that he would come with us, to help us try and find one.

"Dima says we can do a ruble deal for the chopper," Tompkins added, "so it won't cost much. Sounds like a winner, huh?"

"I don't know," Yvon said. "I was kind of set on kayaking the coast."

"Plus, we've put so much work into our plan," I added.

The others were also undecided, but I could see in Tompkins's mischievous grin that part of the appeal was the fact that it *was* a reversal of plans. We were still discussing the merits of the idea when we heard the chopper approaching.

"Come on, it'll be an adventure," Tompkins said.

"All right," Yvon replied. "Let's do it."

"Either plan is OK with me," Peacock added. "I just want to get away from these extortionist KGB motherfuckers."

Before the extortionist motherfuckers knew what was happening, we closed a deal with the pilots that included the two cartons of Marlboros we had brought as barter. We quickly loaded our gear into the chopper, sat ourselves between three-foot-high cans of milk, and took off for someplace called the Bikin River.

* * *

At least we had a good map. Soon we were crossing untracked forest. The mountains were low and rounded and looked old, like the Appalachians. It was hot and humid inside the helicopter, and we opened several port windows that were round, just like those on a boat. Peacock consulted our map, holding it open between his hands, then leaning forward to look out the window to compare map to terrain. Suddenly the map ripped and pieces of it were instantly sucked out the port. Peacock was left holding two panels, one where the trip started and the other where the trip ended.

"What are we going to do without a map?" Tom asked, his alarm evident on his face.

"Remember, Tom," Yvon said with his impish smile, "it's only an adventure when things start to go wrong."

"It's better without a map," Tompkins agreed. "We'll figure it out."

"No one worries!" Dima said, waving his hands for added effect. "I know where to go!"

Dima was behind the pilot's seat, giving them directions as we crossed what to me looked like an endless tract of rounded mountains carpeted uniformly with dense forest. Soon the helicopter banked, however, and we could see a log cabin next to a small river with an adjacent clearing big enough to land.

"Udege hunting camp," Dima said. "This is where the Bikin River begins."

* * *

The flat water of the Bikin River was perfect for our collapsible sea kayaks and the paddle raft that Dima brought. **Rick Ridgeway**

The Udege are the indigenous people of the Sikhote-Alin Mountains, and they had a hunting camp on a headwater tributary of the Bikin called the Zeva. The next morning, we assembled our collapsible sea kayaks, said goodbye to the hunters, and started our descent. The current was swift but the water was flat, so that even though we paddled slowly the forest of old-growth larch, fir, and spruce sped by. On the second day we reached the confluence with the Bikin, and now there were occasional rapids, but they were easily navigable. On the fourth day we pulled the boats ashore to follow a game trail in the hope we might find a tiger.

We knew there was only a slim chance we could see a tiger since it was the middle of the summer and the deciduous forest was dense; you have a much better chance of seeing a tiger in the winter, when the forest is open and snow makes it easy to follow tracks. But maybe we could find a print? Our hope was realized in less than an hour, when we found the prints of a large adult. They were less than an hour old, perhaps much less. Peacock took out of his pack several rubber Halloween masks he had purchased at a variety store before leaving the States.

"Wear these on the back of your heads," he said. "It'll reduce the chance of getting attacked from the rear."

We put the masks on backward, as instructed. Ahead of me was Mikhail Gorbachev, and in front of him was Ronald Reagan. Dima was in the lead, and in a few more minutes he stopped at a tree that had deep claw marks six to seven feet off the ground.

"The tiger is marking its territory," he said with a grin.

There was a strong scent of fresh cat urine where the tiger had peed on the tree, and the stain on the bark was damp.

"How close?" I asked.

"The tiger watches us now," Dima answered.

We never saw the tiger, but we did decide that Dmitry was an honorary Do Boy. Tompkins had picked up on that the moment Dima had told him we should hire the helicopter to take us to the Bikin, both as a good adventure and as a way of saying "fuck you" to the officials. Like Yvon and me, Dima was short, maybe five foot six. He reminded me of the news footage of Nikita Khrushchev I used to see when I was a kid, always waving his arms and hands when he spoke, like he was making karate chops in the air. Dima's face was tanned and weathered from years in the field, and his eyes were always moving, as if he didn't want to miss anything. When he had a point to make, he talked louder and louder until everyone was listening, and while he talked, he never stopped grinning.

I could tell that Doug Tompkins felt an affinity for our Russian guide not only because of Dima's deep knowledge of the wildland we were exploring and its wildlife, but also because of their mutual delight in breaking rules. In another week, we arrived at a bridge that supported the railroad tracks that would take us back to Khabarovsk. It was the end of our river excursion, but Dima proposed an extension to our adventure. In the opposite direction, the railroad went to Dima's hometown, Vladivostok, and if we were to go that way, Dima could show us around the city, and we could meet his family. The only problem was, Vladivostok was home to Russia's Pacific fleet, and strictly off-limits to foreigners, especially Americans.

"We'll all get arrested," Tom said. "That's maybe not a big deal for you guys, but NBC would have a shit-fit."

"No arrests," Dima countered, waving his arms and raising his voice. "On the train nobody say anything. I do all talking. Then in Vladivostok, we buy Russian clothes. You look like Russians. No problem!"

Once again, Doug Tompkins had a grin he couldn't repress. In Vladivostok, we went to a flea market and bought drab Russian shirts and coats. It was Sunday, and Dima insisted we visit the waterfront. The Russian fleet was in full view, including a decommissioned submarine open to the public. Dima, of course, insisted we tour the submarine, and Tompkins, of course, insisted we take up our host on his gracious suggestion.

* * *

A month later I was in New York and went to dinner with Tom Brokaw at a small restaurant he favored. The corner tables were occupied, but this was New York, where the public was used to celebrities, and even though we sat in the middle of the room, no one interrupted us to tell Tom he was their favorite anchorman, as usually happened when I was with him elsewhere in the world. Tom and I discussed the world affairs that were central to his job; from our many conversations, I had concluded that in his profession Tom had interviewed or interacted with more men and women who were directly shaping the major events of the twentieth century than anyone else in the entire twentieth century other than perhaps Lowell Thomas. Yet, as usually happened when we got together—whether it was with Tom, Yvon, or others in our posse—our conversation inevitably led to talking about Doug Tompkins. I realized this was because of our almost hypnotic fascination with watching Doug experiment with one idea and then another as he tried to find his way into the next chapter of his life. I also realized that all of us who were Doug's friends were, at the same time, metaphorically holding our breath as we speculated whether or not Doug *would* succeed in finding his way.

"Think about everything Doug's done to this point," Tom said. "Kayaking and climbing, founding The North Face and then Esprit. He's been enormously successful at all of it, because he's been in control. But tackling the environmental crisis? I'm afraid he might become disillusioned, even depressed."

Tom was right that the jury was still out over whether Doug could find a way to confront the environmental crisis that was effective and at the same time personally gratifying. In Russia, I had watched Doug consider whether or not to get involved in efforts to conserve the taiga forests that were being logged to feed demand for lumber and pulp in China and elsewhere. In Khabarovsk, I had gone with him to a meeting of the local chapter of the Russian Academy of Sciences, and there the Russian forest scientists had told Doug about the illegal logging in the province.

"You should run full-page ads in the Moscow newspapers," Doug told them. "Expose what they're doing!"

"We can't do that. It's against the law."

"All the more reason to do it," Doug countered. "I'll get you the money to pay for the ads."

The scientists demurred, and I could see from Doug's expression that he was mentally writing them off. On our trips Doug also talked about his foundation that made grants that were a major source of revenue for groups like the Center for Biological Diversity and Sea Shepherd, but we could tell, by the way he continued to test other ideas, that being on the sideline as a funder was not as fulfilling as being on the front line as an activist. Maybe his idea of buying estancias in Chile and Argentina and converting them to protected areas would give him what he was looking for.

"I'm not too worried," I told Tom. "Doug's got so many skills he can carry forward. The way he focuses on details, or the way he's always on the lookout for new ideas and people who are doing things differently. You've got to admire him for leaving one chapter of his life and going in a completely new direction. Like Frank Wells did."

"Yes, but Frank went back to the movie business."

"But Frank's not the same guy he was before he spent a full year becoming a climber. Now he's an environmentalist and making a big difference. I don't know, but I think Doug will figure it out."

* * *

What Doug and Frank had in common was a confidence at the height of their careers to change gears and try something completely different. Watching them, I realized that their confidence was rooted in their trust that the skills they had developed in one arena could be used to succeed in a different one. I was reminded of Albert Schweitzer's memoir *Out of My Life and Thought*, which I had read in my twenties. Schweitzer had dedicated his early adulthood to becoming one of the world's great organists and music theorists. At the height of his success, he then did a one-eighty to become one of the world's authorities on the historical life of Jesus Christ. He left that to go once again in an entirely different direction to become one of the world's great physicians.

"Every start upon an untrodden path," he wrote, "is a venture which only in unusual circumstances looks sensible and likely to be successful."

During the three expeditions I had been on with Frank as part of the Seven Summits adventures, I had tried to see things through his eyes, to understand the pluck that it had taken to do his one-eighty. I considered just the facts: after law school, Frank had started as a junior lawyer in an entertainment law firm, then joined Warner Brothers and worked his way up the ladder to the presidency. He was about to turn fifty when he quit his job to attempt the Seven Summits. On the surface, it looked like some version of a midlife crisis, but as I got to know him better I realized that in the back of his mind he knew if he applied everything he had learned up to that moment about how you reach a goal, he might be able to pull it off.

"The reasonable man adapts himself to the world," George Bernard Shaw wrote. "The unreasonable one persists in trying to adapt the world to himself. Therefore, all progress depends on the unreasonable man."

Tom Brokaw was right that Frank was different from Doug because Frank had gone back to the movie business, becoming president and COO of The Walt Disney Company, and it was beyond the pale to imagine Doug returning to the rag trade. After Frank got his new job, however, I watched how he entered his next chapter with an expanded sense of purpose that was rooted in his experiences spending time in the mountains.

Sometimes he would drive up to Ventura to have dinner with Yvon and me. Dan Emmett and his wife, who lived just up the beach, would sometimes join us, and sometimes we would have dinner at Dan's house. Frank was often exhausted from his long days, and he relished reconnecting to the life he'd had during the Seven Summits year. On the beach we pried mussels off the rocks and in the kitchen scraped off the barnacles. Yvon would steam the mussels in a large pot and we would eat them with a seaweed salad foraged from the tidepools. Frank would grin widely, mussel juice dripping onto his oxford shirt, and for an hour or two he would return to his one-year sojourn as a Do Boy.

At our dinners our conversations inevitably meandered to the environmental crisis, just as they did inside our tents during our climbs. For Frank, doing something about the degradation of nature had become a personal goal, as important to him as

Dick Bass (left) and Frank Wells at the black-tie Seven Summits
celebration at the top of the tram at Snowbird. **Rick Ridgeway**

his professional responsibilities at Disney. This conversion was
the result in part of the months Frank had spent in wild nature,
but also of having spent those months in the company of people
like Yvon and Dan.

During our Seven Summits climb of Aconcagua, Frank
and Dan had hit it off, and Dan had gone on to join Frank on
his ascents of Kilimanjaro and Elbrus. They had become close
friends. Frank was a Democrat and Dan was a Republican, but
Dan was one of those Theodore Roosevelt Republicans who
understood that the root of the word *conservative* is *conserve*,
and for Dan that meant the conservation of nature through the
reduction of the human impact on nature. As a lawyer, Dan's

focus was advancing environmental law, and he founded the Emmett Institute on Climate Change and the Environment at the UCLA School of Law.

For his part, Frank founded an NGO called Environment Now that eventually would hire a prominent Californian environmentalist named Terry Tamminen as executive director. A few years later, Terry would leave Environment Now to become head of California's EPA under Arnold Schwarzenegger, and Terry and Dan Emmett would sit down and use Environment Now's action plan as the framework to develop the environmental goals for the state of California. Nearly all those goals would become reality, and one of them would evolve into the idea for a cap and trade scheme to limit greenhouse gas emissions that today is one of the world's leading models of how governments can address climate change, and a model that you can trace upstream all the way to Frank's expeditions into the wilder parts of our world.

* * *

Two years after the kayak trip to the Russian Far East, when Frank was still coming up to Ventura occasionally to have dinner with Yvon, Dan, and me, Jennifer and I took all three kids to celebrate Easter at my mother's house. The living room was pandemonium with kids playing. The TV was on but the sound was off. Out of the corner of my eye I saw Frank's face on the screen.

"Sweetheart, Frank is in the news," I called to Jennifer above the cacophony.

I reached for the remote, but before I could turn up the volume a chyron appeared below Frank's face.

Frank Wells, 1932–1994

I put the remote down and slowly sat down on the couch.
"Sweetheart," I said.
"Yes?"
"Frank is dead."

Frank and Dick, along with Clint Eastwood, Mike Hoover, and Mike's wife Bev Johnson (whom I had known for twenty years, and who was a pioneering American rock climber and the first woman to solo El Capitan), had been on a heli-skiing holiday in the Ruby Mountains of Nevada. Because of the size of the group, they'd had two helicopters, and on the last run, Dick and Clint had loaded into one while Mike, Bev, and Frank climbed into the other. The pilot of Frank's chopper set down briefly to wait for a cloud to pass, and we would learn later that the rotor wash had swept snow into the intake manifold. When the chopper took off, it was airborne for only a few seconds before the engine shut down. Frank, Bev, and the pilot were killed. Mike survived, but his leg was broken so violently that his bone drove through his ski boot.

Frank's family planned a service at a large auditorium at Disney's headquarters in Burbank, and they asked Yvon and me to speak. It seemed like all of Hollywood was there. Yvon and I, with Malinda and Jennifer, were ushered to seats in the second row, so we could more easily get to the podium when it was our turn to speak. We sat behind Stanley Gold and his wife. Gold was the film industry kingmaker who had called Frank to offer him the job of running Disney the day that I had been at Frank's house, working with him on our book *Seven Summits*. As we were all waiting for the service to start, Jack Nicholson walked up to Gold and whispered in his ear. He left, and Gold's wife leaned to him and said, "Who was that?"

"Just some actor."

At the podium Michael Eisner talked about his partnership with Frank, but he had to stop several times to gather himself. Robert Redford told the audience how Frank had supported his career. Then it was Clint Eastwood's turn.

"I knew Frank for thirty years," Clint said.

He then told a story of accepting an invitation to play tennis at Frank's house. Clint was surprised both by Frank's skill as a player and his competitiveness.

"I walked to the net to pick up the ball, and I looked directly at Frank, and lowered my visor and narrowed my eyes. And that's something I know how to do."

Clint paused and then said, "When you skied with Frank you had to ski fast or you skied alone. It was a wonderful day, that Saturday. Frank was in a wonderful mood. We all were. I remember before that last chopper ride, I heard Frank singing 'Hey Jude.'"

He paused to compose himself, then alone at the podium, with no instruments, no backup, Clint Eastwood sang "Hey Jude."

"Hey Jude, don't make it bad. Take a sad song and make it better . . ."

When he finished, voice breaking, he said, "I'll miss you, pal."

Dick was too upset to speak at length, but Yvon and I shared stories about the Seven Summits adventures. I told the gathering how I'd worn my aloha shirt and flip-flops the first time I met Frank.

"When we made that first climb in South America," I said, "Frank was close to helpless. He couldn't set up a tent, pack his gear, start a stove, much less boil water. He slipped, fell, struggled—at one point he even crawled. But he made the top, and by the end of that year he had metamorphosed: he built snow walls, pitched tents, sharpened crampons. He was lean and strong. On the way out from the Antarctica climb, forced to wait out a storm at an American station named Siple, he even learned to cook by heating soup in the base's microwave. When he got home, he couldn't wait to tell his wife. 'It was fantastic. You just push these buttons and, presto. Darling, we've got to get one.'

"'Frank,' his wife answered patiently, 'we've had one for ten years.'

"When the climbing year was over a reporter asked Frank why he climbed, and Frank quoted the last line of his favorite Robert Service poem that he had learned from Dick. 'I want to see it all,' he said. To do that, he made the commitment, just as he turned fifty, to leave the road he had been on all his adult life and take an entirely new one. No maps, no signposts, absolutely no guarantee he would reach the destination. How many among us has the courage to do that?"

In Memory of

Frank G. Wells
1932-1994

The cover of the program at Frank Wells's service. **Rick Ridgeway Collection**

Hobgoblin of Little Minds

Doug Tompkins bought the 37,500-acre estancia called Reñihué, located in the fjords of southern Chile, and built a house for himself as well as outbuildings for the staff he envisioned hiring to help him convert the place to a nature sanctuary. Those of us who were Doug's friends knew he had answered his own question of what he was going to do with his life when he sold his house in San Francisco to move to Reñihué, and it was doubly confirmed when he also sold the art collection he prized, putting the many millions from the sale of the house and the art into his foundation, which now shifted focus to buying more estancias in Chile and Argentina to create even more protected areas, and maybe even converting them to parks that could someday be gifted to the two countries.

Doug then purchased the estancias contiguous to Reñihué, and then the estancias contiguous to those estancias, nearly 800,000 acres total. He constructed a restaurant, visitors center, lodge, campgrounds, and miles of hiking trails, and opened the park, then called Pumalín, to the public.

At the same time, Doug was courting Kris McDivitt. He kept trying to persuade her to visit him in Chile, and she kept saying no, until finally she said yes, and what she anticipated would be a one-week trip turned into five weeks. A few months later, in 1994, Kris and Doug married. She resigned from her position as

Kris and Doug Tompkins shortly after Kris left Patagonia, Inc.,
married Doug, and moved to southern Chile to join him in
creating new national parks. **Tompkins Conservation**

CEO of Patagonia, Inc., sold her house, and moved to Reñihué to join Doug. Over the next twenty years, the two of them would create dozens of protected areas, an outcome that, measured by acreage, would be the biggest achievement by private individuals in the history of conservation.

* * *

When Doug bought Reñihué it came with its own volcano. Michinmahuida was not just any volcano, but a broad dome covered by thirty square miles of glacial ice. In 1997, on my first visit to Reñihué, I stood at the south-facing window at Kris and Doug's house. It was a clear day—unusual in the Valdivian rainforest of southern Chile, where annual rainfall can be more than 200 inches—and Michinmahuida dominated the view. I made a mental note that one day I would come back and climb it.

Chile's southern coast is enchained with volcanoes, and when Doug first arrived, many of them had not been climbed, including the next major one south of Michinmahuida called Corcovado. It was a classic cone with a near-vertical plug of volcanic rock at the top. Doug had conscripted a Chilean friend with some climbing experience to attempt it with him. When his rope partner lost confidence at the base of the near-vertical section, Doug continued alone, unroped, to the top.

The next volcano to the south was Melimoyu—a massive dome similar to Michinmahuida except it had two rock spires at the summit, like the ears of a rabbit. It remained unclimbed, and this time Doug recruited me to join him in giving it a shot. Like most of these volcanoes, the hardest part was not the climbing but the approach. The understory of the forest was so thick with a cane-like plant called *quila* that you couldn't see your companion twenty or sometimes even ten feet away.

From Reñihué we flew south in Doug's Cessna, landing in a small coastal village where we hired a fisherman to take us upriver in his small boat and let us off at a tributary that Doug had scouted from the air. We spent the first day crawling through *quila*. It was raining and the forest floor was a mud bog. We had a machete, but it was usually faster to use your body weight to push through the cane. Other than a short stop for lunch, we struggled on our feet, knees, and bellies for six hours.

Suddenly we encountered an opening. Not exactly an opening, but a line through the *quila* that had been pushed open, like the line we had been making for the last six hours. Was it made by an animal? Other than cougars, the largest animal in this forest was a miniature deer the size of a Labrador retriever. By humans? But who else would be here? Then we saw a footprint in the mud. It was one of our footprints. We had gone in a wide circle, and we were back where we had started.

* * *

Doug said he would do some more surveys in his plane to try and figure out a better approach to Melimoyu, and that I should come back next year and we would attempt it again. Before I went home, however, he had an idea for us to try another volcano called Yanteles.

"Some guys are cutting a horse trail up a valley that leads to it, so the approach should be easy," Doug said.

The area was part of a 200,000-acre property that Doug had purchased along with another Esprit alum, Peter Buckley, who also had cashed out and devoted himself to conservation. Peter had come down for a visit and planned to join us on the attempt.

Not only did the horse trail eliminate most of the bushwhacking, but we arranged for horses to carry our packs most of the way. We camped above tree line, and from my tent I listened as Doug explained to Peter how to use an ice ax. The next morning, at the base of a glacier, we showed Peter how to strap on crampons and arrest a fall. With that, we were ready to start the ascent.

"Aren't we going to rope up?" Peter asked.

"No need to," Doug replied. "This is easy."

"What about crevasses?"

"They're probably all exposed. Anyway, I'll go first."

Doug Tompkins piloting his beloved Husky aircraft over Pumalín. **Scott Soens**

We were in an upward traverse on hard snow when Peter tripped and started sliding. Because of the angle I couldn't move fast enough to stop him before he slid past me. Worse, he was turned turtle, on his back.

"On your belly! Dig your ax in!"

Peter turned over, but he was gaining momentum fast. The slope eased as he slid into a short bowl before it steepened again, and I held my breath as he slowed and then stopped. I ran to him as fast as I could.

"You OK?"

"I might have hurt my leg."

I pulled up his pant leg and there was a hole in his flesh where he had skewered himself with his crampons. I bandaged the wound and helped him to his feet, but he was shaken.

"What do you think?" Doug said.

"I think I should go down," Peter replied.

We helped him back to the beginning of the glacier and told him we would meet him at the tent later in the day. We regained our high point and continued upward. Fortunately for me, Doug was a little out of shape, but even then, I found myself breathing hard to keep up. At noon we dug a small platform with our axes and had lunch. The sky cleared, and by midafternoon we reached the summit.

Below us there was a smoldering caldera of yellow-green rock with fumaroles of seeping steam and the smell of sulfur. In the middle distance rose the near-perfect cone of Corcovado, the peak Doug had climbed solo. To the north, the horizon was wilderness as far as we could see, all of it encompassed within the Pumalín Sanctuary.

"Hard to imagine," I said. "All that wilderness now protected because a lot of women bought a lot of dresses."

"A lot of dresses they didn't even need," Doug added.

* * *

The next year I returned for a second attempt on Melimoyu. I went down a week early, in order to catch up with Kris and Doug on how their conservation projects were going. In addition to Reñihué, Doug's foundation had purchased other ranches to convert to more protected areas. As the purchases had accumulated, so had the controversies attending a *norteamericano* who now owned so much land that the holdings went from the border to the sea, literally cutting the narrow country of Chile in half. As the conspiracy theories proliferated, so did the headlines in Chile's populist press:

"Tompkins Acquires Land to Create International Center for Abortion."

"Tompkins Is Suspected CIA Agent."

"Tomkins Acquires Land to Create a Jewish State."

"Tompkins Acquires Land to Create a Nazi State."

Doug was confident that over time he could convince Chile and its citizens he meant what he said about someday giving the land back to the country. He was petitioning the government to support legislation to designate Pumalín an official nature sanctuary, and even though that was advancing, the contro- versies continued. The day I arrived, a writer for *The Atlantic* was wrapping up a visit for a profile of Doug, and Kris had her fingers crossed that he had gained an understanding not just of Doug's detractors, but also of his emerging cohort of supporters.

The writer left, and Doug returned to his list of daily chores, which included training a new personal assistant, the wife of the project's resident pilot. On the to-do list was an inspection of some of the construction projects around Pumalín; Doug figured he could give me an update and the new assistant some training if both of us came along.

We started with a new building sheathed in hand-split shin- gles made from dead-felled alerce wood.

"They've got these shingles mismatched," Doug said to the assistant. "Look, they have the gray ones all grouped here and the red ones in a block there. They need to be spaced in a mosaic pattern. See?"

"No problem, Doug. I'll make sure it gets fixed."

"This light switch is too close to the doorjamb. You've got to squeeze your arm like this to flip it."

"We'll get it fixed."

We then walked to a grass landing strip where a crew was beginning construction on a new hangar for Doug's three small aircraft.

"This is positioned too close to the landing strip. You need a lit- tle more room for the planes to taxi. Good thing we came along!"

"See," Doug said to his new assistant, "we have to spell out things clearly. Also, remind me to get you a tape measure. Always have a tape measure."

I thought of a sign Doug used to have above his desk at Esprit: No Detail Is Small. The next day Doug and I took a launch to Caleta Gonzalo, a pier at the head of the Reñihué Fjord where a ferry docked to load and off-load cars navigating a break in the north-south highway caused by a series of deep fjords. Caleta Gonzalo was also the launching point of the Carretera Austral—the Southern Highway—and it was where Doug had built the visitors center, restaurant, small cabins, and hiking trails, including one loop hike through a nearby forest of giant alerces, the southern equivalents of California's redwoods that, like their northern cousins, can live to be 2,000 years old and more. The hike included interpretive signs designed to teach visitors how Pumalín was protecting these national treasures that otherwise were being illegally cut down by loggers.

Before leaving the States, I'd been in touch with a friend named Michael Wadleigh, who was traveling through South America; he and I expected to be in Pumalín at the same time. Sure enough, I spotted him at the ferry ramp. Michael was a filmmaker who had won an Oscar for *Woodstock* and a social critic who stayed on the leading edge of developing trends.

"I'm visiting your park to photograph it with my digital camera," Michael told Doug, pointing to the camera around his neck. "No more film, no more chemicals. Just ones and zeros."

"That so?" Doug answered.

"And you've no doubt heard about the worldwide web? I have what's called a website, kind of like my personal plot on the web. I'm going to put my photographs on it as a travelogue of my trip."

Doug was dressed in khakis and an Australian oilskin canvas raincoat that was open in the front, exposing his hand-knit sweater made from locally produced wool. I wondered if Michael was picking up on his skepticism.

"I can see you're skeptical," Michael said a moment after I had the thought. "Do you keep up with technology developments? The personal computer?"

"My daughter used to date Steve Jobs," Doug answered. "Every time he came over, I got into an argument with him about personal computers. He never could see the big picture. I'm sure he still doesn't."

I was afraid the conversation was about to go south, but Doug invited Michael to join us in the restaurant for tea.

"Personal computers are what I call 'compulsory technology,'" Doug said after we had been served. "You are forced to use them in order to function in society. But then they become another cog in the wheel of the global economy that is ultimately overusing the planet's resources, reducing habitats, and making species go extinct."

"But you don't see the benefits of personal computers? Bringing us information? Making our lives more efficient?"

"Sure, they have personal benefits. I remember Steve coming over one day with a piece of paper listing all the benefits, you know, trying to win the argument. But he was allowing those benefits to cloud his understanding of the larger impact."

"If personal computers are compulsory," Michael said, "then you'll be forced to use one yourself."

Michael was a playful teaser, and I hoped Doug sensed that.

"You're probably right. More inconsistencies."

"You should get a website for Pumalín. I'll help you build it."

"I'll probably be forced to get one of those too. See what I mean? Compulsory!"

* * *

By the time we made it back to the base of Melimoyu, the daily and nightly rains had increased to such an extent that it was impossible to wade across a river we needed to cross to gain the upper part of the mountain. Attempt number two: defeated before we actually started.

Several months later, back in California, I had dinner with Kris while she was visiting her mother and family. *The Atlantic* article, "Eden: A Gated Community," had come out, and it was mixed. "The plot contains elements of *Lost Horizon* and *Heart of Darkness, Fitzcarraldo* and *The Tempest*," the subheading read. "After making a fortune as founder of North Face and Esprit, Douglas Tompkins embraced the principles of deep ecology. Then, forsaking civilization, he bought a Yosemite-sized piece of wilderness in Chile, where only he and a like-minded few would live."

I told Kris the subhead was written by editors who were no doubt thinking how to sell magazines, and that the article itself did a pretty good job of capturing the complexities of Doug's personality. I was thinking specifically about a line describing Doug as "suffering from an abundance of certainties."

"I know," Kris said, her exasperation revealed in her inflection of "know."

"The writer was also pretty accurate about the inconsistencies. Doug's penchant of criticizing things that he does himself."

"Well, we're all guilty of that," Kris said. "Like Yvon says, we're all going to hell, if for no other reason than our personal carbon emissions from all our flying."

"On the other hand," I offered, "maybe Emerson was right: consistency is the hobgoblin of little minds."

Life in the Food Chain

I love long walks, and, if forced to choose, I would trade the life I have spent as a mountaineer for them. When I was in Punta Arenas with Reinhold Messner waiting for the weather to clear to fly to Antarctica, he had told me the same thing.

"It's the long walks that attract me now," he said. "The long walks across open places."

Once, while in East Africa, I had a chance to make a short walk through the open thornbush country that parallels the coast with Iain Allan, a climbing friend and safari guide. Iain had extended his services to include foot safaris through the Tsavo bushlands, and he told me about an idea he had to make a trek from the top of Kilimanjaro all the way to the sea, crossing the twin parks of Tsavo West and Tsavo East.

Two years later I returned to make the Summit-to-Sea walk with Iain. Two more of Iain's friends, the brothers Danny and Bongo Woodley—both senior wardens in the Kenya Wildlife Service—joined us, as well as their Wildlife Service colleagues, rangers Mohamed Hamisi, a six-foot-seven-inch Samburu, and Lokiyor, a six-foot-four-inch Turkana. We would be walking for a month, a total of over 300 miles, nearly all through wild country where every day we would be eye level with big animals that placed us several rungs down the food chain.

My previous encounters with top predators had always been

Mohamed Hamisi, in the lead, shortly after our Kilimanjaro Summit-to-Sea foot safari crossed into Tsavo West National Park. **Rick Ridgeway Collection**

285

brief, but I knew how they triggered a hyperalertness, a warning buzzer in your ear that connects you to the animal side of yourself. For most of us, that connection to when we ourselves were lower in the food chain is buried so deep that when it does surface, we fail to recognize it.

* * *

Iain, Bongo, Danny, and I climbed Kilimanjaro from the Tanzanian side, following a little-used track to the summit, then descended the Kenya side, where we met Mohamed and Lokiyor, who had brought weapons for everyone . . . except me. I didn't have a gun permit, and I needed to carry a camera for a TV show I was making. We were an officially sanctioned wildlife patrol, and the guns were to protect us against encounters with dangerous animals as well as armed poachers.

From the base of Kilimanjaro, we walked another two days before crossing into Tsavo West. The border of the national park was unmarked, but we could tell the difference immediately. With no livestock in the area, the grass was high and wildlife was everywhere.

We were walking in single file behind Mohamed when he stopped suddenly and lifted his hand, motioning us to stop and be quiet. He raised his gun across his chest, and the others did the same. Through the thornbush I saw a vague dark shape that took me only a single heartbeat to recognize as a large Cape buffalo, the most aggressively temperamental of Africa's megafauna. The animal stood motionless, baleful eyes locked on us. We waited, ten, twenty, thirty heartbeats. Suddenly the beast snorted, turned away, and galloped in a crash through the bush. That triggered more crashing, and we realized there was not one buffalo but a full herd. Our only movement was a slight turn of our bodies as we tracked the sound of crushing bush and beating hooves. Then ahead, through an opening cut by our trail, we glimpsed each one as it ran past—ten, twenty, thirty animals, a thunder of hooves and rising dust.

For the next week, we followed game trails paralleling the Tsavo River as it flowed along the southern terminus of the Chyulu Hills. Each day brought encounters that I knew would imprint indelibly in my memory. I paused to watch two giraffes, their necks fringed by backlight, lope into a fever tree forest with what Karen Blixen in *Out of Africa* described as "queer, inimitable, vegetative gracefulness."

One day we left the riverbank to shortcut a bend, crossing a tongue of lava that had flowed out of the Chyulus during an eruption only 200 years ago. It was hot. We left the lava, dropping into a gully where a pair of bush shrikes scolded like seagulls. The thick acacia opened to a spring-fed meadow framed by *Phoenix reclinata*, a handsome date palm native to tropical Africa that grows in dense clumps of slender trunks that bend and recline, hence the name. We crossed an emerald lawn of Bermuda grass cropped by grazing animals, passing the skull of a Cape buffalo that Danny said would have been taken down by lion.

"This is a perfect setup for lion," Iain added. "They lie in ambush in the tall sedge over there, waiting for game that wouldn't be able to resist this grass."

We left the meadow, following a game trail through thickets of *Acacia mellifera* and wait-a-bit thorn, past quartz rocks with crystals that flashed in the sun.

"This is the time of day when we're not alert," Bongo said. "When our guard is down. That's often when it happens. When you get charged."

I took a deep breath and opened my eyes wide and forced myself to stay alert. This was *not* a backpacking trip in the High Sierra. It wasn't even like a hike I once made in the Bob Marshall Wilderness in Montana where I had to keep an eye open for grizzlies. There you might have a close encounter with a bear once or twice a month, but here we were having close encounters—with a hippo or a buffalo, an elephant or a lion, a snake or a crocodile—several times a day, and the encounters were producing a tension that forced me to hike with all my senses honed. It was a tension, however, that felt like something I was meant to own, like something I had lost but now recovered, and consequently it was something that I valued.

"Natural Selection has designed us," Bruce Chatwin wrote in *The Songlines*, "from the structure of our brain-cells to the structure of our big toe, for a career of seasonal journeys *on foot* through a blistering land of thorn-scrub or desert."

In a back issue of *National Geographic* I once found a photograph of a set of fossilized footprints that were discovered on the Laetoli Plains of Tanzania, to the south of the celebrated Olduvai Gorge. They were the prints of upright primates, two adults and one child, walking side by side, made 3.6 million years ago, near the dawn of our emergence as a species.

Now, as I walked through the thornbush, I again thought of those footprints in stone. I watched my feet leave prints in the red earth, and I felt a palpable connection. My mind flipped through the generations like calendar pages in a period movie—20,000, 50,000, 100,000 generations—and there was my ancestral family walking across this same thornbush land, with the same savanna trees and only slight variations of the same animals, leaving their prints in the soft mud as they strode bipedally forward in their eternal gait.

* * *

One morning during the second week I was awakened by a series of deep, throaty exhales that could be made only by a large animal. As my mind came to attention, I remembered that this was the sound made by a lion. I listened, but then it was quiet. Now awake, I remembered an incident on my first trip to Africa, when I was climbing Mount Kenya with Iain and we ran into Bongo, who was then chief warden of Mount Kenya National Park.

"We had a bit of a mix-up last night," Bongo had said. "In the camp just up the trail."

He nodded his head, indicating the direction in which we were heading. He had a rifle slung over his shoulder with a bore the size of an elephant gun; in fact, at second glance, I could see it *was* an elephant gun.

"What happened?"

"Lion. Pulled a poor bugger out of his tent. German chap, going up to climb the mountain."

"Oh dear," Iain had said.

"The guys in the next tent were bush savvy and charged the lion, clanking their dinner pot. That worked. The lion dropped the German and ran off."

"So, he's OK?"

"He'll live. But he lost a leg."

"That's a shame," Iain replied.

"I know the lion," Bongo said. "Big male, crossed over from the Aberdares. It's a problem, now that he's got a taste of flesh. Human flesh."

That evening I had suggested to Iain that perhaps we didn't need to sleep in separate tents.

"Nothing to worry about," Iain had replied. "That rifle that Bongo has, it's a Rigby .458. Belonged to his father, Bill Woodley. One of the great African elephant hunters and the founding warden of Tsavo. Bongo grew up down there, in the bush. He knows what he's doing. He'll track down the lion."

Bongo had indeed tracked down that lion and shot it, and now, as I lay in my tent, I took comfort knowing that Bongo was in a nearby tent where he had next to him the same Rigby .458. I was nearly asleep when the lion roared again, this time from behind our camp. It was circling us. I stared at the night sky through the insect netting that formed the top of my shelter, regretting that we each had separate tents. Surely the others were as awake as me?

Then, again it was quiet, and eventually I fell asleep. The next morning, predators were still on my mind as we crossed the Galana River at a ford adjacent to our campsite. As I entered the water my eyes scanned up- and downstream for any sign of crocodiles. We made these crossings every day—sometimes several times a day—and whenever I found myself getting complacent I recalled Bongo's story of when he was nineteen and a crocodile had pulled his girlfriend from a rock. He had grabbed her under the arms and pulled as the croc surfaced with her foot in its mouth. The animal's tail thrashed violently, and Bongo yelled to the ranger accompanying them to fire. The crocodile let go, and Bongo flew backward with his girlfriend in his arms.

"Her injuries were fairly serious," Bongo had said. "That ended our safari . . . and our relationship."

On the opposite bank we walked through the morning cool and into the afternoon heat, and I struggled, as I did each day, to stay alert. I recalled a passage from Peter Matthiessen, in his book *The Tree Where Man Was Born*: "On foot, the pulse of Africa comes through your boot. You are an animal among others, chary of the shadowed places, of sudden quiet in the air." I found comfort walking behind Mohamed. The Samburu had worked for over a decade as Iain's lead ranger on his foot safaris. Mohamed was also a ranger in the Wildlife Service, and he had been on numerous patrols with Danny and Bongo, fighting elephant poachers. His skin was coal black and his eyes impossibly red. His earlobes were distended with long, tribal gaps in each lobe. He had a scar on the left side of his face the length of his cheek that Iain had told me was a knife wound from a fight with an elephant poacher. Mohamed survived and the elephant poacher did not.

Suddenly Mohamed jumped back and waved at us to stop. Ten yards to our side, under a *mellifera* bush, was a dozing hippo. This was serious. The others raised their rifles to their shoulders, clicked off their safeties, and put fingers on triggers. The hippo looked like a giant sleeping dog with the weight of its head flattening its fleshy jowls. Bongo motioned us to begin moving, pointing to the ground to indicate twigs. I stepped sideways, eyes going from the ground to the hippo to the ground.

Mohamed Hamisi, ranger in the Kenya Wildlife
Service and foot-safari guide for Iain Allan for
over twenty years. **Rick Ridgeway**

When we were far enough away Bongo said in a low voice,
"If he'd woken, he almost certainly would have charged, and we
would have had to shoot him."

If we had had a life-threatening encounter with a hippo—
which, along with crocodiles, are responsible for the deaths
of more humans than any of Africa's other large animals—we
would have shot to kill. In the ten years that Iain had been guiding clients on foot safaris in the West and East Tsavo National
Parks, he'd had to shoot six hippos. At the beginning of our foot
safari, Bongo had pointed out that they would shoot to kill an
elephant only if absolutely necessary, and that they would not
shoot a rhino, even if it had killed one of us.

Danny Woodley (left) and Iain Allan as we pass an elephant family group. **Rick Ridgeway**

I tried to think this through. Part of the reasoning was the ethics of valuing the lives of rhinos and elephants over those of crocodiles and hippos: rhinos because they were nearly extinct in the wild; elephants also because of the threats to their survival, but additionally because of their intellectual and emotional intelligence. The other part was the existence of an alternative to foot safaris, which was viewing wildlife from a vehicle, as nearly all visitors do. But that was like seeing animals in a zoo, with you in the cage, and it removed what to me was the most primordial connection we humans can have with wildlife. But was that connection worth the potential loss of the life I was seeking to connect to?

* * *

The sun rose in an orange ball behind a line of Tana River poplars that grew like a giant hedgerow along the gravel bar behind camp. The morning air was cool, but it was a cool that was like a medicine that only masks instead of cures a pain because, under the cool, just below the surface, we could already feel the heat.

By midmorning the temperature was approaching a hundred degrees. There was no wind, and under my shirt I felt drops of sweat running down my skin. To the north, the savanna stretched flat and forever, open save for a few dead acacias with bone limbs that contrasted with apocalyptic nakedness against the dry blue sky. To the east, ahead on the horizon, a long line of zebras shimmered through the heat waves.

A steep bank forced us into saltbush, and everyone with rifles raised their weapons to their chests. We left the bush and once again entered open plain. A breeze began to fill, and I lifted my arms to cool my torso. A hundred yards to our left we saw a group of elephants.

"We're better to stay wide and downwind," Danny said.

Soon we encountered two juvenile male elephants browsing in doum palms. I stopped to videotape them when suddenly one of the males lifted his head, fanned his ears, and extended his trunk directly at us. The others shouldered their rifles as we all stepped backward. The elephant quickly stepped directly toward us and I felt every fiber in my body tense as I prepared to run. Then he snorted, shook his head, and turned back into the palm grove.

"That was close," I said.

Danny paced it off, turned, and replied, "Fifty feet. But there was no need to worry: he was just a teenager and it was a mock charge. You can tell, the way he held his head and his trunk up, fanning his ears. When an elephant has its ears back, head and trunk down, and is coming straight at you without trumpeting, that's when the elephant means to do you harm."

We continued along the game trail paralleling the river, now a hundred yards to our right and hidden by a channel lined with riverine bush. We walked another quarter mile and spotted the head of an elephant above the bank of the river. Suddenly, it rose above the bank. It was a large matriarch, head and trunk down, ears back, and as she cleared the bank she started to charge straight at us.

"Fall back!"

The matriarch was 200 feet away. We ran as fast as we could. I glanced back. The matriarch was silent—no trumpeting, no snorting—just a giant animal closing in fast. A hundred feet, ninety feet, eighty feet. Her trajectory and her speed were unchanged. She would reach us in five seconds, four seconds, three . . . Danny suddenly stopped and turned toward the elephant. In the same instant Mohamed spun, dropped to one knee, and shouldered his rifle as the others did the same. In a quick heartbeat there was the sudden lightning clap of rifle fire—ten rounds, twenty rounds—and the matriarch just as instantly plowed her front legs to a stop, veered, and ran at an angle into the bush.

All the shots were aimed over her head and past her ears. From above the bank we saw the full herd emerge—two more female adults, six juveniles, and three infants. The matriarch directed her group away from us, toward the open country to the north, as two more juveniles emerged over the bank and ran quickly to catch up to their family, all who continued to move away, all with trunks raised like periscopes.

"Had we remained in position," Danny said, "the whole herd could have come at us. You have to be very, very careful of that."

"They felt trapped between us and the river," Bongo said.

"That was a serious charge," Danny added. "Hence the shots." He paused, then said, "We had a fright, they had a fright, but they're back together and nobody was hurt."

Iain didn't say anything. We resumed our walk, but I could see he was upset. I caught up to him.

"You don't think we should have fired?"

"It wasn't necessary. Mohamed could have stopped that charge with a loud handclap or a yell. I've seen him do it. Now we've traumatized thirty elephants."

Iain said that the other elephants in the area would have heard the shots and no doubt thought they were once again under attack from poachers. We continued, but as soon as we stopped to rest, I told the others we needed to talk this through.

"These elephants have been to hell and back," Iain said. "Now, after a few years of peace, they've begun to relax, and then we go shooting at them."

"They're not relaxed," Bongo countered. "They're as windy now as they've always been."

"It's actually good that they stay wary of humans," Danny added.

I wasn't sure who to believe. All I knew for sure was the charging matriarch had produced in me a surge of adrenaline that had honed my senses to a razor sharpness that held its edge through the remaining hours of our day's march.

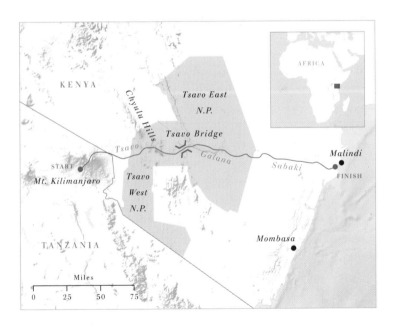

The route of our nearly 300-mile foot safari that went up one side of Kilimanjaro, down the other, then followed the watercourse across the twin Tsavo national parks until the waters of Kilimanjaro emptied into the Indian Ocean.

People of
the Long Bow

The bushlands we crossed on our trek from the summit of Kilimanjaro to the Indian Ocean had been the traditional hunting grounds of a tribe called the Waliangulu. After the end of World War II, when the area was incorporated into two new national parks—Tsavo East and Tsavo West—the Waliangulu were forced to move to villages outside the perimeter of the parks. On top of that displacement, the Waliangulu, who primarily made their living hunting elephants with bows and poisoned arrows and selling or trading the ivory, were suddenly turned from native hunters to scofflaw poachers. They were arrested and imprisoned, and upon their release there was an effort to find them jobs as trackers for wealthy big-game hunters, but most failed to make the conversion to the work-for-hire economy and they drifted back to their villages and assimilated into other tribes. When we began our trek, no one knew if there were any Waliangulu still alive.

* * *

After we left the eastern boundary of Tsavo East, we planned to walk through the villages from which the Waliangulu had disappeared decades before. This was exciting to my two companions, Danny and Bongo Woodley, because in their youth their father, Bill, one of two founding wardens of the Tsavo

The ace Waliangulu elephant bow hunter Abakuna Ise. **Mohamed Amin**

parks, had told them stories about the People of the Long Bow. The Waliangulu were the only native hunting people in Africa who had perfected the exceedingly dangerous technique of killing an elephant with a bow and arrow.

In the late 1940s Bill Woodley and David Sheldrick, the other founding warden, had heard about the elephant hunters when they were first assigned to the new parks and would discover vultures darkening the sky over the carcasses of elephants. They did a survey and concluded that the bow hunters were killing somewhere around 600 elephants a year. How could that be? Were the bows that powerful?

They managed to obtain one of the hunters' long bows, and with several villagers from other tribes watching, Bill nocked an arrow and tried to draw the bow. To his chagrin he couldn't pull it back more than a few inches. The wardens would later learn that to draw a Waliangulu bow you had to lift it over your head, then lower it as you drew the bowstring in one motion. Perhaps the most graphic illustration of the Zen focus required was that occasionally a hunter died drawing his bow because he blew out a blood vessel in his brain or an artery in his heart.

More deadly than the bow's strength was the poison smeared on the arrow. It was derived from a species of *Acokanthera*, a small tree that contains extremely potent toxins called cardiac glycosides, which are used in medicine as heart stimulants. Indeed, only two-tenths of a gram of the *Acokanthera* extract used by the Waliangulu is enough to kill a human, and a typical Waliangulu arrow carried enough poison to kill a 12,000-pound elephant several times over.

David and Bill learned that most of the bow hunters lived in a village called Kisiki Cha Mzungu, a name that translated as White Man's Grave. They began to collect the names of the more active Waliangulu hunters: Barissa Dara, Boru Debassa, Abakuna Gumundi. At the top of the list was an individual whose hunting prowess was referred to reverentially: Galogalo Kafonde.

Eventually, they managed to capture one of the bigger-name hunters. He was about forty years old, and they were surprised when the hunter led them to the tusks he had hidden, and then to the carcass of the elephant he had most recently shot. The hunter had an endearing naïveté. He was affable, polite, and honest.

"How many elephants have you killed in your career?"

"About four hundred."

"What about this fellow Galogalo Kafonde?"

"He has killed fifteen hundred. Maybe more."

Bill and David decided to stage a surprise raid on Kisiki Cha Mzungu. They approached at night and, waiting for first light, they spied Galogalo Kafonde sitting outside his hut, watching the sunrise. If he was surprised when the wardens suddenly appeared, he didn't show it. He was lean and well-muscled, with short-cropped wiry hair and watchful eyes.

He agreed to lead them to his ivory cache. They handcuffed him, walked several miles back to their vehicles, and crossed the park on dirt roads. Then they tied a short length of rope to Galogalo's handcuffs, and the hunter led them into the bush. Night fell, and they continued in the dark toward the river. Suddenly Galogalo lurched forward against the rope. The rangers pulled and then fell backward. Galogalo had slipped his hands through the cuffs and was gone.

Over the next two years Bill and David succeeded in capturing more of the native bow hunters, but Galogalo continued to elude them. They staged another raid on Kisiki Cha Mzungu. Galogalo's hut was empty but there were indications the occupant would soon return. They hid behind a bush and waited. Soon Galogalo appeared, walking toward his hut. But the hunter stopped when he saw his dog standing in front of his hut. The dog looked toward the bush where the wardens were hiding, and Galogalo suddenly turned and ran.

It was as though Galogalo possessed the stalking instincts of a lion and the stealth of a leopard. The two wardens and their rangers continued the campaign to arrest the native bow hunters. They were now in the field for weeks at a time. After one patrol that lasted six weeks, Bill, David, and the rangers were in the bar at a nearby hotel drinking beers when a telegram arrived. David opened it.

"Please arrange to pick up Galogalo Kafonde at the Malindi Police Station."

At first, they thought it was a hoax, but at the station the police said some old man had showed up and turned himself in, saying he was a poacher. Bill and David found Galogalo sitting alone in a jail cell. They drove him back to their headquarters and interrogated him for several days. He told them he had turned himself in because he was getting old and he had grown tired of being chased. David asked him why years before, when he had first been arrested, he had slipped out of his handcuffs and escaped.

"Because you never told me *not* to escape."

They decided not to arrest Galogalo Kafonde. They released him and he walked back to Kisiki Cha Mzungu, and no one heard any more about him. The days of the bow and arrow elephant hunters of East Africa were over.

* * *

It had taken us two weeks to walk across the breadth of the two Tsavo national parks, and once we left the parks and entered into ranchlands with their cattle and goats, the only wildlife we saw was a solitary fox and a small group of oryx. This was in startling contrast to the large companies of ungulates, the herds of elephants, the gatherings of hippos, and a magnificent pair of lions that we had seen all within a day's walk of the park boundary.

The trail was no longer a game track but a path used by humans herding their livestock. We angled toward the river until we reached a gathering of wattle-and-daub huts. We stopped at one hut where a middle-aged woman in a stained lavender and green *kanga* was restringing a bed frame with plaited cord.

"*Jambo,*" Bongo said, but the woman was shy and didn't respond. A man in his midtwenties approached, and we exchanged greetings.

"What is the name of this village?"

"Kisiki Cha Mzungu."

A small crowd gathered around us, and we asked another young man if anyone remembered the old elephant hunters who used to live here.

"Yes," he said, pointing to the ruins of an abandoned hut about thirty feet behind us. "That was the *muji* of Galogalo Kafonde."

"Are there any of the old people still around?"

"Yes, this woman here," he said, pointing to an old woman standing in the crowd. "This is Galogalo's senior wife."

The old woman had short, wiry hair, and her skin looked thin over her small-boned body. She avoided our eyes, perhaps because she was nervous, and put her hand on the head of a young boy standing next to her.

"And this man here, he is Galogalo Kafonde's son, Hunter Galogalo."

We were introduced to a middle-aged man who must have been a teenager when Bill Woodley and David Sheldrick arrested the senior Galogalo in the late 1950s. We shook hands. Under his eyes he had a line of ceremonial beaded scars that extended on each side of his face and small holes in his lower earlobes. His eyes were red, and he seemed shy.

"We have come to find you people," Bongo explained in Swahili. "We want to say hello on behalf of someone who is now dead, but who knew Galogalo well. He was someone who did the same job we now do. He was a game warden."

"Oh, you mean Bwana Bilu," Hunter said.

"Yes, Bwana Bilu," Bongo replied. Then, gesturing toward Danny, Bongo said, "We are Bwana Bilu's sons."

There was a murmur in the crowd. Hunter smiled and seemed to lose some of his shyness. The others also smiled, even those too young to have known Bill but who no doubt had heard stories about him; Bongo and Danny had been told that mothers used to scold their children when they misbehaved by telling them to "be good or Bwana Bilu will get you."

"We have also come to pay our respects to any of the old elephant hunters who might still be alive," Bongo said.

Hunter told us that a couple of the old hunters—Kiribai Balaga and Guyu Mkunzu—were still alive, but at this time of year they were living on the north side of the river and they wouldn't be back until the rains ended. I was disappointed—the river was too wide and too deep to cross—but it was heartening to know two of the long-bow hunters were still alive.

"What about Galogalo?" Danny asked.

"He died in 1989, from being an old man. His grave is there."

"Where?"

"You are almost standing on it."

We turned around, and three feet behind us there was a small headstone and two sticks in the ground at the foot of the grave.

"You shoot fifteen hundred elephants with a bow and arrow," Danny said, "and you become perhaps the best hunter in the world, and it doesn't come to much, does it?"

* * *

In another week, we reached the delta where the Galana emptied into the Indian Ocean. It felt surprisingly wild, with no houses or other indications of human beings. We left our sweat-stained clothes in a pile and ran into the waves. The summit snows of Kilimanjaro seemed an impossible distance away. It had been a gratifying adventure, yet at the same time there were questions that needed more answers.

Bill Woodley and David Sheldrick were long dead, but back in Nairobi I looked up Ian Parker, who was their contemporary and also a warden. He was in his late seventies, lean and articulate.

"The more I learned about the Waliangulu, the more impressed I was," he told me. "Their skill, and the incredible danger they faced hunting elephants. Then look at their bows. They were more powerful than medieval long bows designed to pierce armor; only in their case it was to penetrate elephant hide. Yet for both purposes you have to have metal arrowheads. So, where did the Waliangulu get metal? From trading ivory. How long had they been trading ivory for metal? Go read *The Periplus of the Erythraean Sea.*" (I did read it. The *Periplus*, written in the first century AD, was the sailing directions for the Erythraean Sea, which was the ancient name for the Arabian Sea.)

Waliangulu hunters celebrating their kill of an elephant
with bow and poisoned arrow. **Mohamed Amin**

"The *Periplus*," Ian continued, "makes reference to a tribe
along the East African coast who hunted elephant with bow and
arrows that required two ordinary people to draw them, and
it instructs sailors how to trade iron for ivory. So, you see, the
Waliangulu were not some group of primitive hunter and gather-
ers. They were an elephant-hunting culture geared to providing
ivory to the outside world, and when we came along, they had
already been doing it for at least two thousand years."

Assuming that Bill Woodley and David Sheldrick were right,
and the Waliangulu were killing about six hundred elephants
a year in the Tsavo, and assuming that Ian Parker was right,

and the Waliangulu had been doing that for at least 2,000 years, then you could conclude that they were sustainably harvesting the elephant. Which also meant they were hunters—and not just subsistence hunters but commercial hunters—who were living with their prey animal in a balanced relationship.

* * *

The best journeys answer questions that at the outset you never thought to ask. What I didn't know at the beginning of my foot safari was how the journey would catalyze in me a reflection on our species' relationship with elephants—and by extension with all our brethren wildlife—going back to our coevolution on the plains of Africa, and then to what happened to that relationship once we began our diaspora across the planet.

Once home I continued my research, learning that after the Waliangulu were removed as elephant hunters from the Tsavo, the elephant population exploded, and the animals began to eat themselves out of house and home. The Tsavo was turning into a desert. There was a bitter debate about culling them, but then a drought hit, and the population plummeted. With dead elephants littering the landscape, a gold rush of sorts began, as tribes from as far away as Somalia scoured the Tsavo for deadfall ivory. When that was all gone the tribes remained, especially the Somali. Once the drought ended the poaching resumed, but now instead of bows and arrows the poachers, mostly Somalis, were shooting elephants with semiautomatic rifles acquired during their civil war. The poaching wars that ensued have continued to this day, and so has the steady decline of elephants.

Would the Waliangulu have hunted the elephant to extirpation if they had been given AK-47s to replace their bows and arrows? Even with primitive technology, there are stories of how early humans decimated wildlife once our species left Africa.

To learn more, I visited the La Brea Tar Pits in Los Angeles. I stood under the skeletons of the mammoth and mastodon, alongside the saber-toothed cat and the short-faced bear. The Los Angeles Basin was once a Serengeti, with three species of elephant, vast herds of camels, and zebra-like horses and antelope, cheetah-like cats, and lions that looked just like African lions, only larger. Yet when human beings arrived about 12,000 years ago, 80 percent of all these large mammals—up to thirty-five genera in total—went extinct within 2,000 years (most within 500 years), a period that paleontologists called "a geologic instant."

Who or what caused the Pleistocene extinctions has been for decades a hotly contested debate. From my research, I was swayed by what *didn't* happen 12,000 years ago. If climate change was responsible, as some argue, why did no amphibians go extinct? Why was the only insect that disappeared the dung beetle? Why no birds other than two of the eleven species of vultures that once flew over the Los Angeles Basin?

What about the moas, the several species of large flightless ratites—the order of bird families that includes ostriches—that disappeared shortly after the Maori arrived in New Zealand? The extensive assemblage of marsupials that went extinct shortly after aboriginal peoples arrived in Australia?

I recalled when, during my journey to the High Arctic with Doug Peacock, Doug Tompkins, and the team trying to "talk to belugas," we asked the Inuit hunter accompanying us if he would kill the last whales even if he were told there were only two left, a male and a female. He said he would, because he had a *right* to hunt them.

I came to the conclusion that our basal response, whenever we have the opportunity combined with the technology, is to hunt our brethren wild creatures into oblivion. It is sometimes said that, like other wild creatures, we, too, have three imperatives: to eat, to not be eaten, and to procreate. I would add a fourth: our imperative to have purpose—our need for art, for beauty, for understanding how we fit into the universe, and, closer to home,

how we fit into the web of life that surrounds and includes us. Therein lies the hope: that we might allow the fourth imperative to counter the instincts we have carried with us out of the plains of Africa.

Trapped in Time, paleoartist Mark Hallett's depiction of the Los Angeles Basin in the late Pleistocene, before the arrival of human beings. This mural is on permanent display in the museum at the La Brea Tar Pits, and it is the baseline for how I measure our species' impact on my home region of Southern California. **Mark Hallett**

The Two Burials of Jonathan Wright

The Konka Gompa monastery was perched on a small bench of an otherwise steep hillside overlooking the terminus of the glacier that descended the west side of Minya Konka. I knew that on a clear day there was a stunning view of the nearly 24,900-foot peak, but that afternoon the mountain was shrouded in monsoon clouds. In the last light of a dim day, I stood beside Asia Wright, both of us leaning on the rail encircling the second floor of the monastery, looking at the prayer flags that hung like bunting under the eaves. At the altar in the center of the courtyard, a smoldering bough of juniper released into the still air a single tendril of smoke. From the prayer room, we heard the chant of the senior monk, who was old enough to have lived in the original monastery before Mao's Red Guards destroyed it in the 1970s.

The Khampas, the ethnic Buddhists of eastern Tibet, had done an admirable job rebuilding the monastery, but even so, I could see it didn't match the original. Twenty years before, we had camped next to what was left of the old monastery, and Yvon Chouinard, Jonathan Wright, and I had spent the afternoon checking out the ruins, admiring the fine joinery in the remains of the beams and joists.

Now, nearly two decades later, I was in the same place with Jonathan's daughter, who had just turned twenty, and who was with me not on a journey but a pilgrimage. That night I lay in bed,

Me and Asia Wright during our two-month pilgrimage across Tibet to follow her father's footsteps that lead to his grave. Rick Ridgeway Collection

309

writing in my journal by the light of a candle secured in a pool of wax atop my bedpost. My bed was along one end of the room, Asia's in the middle, and the old monk's (he was sharing his room) on the opposite end. He was chanting sotto voce as he arranged his belongings on his nightstand: prayer beads, a bell, and two portraits of lamas, each in a hand-carved wooden frame. Asia was also awake, the cone of light from her headlamp illuminating the photocopy of her father's journal she had brought with her.

So many times on the trip with Asia I had the sensation of the past melting into the present. The sight of her hiking in front of me would carry me back in time, and there he would be, Jonathan, walking ahead on a day long in the past. She had her mother's dark hair and Japanese eyes and high cheekbones, but she had her father's long legs and fair skin. She wore a Tibetan necklace of turquoise and coral given to her by a friend for good luck on our journey, and she carried her father's Tibetan prayer beads. The day before we left, my sixteen-year-old daughter had cut Asia's hair, the two of them giggling on our veranda, as the long locks of black hair fell to the tile floor.

When we began our journey—our pilgrimage—I worried about Asia's asthma, her vulnerability to cold, her phobia of bugs. At first there was a kind of cautious formality between us, but after a week we had grown more comfortable around each other. I was confident that when the pieces of the trip fit together it would give her a clearer picture of her path forward. It was my idea for our journey to be just the kind of trip her father would have taken her on. Now, lying in bed in the Konka Gompa monastery, I decided to test my assumption.

"Asia, what's the most important thing you think you're getting from your father's journals?"

"I think his ability to always improve himself and maybe realize it's a job that never ends. But to be honest, I think you're getting more from his journals than I am, because you knew him."

"You've got a good point."

"You're real to me. And your stories—I'm learning from them."

In the courtyard of the Konka Gompa monastery. I gave the lama my camera and asked him to take our picture. **Rick Ridgeway Collection**

"Thanks for telling me that."

"Good night, Rick."

She turned off her headlamp. The old monk was in his bed, asleep. I took off my parka and blew out my candle, and in the darkness I cozied into my sleeping bag. I thought of some of the stories I had told Asia during our journey, about standing on the summit of K2 not as a victor but as a survivor, about coming home and over time realizing that if I could do that, I could do a lot of things. About meeting Yvon and then Doug, and what I had learned from them, things like sitting at the base of a nearly unknown massif in Bhutan and burning the maps we had worked so diligently to draw.

In the darkness I could hear the rush of the river below the monastery. Before I fell asleep, I had one more thought: *If somehow today I were caught in the same avalanche, now that I am*

*fifty years old, would I have the wisdom to ride the cascading
snow not in fear but in wonder?*

* * *

In the years following Jonathan's death, I had continued to
connect with Asia and her mother every two or three years. Asia's
mother had never remarried, and they remained a household of
two. When Asia was fourteen, I stopped in Aspen to see them.
Asia's cheeks had freckled, and she was growing into a beautiful
young woman. At first she was shy, even distant. Asia was on
the JV volleyball team at her high school, and her mother and
I sat in the bleachers and watched her play. Afterward, I offered
to take Asia and some of her volleyball friends to dinner. They
asked to walk to the restaurant, and I was sure it was so Asia
could tell them about me.

Waiting for them at the restaurant, I asked Asia's mother if
the two of them talked very often about Jonathan.

"Not really," she replied. "I gave her a framed photo of
Jonathan getting on the plane, when you guys left to Minya
Konka, but I don't know what she did with it. She's bitter about
growing up without a father."

Asia and her friends arrived, and after a while she began
to open up. She told me she was an avid snowboarder (later she
would make the US Junior team). She said she was also interested
in learning to rock climb.

"Maybe this summer Yvon and I can take you up the Grand
Teton," I said. "First we can give you a lesson on a practice climb
called Baxter's Pinnacle."

"Wow, that would be terrific," she said.

I got busy with other things, though, and I never followed
through. Toward the end of her freshman year at the University
of Colorado, Asia called to say she hoped to come to California
for the summer and was wondering if she could stay with us in
Ojai. Her ambition was to follow in her father's footsteps and
become a professional photographer. By then I had started an

agency representing outdoor photographers, so that summer she worked part-time for my company.

After she had been with us for a couple of weeks, I took her to a café for lunch. I told her about the avalanche: how the four of us roped together were trapped in the tons of cascading snow sweeping down the steepening slope; how as the snow catapulted over a cliff I knew I was dead; how it then slowed and stopped, and started again, and finally stopped; how I was somehow still alive but the others—Yvon, Kim, and her father, Jonathan—were all injured to varying degrees. I told her how I had held her father in my arms, locking eyes with him and telling him it would be OK, we were all still alive; how his eyes had rolled back in his head and his breathing stopped and I breathed into him and it started and stopped. I told her how we had carried her father's frozen body to a nearby promontory and covered him with rocks and strung prayer flags above his grave.

"I don't know," she said after I finished speaking, shaking her head. "Somehow it still seems like a story. All my life, people have asked, 'What does your father do?' and I've answered, 'He was a *National Geographic* photographer, but he was killed in an avalanche when I was a baby,' and they answer, 'Wow, that's incredible.' It doesn't sound real to them, and, in a way, it's never been real to me.

"My mother didn't want to talk about him," she continued. "The only connection I ever had were his photographs, mostly pictures of Nepal and the Himalayas. I knew that was his favorite place, and that's why he gave me my name. When I was eight, I had this idea that if I could somehow go there, I would be able to figure out who he was. I still want to go."

I assumed she was going to ask me to help her get to Nepal. I was already forming my answer—that I could contribute half, but she would have to work for the other half—when she told me what she had in mind.

"Would you take me to Tibet?" she asked. "To Minya Konka? To climb up the side of the mountain and find my father's grave?"

313

* * *

I didn't give her an immediate answer; I had to talk to my wife. "Of course you're going to take her," Jennifer said. "Asia isn't just asking you to help her find her father. She's asking you to *be* her father."

I remembered the journey Jonathan and I had planned to take following the Minya Konka climb, when we intended to travel overland across Tibet and then to Everest, to do the story for *National Geographic*. What if I did the same trip with Asia, in reverse? We could start in Nepal, hiking to Everest Base Camp, going with some of the same Sherpas who had been her father's friends. Then we could go overland to Tibet. Maybe we could climb a peak? But the snow on the mountains in eastern Tibet was often wet with monsoon moisture, creating avalanche conditions; even considering that gave me goose bumps. But in western Tibet the snow was dry and stable. If we went there, we could also join the pilgrims making the *kora* around Mount Kailash, the circumambulation of the most sacred mountain in Asia, and something Jonathan had dreamed of doing. We could continue to the remote Chang Tang Plateau, perhaps to the Aru Basin, the area where for nearly a century the only Westerner to see it had been the famed wildlife biologist George Schaller, whose books and articles I had devoured. What if I reached out to Dr. Schaller? Maybe he would help me find a mountain there to climb in what he had named the Crystal Mountains. I knew it was an entire range in which no mountaineer had ever set foot. Then Asia and I could recross Tibet, to Minya Konka, to climb the flank of the mountain and find her father's grave.

Her reply was instant. "Yeesss!" she exclaimed with the same enthusiasm her father had used—"Wuuwee!"—whenever he encountered anything that delighted him.

Our journey to Nepal and Everest, across the open alpine steppe of the Chang Tang Plateau in western Tibet to the mon-soon-swept mountains of eastern Tibet, took two months. In the

The plateau of northwest Tibet, during my 1,000-mile off-road excursion with Asia Wright. **Rick Ridgeway**

Khumbu, on the south side of Everest, we hiked with the Sherpas who knew and revered Jonathan. We joined hundreds of Buddhist pilgrims making the three-day trek around Mount Kailash. In the Crystal Mountains, we reached the summit of an unclimbed, unnamed 21,000-foot peak. Returning overland to Lhasa—an off-road drive of more than a thousand miles—we flew to Chengdu and arranged for a vehicle to take us on the three-day drive to the trailhead leading to Minya Konka.

* * *

When I woke in the Konka Gompa monastery in the small room with Asia and the old monk, it was still dark, but the parchment window carried a faint glow. There was no sound of rain, only the rush of the river, but even at a distance it was an undertone that left a disquieting power. I quietly unzipped my sleeping bag and, with my envelope of travel notes and binoculars, I descended the steep stairs to the courtyard. Outside the monastery, I could see that a gray blanket of clouds obscured all but the lowest flanks of Minya Konka. I removed photographs from the envelope and studied them. I had circled on one of the photos the place on the buttress where we had buried Jonathan, but there were too many clouds to see it now.

Over breakfast Asia and I formed a plan. We would take a minimum of equipment and food and hike up the lateral moraine of the glacier to camp in the same alpine meadow where, in 1980, we had set up Base Camp. Then the next day, weather permitting, we would try to find her father.

The monks gathered in front of the monastery to wish us good luck. In a half hour we reached the river rushing over glacial boulders. It was too wide to cross. Scouting upriver, we found a single wet log spanning a narrow. On the other side, we climbed a steep slope thick with rhododendron, dewy in the heavy fog. We twisted through the thicket, careful not to grab the thorny branches of wild rose.

We gained the crest of the moraine and followed it for an hour. There was a dark squall approaching. I wasn't sure where we were, and, reaching a narrow flat, we decided to camp. We had just finished pitching the tent when the squall hit. Inside, through the nylon fabric, I could see a flash of lightning, and it brought back a memory of the hours after the avalanche, when I had descended to Base Camp and everyone had then grabbed their packs and left to help Yvon and Kim. I was alone, and there was lightning and then thunder that seemed to sound for the departure of Jonathan's soul.

All night, I listened to the sound of the rain hitting our tent. I found my headlamp and shone it on my travel alarm: 4:00 a.m. Pointing the beam out the tent door and onto a small bush at river's edge that I had identified earlier as a marker, I could see that the river was within an inch of jumping its bank and flooding our tent. *In this weather,* I thought, *I could never find the grave.* Still, I went through my mental checklist—compass, headlamp, lunch, camera, film, reference photographs, binoculars—and started the stove to make tea. I handed Asia her mug, and she sat up and thanked me. Then the rain stopped.

"What do you think?" she asked.

In the moonlight I could see the tip of a lateral glacier hanging like a tongue out of the clouds.

"It's starting to thin," I answered. "Maybe we can pull this off."

By dawn we were on our way, following a yak trail paralleling the river. The last time I had walked this path, my arm was in a sling. Yvon was behind me, his breath shortened by pain in his ribs. Kim was farther back, with an injured back and knee; he moved in halting steps, his lips tight. His blue eyes, clouded with morphine, seemed to focus on the middle distance, even when you talked to him.

The moraine squeezed against the river, and Asia and I were forced to hop from boulder to slippery boulder. We decided to climb the loose moraine, where at the crest we found a faint trail. Ahead I could see three parallel buttresses descending out of the clouds, one of them vaguely familiar. Looking through binoculars I compared what I saw to the photographs.

"Do you know which one it is?"

"I'm not sure," I answered. "It doesn't look the same."

Then I realized what had happened. In twenty years, because of global warming, the lateral glaciers had receded so much that I didn't recognize them.

"Look," I said, pointing to the photograph. "The glacier was here in 1980, and now it's way up there. But see these rocks? I think this is the one where the avalanche stopped. We buried your father just to the left, right about here."

* * *

The crest of the moraine sharpened, and for balance I walked with my arms extended. Asia was about fifteen yards behind me, seemingly as absorbed in her thoughts as I was in mine. I was reliving that day I had carried her father to his burial platform, how the sun had warmed one side of my face while his frozen body cooled the other side.

Ahead I recognized the meadow where we had set up our Base Camp. Looking up, I could see the route we had taken to the base of the buttress. I angled toward it, keeping a steady pace, looking back to check on Asia. She was maintaining our separation, and I had the feeling she wanted it that way, maybe to collect her thoughts. The layer of clouds that had filled the valley continued to lift. In an hour I reached the top of the scree and stopped to drink from my water bottle. Asia arrived and we were quiet. I could see a few hundred yards above us the place where the avalanche had stopped, and, over to the left, where we had buried Jonathan.

I studied the area with binoculars. If his grave was still there it must have been hidden behind the foreground cliff. There was a route upward to the right, but it was under a sérac that teetered at the end of the glacier. I had no memory of the terrain being as difficult as it appeared. We continued to the base of the steep section.

"I'm scared."

"It only looks hard," I said, putting my hand on her shoulder. "I know you can do it."

"It's not that. I'm scared of what we're going to find."

"Do you still want to do this?"

She nodded her head.

"You go first, so I can spot you," I said. "There's a foothold here, then two handholds right there. Go up a few feet, then we'll go left into that little dihedral."

"OK."

"I'll be right behind you."

Asia placed her boot on the first foothold, then reached for the handholds and moved up. I didn't know for certain what was going through her mind, but her body moved with athletic

The sullen rain, the swollen river, the slick rock ... it all added to the
tension as we moved closer to her father's grave. **Rick Ridgeway**

grace. I followed her, mindful to move only one hand or foot at
a time to maintain a firm grip so I could stop her if she slipped.

"You're doing great. Now traverse left, to that dihedral."

The dihedral, an inset corner in the rock face, looked tricky,
but my larger concern was down climbing it, especially in the
rain. *Should I turn back?* I decided to keep going. At the top of the
dihedral I led again, through a slope of loose rocks. The crest of
the rib was now only ten feet away. I made five steps and looked
up. I recognized the slope immediately: it was the place where
the avalanche stopped and where Jonathan had died.

I took off my pack. Asia was about fifty feet below me, moving
steadily. I looked up and to the side. There it was. Jonathan's grave.
How could it be so close? It had seemed so far the morning we carried him on our shoulders. But something was different. The grave

wasn't as high as we had built it. *What had happened? Had it collapsed as his body had withered? What was that sticking out of the side? Faded nylon? Yes. And at the end? His climbing suit? Yes.*

Asia was now only a few feet away, but she was looking down, focusing on her foot placements.

"Asia?"

She stopped and looked up.

"I see your father's grave. Please prepare yourself because it is not intact."

She looked past me, and her eyes froze on her father's broken bier. Then she looked away and didn't say anything. Neither did I.

"I don't want to go up there."

"Come to where I am. It's a good place to rest."

She climbed the last few steps and stood next to me and started to cry. Her shoulders rose and fell, her tears coming from deep inside. I held her head next to mine and looked past her to the place where I had held her father in my arms as he died. I was now with him again, with his head in my lap, as I held his daughter and she continued to cry.

"Why don't you take off your pack and sit down."

She wiped her tears and sat on a rock.

"I'm going up there, to have a look. Are you OK here?"

She nodded her head, still wiping at her tears. I stepped slowly toward the grave. I could hear the clink of the flat stones under my boots and remembered again how cold he had been on my shoulder. Then I was at the grave. One leg of his climbing suit was exposed. The nylon looked old, faded, and brittle. The other leg was still covered by the stones, but parts of his jacket showed. I reached down to the exposed leg and moved the fabric and . . . he was not there.

Maybe a snow leopard? It would have taken something powerful to move the stones. But then the griffins would have finished the job. I bent and lifted another stone, and there was his long underwear, still bright blue as though it were new. And the label, the old, oversized chest label that said Patagonia. Where the underwear was torn, I saw parts of my friend: his backbone and his ribs and his collarbone. I shifted another rock. His skull was gone but his hair was still there, in good condition.

I rubbed the strands between my fingers and was back in time, fingering his hair and looking up at Yvon, who didn't understand, and saying, "Yvon, Jonathan just died." I was in the past and I was in the present and then I was crying.

"Jonathan, my old buddy."

I cleared my eyes and stood. I would have to bury him again, replace the stones over his remains, and set up the new prayer flags we had brought. Maybe then Asia would come up, to be at the grave. Then I looked down, and to my surprise she was already heading toward me.

"Asia, your father's clothes are here. But some of his bones are gone. You sure you want to come up?"

"I'm coming."

We rebuilt the grave and secured a brass plaque Asia Wright's paternal grandparents had sent with us. Then, just as I had done twenty years before, Asia positioned the last stone. **Rick Ridgeway**

Chapter Twenty-One

Across the
Big Open

Two hours before dawn I zipped open my tent and peered out. The beam from my headlamp illuminated six inches of snow. The previous night, when the ground was clear, my three mountaineering buddies—Conrad Anker, Galen Rowell, and Jimmy Chin—and I had decided to get an early start. We wanted to pull our rickshaws, each weighing about 250 pounds, as many miles as possible before the sun melted the hardpan into soft mud. Now it didn't matter; pulling through snow would be just as difficult. I reminded myself that tenacity is easier when you don't have a choice.

I maneuvered out of my warm bag and into my cold pants and considered the work in front of us. We were on day five of what we judged would be a thirty-day trek during which we were unlikely to see any other humans. Using historical records, my mentor and guiding light George Schaller had traced on a map the route of every Western explorer—himself included—who had traveled through this northwest section of Tibet; none had crossed the central part of our planned route. It was so desolate and high—with an average elevation above 16,000 feet—that even the Drokpa, the leather-skinned nomads of western Tibet, didn't venture there.

Dr. George Schaller is commonly regarded as the most influential wildlife biologist of his generation, and when I had

For 275 miles there were no signs, not even neolithic artifacts, that human beings had ever lived in this remote corner of the planet. Galen Rowell

suggested to Asia Wright that she and I could journey across Tibet on our way to find her father's grave, it was Schaller's articles and books that had given me the idea of climbing a mountain in the Chang Tang, the section of northwest Tibet where Schaller had conducted many of his surveys of the region's wildlife.

When I had written to Dr. Schaller asking if he might help me plan my trip with Asia, he was already in my personal pantheon of individuals who had inspired my combined commitment to adventure and conservation. I first read about him in *The Snow Leopard*, Peter Matthiessen's National Book Award-winning account of his trek with Schaller into the remote Dolpo region of Nepal. Schaller had himself won the National Book Award for *The Serengeti Lion*, one of his many books describing his extensive fieldwork that included foundational studies of some of the world's most iconic species: jaguars, tigers, gorillas, and pandas.

I met him in his office at the Bronx Zoo, where I shook hands with a lean and fit man in his midsixties who not so much walked as bounded gazelle-like around the room. He unfolded large maps, well worn on their crease lines, and showed me the route to the Aru Basin, a journey by vehicle that required nearly a thousand miles of off-road driving. We spent an entire morning going over maps and notes, then he offered to drive me back to the airport. At the terminal I thanked him, and had turned to leave when I heard him call my name. I walked back to his vehicle. The passenger window was still rolled down, and he was leaning across the seat.

"Remember," he said, "as soon as you stop moving, you start rusting."

Dr. Schaller had asked me to keep notes of all the wildlife I observed during my trip with Asia Wright, logging numbers and positions. He was particularly interested in an ungulate called the chiru. Standing about three feet at the shoulder, chiru are actually more closely allied to goats and sheep than to antelope. But they've evolved for so many millions of years on the high alpine steppes of Tibet that, by what biologists call convergent evolution, they have acquired antelope-like features. "Chiru look as if they have somehow strayed from the African plains," Schaller had written. "Their lanky legs seem designed for striding toward the horizon, and their large, bright eyes are ideal for sweeping the steppe for danger."

Schaller had been the first to link the poaching of chiru to the production of very expensive shawls called *shahtoosh*, and at his persuasion the Chinese government established the 129,000-square-mile Chang Tang Nature Reserve. But with few patrols over such a large area, poaching remained rampant and chiru numbers continued to decline. A species once thought to number in the millions was now reduced to an estimated 70,000 survivors.

Early in his studies Schaller had observed that the females of the western herds—the largest population of chiru—left their southern range each year in late May to early June and headed north, toward the Kunlun Mountains. They returned in early August with their calves after "following an ancient migration route to some mysterious place to give birth," Schaller wrote in *National Geographic* in August 1993. "It is a place so remote that even nomadic herdsmen do not venture near it. It is so bleak that the animals find little more than the dry leaves of a sharp-tipped sedge to eat. We tried to follow the herds, but severe blizzards stopped us."

When I first read those lines, I had taken a pen and underscored them, writing in the margin, "Great challenge for a future expedition." Once I returned from my trip with Asia Wright, I met with Schaller to review the notes I had kept, including all my sightings of chiru.

"I still need to find those calving grounds," he said.

"What if you tried to follow the migration on foot?" I asked. "Let the chiru lead you to the calving grounds?"

"That area is completely uninhabited, so you would have to carry your own supplies, including water because in places it's two or three days between streams. Each person would need to carry well over a hundred pounds. With camera gear it would probably be closer to two hundred."

We both knew that was beyond what anyone could carry in a backpack for any length of time. Still, I couldn't let go of the idea. I was in my early fifties, but I had kept moving and I was far from rusting. I had successfully sold my photo and film agency to focus on making films about outdoor sports, but that wasn't as fulfilling as it had once been. I had written a book about my trip with Asia to find her father's grave, and I felt good about that. But I was watching my friends increasingly dedicate themselves to wildland and wildlife conservation, and I felt inspired to do my part. Doug and Kris were busy buying estancias in Argentina and Chile, and Yvon was doubling down on Patagonia's commitment to environmental protection, giving away 1 percent of the company's sales—not profits, but sales—to environmental nonprofits, so that rain or shine, good year or bad, the company was paying what Yvon called its "Earth tax."

Using my mountaineering and adventuring skills to try and help save an endangered species seemed like just what I should be doing with my life. But even with my skills, how could you traverse without any outside support an uninhabited plateau 300 miles across? I was still pondering this dilemma when I went to Salt Lake City to attend the biannual Outdoor Retailer trade show. Sitting in the lobby of the Marriott Hotel across from the Salt Palace, I noticed a bronze statue of a man with his wife and kids. It was a nineteenth-century Mormon family, and they were on foot, crossing the Great Plains on their way to Utah, and the man was pulling a rickshaw loaded with their belongings.

* * *

By dawn of day five we were ascending the flank of an unnamed 20,000-foot peak, straining against the waist harnesses of our high-tech rickshaws as their mountain-bike wheels traced deep furrows in the virgin snow. The sky brightened and a snow finch sounded its morning chirp. The sun feathered through a reef of clouds. Behind us, the slanting rays painted the hills pink. Ahead, the early light dispersed through an icy haze into a long band of purple, green, yellow, and red.

"A circumhorizontal rainbow!" Galen Rowell exclaimed. "It's in ice crystals, not water vapor like regular rainbows. You see it in high mountains every once in a while."

Galen was widely known as a photographer and a mountaineer, but among his friends he also had a reputation as a font of factoids regarding natural history. A little over a year before, I was having lunch with Galen and Conrad Anker when I told them about Schaller's need to discover the calving grounds of the chiru, and my idea to follow the migration pulling rickshaws. They immediately signed up, and Conrad later suggested inviting another up-and-coming young climber named Jimmy Chin.

Conrad and I had been friends since we had met several years before when I was hired by *National Geographic* to film an ascent of a 2,000-foot rock spire in a remote corner of Antarctica called Queen Maud Land. Conrad and his climbing partner Alex Lowe were the lead climbers, and if they succeeded it would be the first big-wall climb ever done in Antarctica. At the time, Conrad and Alex were considered the top alpine climbers in the world. There were six of us altogether on the small team, and even though we were on the wall for a couple of weeks, it was the only expedition I had been on where there was not a word of contention between anyone. We marveled at our surroundings, a panorama in three panels like a giant Rothko painting: the gray granite and the white ice and the blue sky. The wall was actually beyond vertical; after reaching the top, back down at our high camp—three hanging tents with nothing but air under them—we had packed our sleeping bags in a haul bag and let it go. It dropped in a plumb line straight down 2,000 feet without hitting anything, until it landed about 300 feet *away* from the base of the wall.

During the climb a storm had forced us off the wall and into our tents at the base of the spire. It was a welcome respite, and

we spent the hours in our community tent drinking coffee and telling stories. Conrad said he had a story he had been waiting to tell me. He had been raised in a rural area of California, near the entrance to Yosemite National Park, and seeing the climbers on El Capitan had captivated him. Then one day he got his parents' copy of *National Geographic* in the mail describing my ascent of K2. On the cover was a photograph of me crossing the knife-edge.

"When I saw that cover photo of you on K2," Conrad said, "I looked at it and I knew that's what I wanted to do."

I told Conrad my story of being about the same age and getting my copy of *National Geographic* with the story of the first American ascent of Everest and the photograph of Jim Whittaker on the summit, and me telling myself, *I want to be THAT guy.*

A year after our Antarctica trip, my *National Geographic* arrived in the mail with a story about our big-wall climb in Queen Maud Land. On the cover, there was a photograph of Conrad, sitting on a rock precipice peering over the ice cap to the distant mountains. I called Conrad on the phone.

"Congratulations on being the cover boy," I said.

"Thanks."

"You know what this means, don't you?"

"I think I know what you're going to say, but tell me."

"It means that there is a young twelve-year-old girl or boy out there somewhere, just now opening their parents' copy of *National Geographic*, and looking at you on the cover and saying, '*That* is what I am going to do with *my* life.'"

* * *

Jimmy Chin would tell me later that when Conrad had asked him to join our team his initial thought was, *Wow, what did I do to deserve this?* He would also tell me that on about day five of the trip, as we struggled like beasts of burden to pull our 250-pound rickshaws up a mile-long slope at 16,500 feet, he asked himself, *What did I do to deserve this?*

Scaling that rock wall in Antarctica was as close to being on another planet as you could be on our own Earth. **Gordon Wiltsie**

We told Jimmy he would shoot video. A still photographer whose inspiration had been Galen himself, Jimmy had never shot video or made a film. On the long flight to Asia, we elders had leisurely read our novels while Jimmy had fallen asleep reading "Operating Instructions for the Canon X-1."

Now on day five the concern was less the mud and snow than the fact that we still hadn't encountered any masses of chiru. We had seen a few groups of ten to twenty, but not the long procession of animals walking in the deep grooves of an age-old migration. Had the migration already passed? Or had its route shifted since Schaller's last visit? Worse, had the poaching been so severe that only a handful of chiru had survived to make the trek?

By two that afternoon the snow was gone.

"It didn't melt," Galen observed. "It sublimated into the dry air."

We were still an estimated two days south of Heishi Beihu, or Blackrock Lake, crossing an utterly flat steppe we called Kansas. In the distance, a rain squall moved like a dark curtain across a stage and the horizon shimmered through the rising waves of warming air.

"Animals!" Jimmy shouted. "Hundreds of them."

I raised my binoculars, but when I brought the animals into focus I saw instead dozens of black rocks distorted by air convections. Jimmy took the news with a grin. At twenty-eight, he was young enough to be my son, but I could tell he was already a peer in mental determination, with built-in curiosity and a sense of humor. "I'm looking forward to learning from the old goats," he had said at the beginning of our trip. "Oh, excuse me. I mean, from my mentors."

The next day we continued across the steppe, stopping at the base of a basalt ridge for an early lunch: a small packet of nuts, dried fruit, jerky, and an energy bar. It was the same thing we'd had the day before, and it would be the same thing we would have the day after. Each day we were expending more

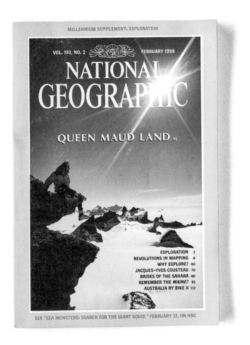

The February 1999 issue of *National Geographic*
with Conrad Anker on the cover. **Gordon Wiltsie/
Courtesy of the National Geographic Society**

calories than we were eating, and already we were starting to
lose weight.

We climbed the ridge, each step like a weightlifter's leg press,
but when we reached what looked like the pass, we saw another
ridge behind it that was still higher, and we soon came to yet
another beyond that one. Still no chiru. I had developed a persis-
tent cough and my lungs ached. By the time we reached the final
pass, my legs were cramped, and I wondered whether at age fifty-
two I could make it to the finish line. We chose a campsite nestled
between basaltic boulders, unbuckled ourselves from our carts,
and walked toward a rock ridge we hoped would give us a view.

Near the crest, Galen motioned for us to be quiet. He had
spotted a few chiru. We crab-crawled until we could peer into
a valley bordered by low-angled hills covered in pale-yellow grass.

Below us, seventy chiru were walking in a line. As some disappeared to the north, more appeared from the south. We had found the migration.

* * *

We reached the icy shore of Heishi Beihu and, now walking with the chiru, we were confident we could follow them to their calving grounds. The animals were skittish—no doubt from having been shot at so much by poachers—but if we stalked them carefully we found we could get close enough to see the white markings on the insides of their alert ears, the dark eyes framing their pug snouts, the sheep-like texture of their fawn coats covering the bulges of their bellies.

As we pulled our heavy carts, we could empathize with the pregnant females on their 200-mile migration. Why did they do it? It couldn't be for grass or browse; that was more abundant in the southern part of their range. Maybe there were fewer predators in the north. But wouldn't the stress of such a long migration outweigh that benefit? Schaller believed the migration was a vestigial behavior tied to a time when it was "nutritionally adaptive" for females to move north. Pollen profiles and ancient shorelines suggested that 5,000 to 13,000 years ago, the Chang Tang was relatively lush.

For us the mystery made the migration even more compelling. For the next two days we followed the chiru northward, crossing the border into Xinjiang and leaving the animal's safe haven in the Chang Tang Reserve. In the distance I could see chiru all going in the same direction, at the same speed.

When it was flat, we often pulled our carts side by side, like cowboys in a Western film trotting across the plains, and our conversations often veered to the wild places we had visited. Galen told us there were places in Eastern Europe where people still lived in many ways as they did in the Middle Ages; in the Carpathian Mountains he once encountered, on a remote farm, two brothers who shared the same wife.

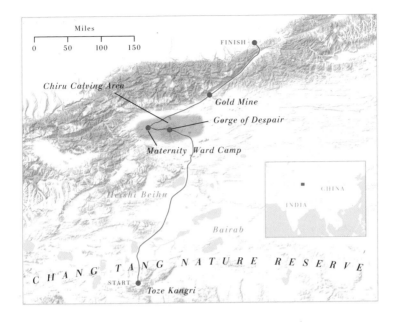

Three years before our traverse, George Schaller had traveled by camel-and-donkey caravan crossing the Kunluns from the north in an attempt to confirm the location of the calving grounds. The excursion was so arduous some of the animals died, and Schaller had to turn back before confirming the chiru were giving birth. From the notes of his explorations, we knew what the beginning and end of our route looked like, but no outsider had ever seen the middle part.

"I guess you could say that's what I'm doing," Conrad said. "Married to my best friend's wife."

Conrad was referring to his best friend, Alex Lowe. Since our climb of the rock spire in Antarctica, three events, each individually improbable, had punctuated Conrad's life. The first happened a couple of years after our Antarctic climb, when Conrad returned to Everest on an expedition to reconstruct what had happened to George Leigh Mallory in 1924 after Mallory and his partner, Sandy Irvine, disappeared into the clouds on a bid to reach the summit. The year of Conrad's Everest trip was an unusually dry one in the Himalaya, and there was less snow than normal. Conrad was alone traversing a slope at the 8,200-meter contour when he saw what he knew was a body.

"The exposed skin was white, but it was a different hue than the snow," Conrad later told me. The others in his party were traversing above him, and before calling them on the radio he sat alone next to the body. He could tell by the wool clothing it was old, and because there were only two climbers from that period who had disappeared at that extreme altitude, he knew the body had to be either Irvine or Mallory. He could also see the climber's leg was broken.

"I've been on enough search and rescue missions to know what a body looks like when it's unconscious after a fall," Conrad said, "and by his repose I knew he hadn't been killed outright. He was face down and his arms were extended, gripping the ground. He had fight left in him to the end."

Conrad sat next to the right hand of the dead climber. After a few minutes, he called the others. When they arrived, they examined the body and found an envelope in the wool jacket, with letters inside. They were addressed to George, and they were from Mallory's lover, Stella, back in the United Kingdom. They also found a pocket watch with the initials "GLM" on the inside of the clamshell cover, confirming the body was George Leigh Mallory.

Before the others had arrived, Conrad had felt an eerie connection to the dead climber. "Mallory and Irvine had set the stage," he told me, "for expeditions that followed in 1933 and 1934. Tenzing Norgay was on those expeditions as a young man, and then Tenzing went with the Swiss in 1952 and with the British in 1953, when he and Hillary were the first to reach the summit. That set the stage for the first Americans in 1963, then for your trip on the Bicentennial Expedition in 1976. Then the 1980s and then my first expeditions to Everest in the 1990s. It was eerie because I realized if it hadn't been for Mallory and Irvine paving the way, I might not have been there, sitting alone with Mallory's body."

Conrad felt another connection to the man whose body was next to him, the man who had defined for the generations the lure of reaching the summit when he had answered the perennial question "why" with the pithy answer "because it's there." It was that Mallory had died utterly alone. Where now a climber almost certainly would have a radio to call for help, Mallory had no one but himself. Yet he had continued to struggle, whether for his teammates, for his Stella, or for himself, it didn't matter, because what mattered was that he had not given up. That was the quality that did not need to be passed between generations, because it was the quality that most climbers already owned when they ventured to the high mountains.

Later that same year, Conrad and Alex Lowe were climbing Shishapangma, an 8,000-meter peak in the Himalaya, when an avalanche broke off below the summit. They were with a third friend, and each of them ran in a different direction. When the blast hit, Conrad went into an arrest position with his ice ax. Once the avalanche cloud passed, Conrad was OK, but Alex and their friend were dead.

Back home Conrad comforted Alex's wife, Jenni, and their three boys as best he could. As Conrad spent more time with the family, he and Jenni fell in love, and announced their wedding. A year later, my son Connor and I joined Conrad and Jenni and the boys on a family trip to Mongolia. I watched how Conrad dedicated time each day to the boys, playing with them, reading to them, hiking with them, verbally disciplining them when needed.

On a clear day under a blue sky, Jenni and I went on a hike through a broad grass valley above our camp. She reached down and picked a tiny blue flower.

"An Alpine forget-me-not. Alex used to pick them for me."

She wiped a tear and said, "Conrad is so good to me and the boys. I don't know . . . you lose and then you gain, and you count your blessings."

She gave me the flower and I placed it in my journal, a reminder that love is the truest balm against the pain of the loss of love.

* * *

On day twelve, the migration scattered in multiple tracks across a snowy plateau, all hoofprints pointing toward a ridge of low hills. We followed what on our topographical map appeared to be a moderate passage through the hills toward the Shar Kul basin. We found the prints of about a hundred chiru frozen in mud, but now we were less concerned about whether they were leading us to their calving grounds than whether we were following them into an impassable canyon.

Instead of mud and gravel bars we were now pulling our carts over sofa-sized rocks. Each time the wheels hit a rock, we had to triple-team the cart over it—one pulling while two pushed. We were all listening to the caution alarms sounding in our heads. Would the canyon become impassable, forcing us to reverse course? If it did, would we run out of food?

Conrad scrambled up to the canyon's rim to assess the alternative, but reported seeing a series of steep hills that looked more difficult to traverse than the canyon. We trudged on, fighting for each yard. By day's end, we had made less than two miles. The following day, the gorge narrowed further. We pulled the carts through the icy stream, our feet numbing. At one point the walls of the gorge squeezed to only ten feet apart for more than fifty yards. Suddenly we heard a loud *whumpf* as a basketball-sized rock smashed into the streambed twenty feet away. With the warming sun, there would surely be more rockfall. Conrad took a photograph of Jenni and the boys out of his pocket notebook and, in the manner that Tibetan Buddhists venerate sacred objects while praying for good fortune, held it to his forehead for several seconds.

"The Gorge of Despair," I sighed.

When we stopped to rest, I discovered the wheel frame on my rickshaw had two cracked welds. Conrad's had four cracked welds. One of the welds on Jimmy's cart had broken through. We had no choice but to portage our supplies, then carry the empty carts over the bigger rocks. We loaded our backpacks until they weighed sixty pounds or more; even then, it took two shuttles.

Jimmy Chin (left), Conrad Anker, and me (in the middle) struggle to get our rickshaws through the Gorge of Despair. **Galen Rowell**

A baby chiru shortly after its birth. **Galen Rowell**

In midafternoon we spotted a well-worn trail leading out of the canyon, and we surmised it was the chiru route to the calving grounds. But the hillside was steep, and we would have to use ropes to get the carts up. We decided to stay in the canyon with the hope of finding the calving grounds once we got to the basin. It was nearly 6:00 p.m. by the time we found a small bench fifteen feet above the river. Conrad suggested we camp, but Galen countered that we still had four hours of daylight, perhaps enough time to get out of the gorge.

"Otherwise we're still exposed to a flash flood."

"But we're tired," I countered, "with a higher risk of spraining an ankle."

"I'm going to scout," he said. He disappeared down the gorge and was back in an hour.

"There's one more narrows. It'll be hard with the carts, but we can definitely get out."

I held firm to my opinion, and Conrad and Jimmy agreed
with me.

"I'll go with the majority," Galen said, "but I'm portaging my
camera gear and film out of here today."

"Why don't you do that in the morning," I suggested.

"Because I don't think it will be safe in the morning."

I watched him load his pack and disappear down the gorge
and I asked myself, *Where did he get that ability to push himself
when the rest of us have thrown in the towel? What is his secret?* But
I knew there was no secret. There was only passion and willpower.

* * *

The next morning, Conrad unzipped our tent door to tell
Galen and me the coffee was ready. We hadn't heard him over
the sound of the river.

"It came up during the night," Conrad said. "It's nearly twice
as high as yesterday."

I could see he was concerned, and I could also read in his
expression the acknowledgment that Galen had been right. It
took until midday to complete our shuttles, but finally we escaped
the Gorge of Despair and reached the broad Shar Kul basin.
We spent another hour reinforcing the carts with wire and tape.
"Let's see if this works," Conrad said. No one suggested what we
would do if it didn't.

We felt even luckier when we began to see chiru, at first in
groups of 20 to 30, then a herd of 130 animals, so many the slope
appeared to shift like wind blowing across tall grass. With binoculars I scanned the foothills, bringing into focus what looked
like scores of rocks peppering the hillsides. They shimmered in
the heat waves as suddenly one rock, then another and another,
moved in a slow amble.

"The hills are covered," I called to the others. "Covered
with chiru!"

We had found the calving grounds. In one sweep of my eyes
I estimated there were 1,300 animals. In the larger area, we

estimated another 3,500. Now we had to document their birthing. We set up our two tents, christening the site Maternity Ward Camp, and reassessed our food supply. We had enough to stay for two days, so we had to make each hour count. To get close enough for good shots, Galen reminded us to approach the chiru slowly and quietly, using hills and gullies for cover.

The following morning, Conrad and I stayed hidden while Galen and Jimmy, draped with camouflage netting, stalked up a ravine. Soon they inched forward on knees and elbows toward a crest where earlier we had spotted a herd of chiru. Galen and Jimmy dropped to a belly-crawl and as they peered over the crest they saw the herd quietly grazing. They were all pregnant females—except one with a newborn suckling. The mother moved a few feet, and while Galen and Jimmy's cameras hummed and whirred the fledgling tottered on skinny legs to rejoin its mother.

A day later, alone on a hillside, I watched a group of eighteen pregnant females, their bellies bulging, and a single mother with a tiny calf. They didn't see me, but they raised their heads in the direction where an hour earlier I had seen a large wolf. The chiru still had to be wary of natural enemies, but at least for the few weeks they were here they could birth their young without concern of poachers. Elsewhere across the Chang Tang, hunters were killing what Schaller estimated were as many as 20,000 animals a year. Even if we did manage to create a new reserve around the calving grounds, the challenge had to be met by everyone in the chiru wool trade, including the women in New York, Paris, and Milan buying *shahtoosh* shawls.

First things first. We still had a hundred miles to walk to rejoin civilization. Then, three days later, day twenty-five of pulling our rickshaws, civilization suddenly came to us. Rounding a bend, we were startled to see a large mine. Through binoculars I could see fresh tailings, bulldozers, a crane, and dozens of people where only a year before George Schaller had found wilderness.

The miners were friendly, offering us food and tea. More than a hundred of them were working a placer operation they hoped would yield 2.8 million ounces of gold. They were proud of what they had accomplished in less than three months, including construction of a sixty-mile dirt road from the nearest highway.

The same dirt road gave us an easy way home, as we pulled our carts on the comparatively smooth surface. But it could also give poachers easy access to the calving grounds. From the mine we estimated a four-wheel-drive vehicle could make it cross-country in two days—disheartening when we considered that from the other direction, it had taken us more than a month.

Two days later we reached the first village we'd seen in more than 400 miles. There was our vehicle, waiting for us as planned. We loaded our carts into the back, and as we drove away I leaned out the window to look in the side mirror, discovering with some surprise that I was just as grizzled as my companions.

The end of the trek. Conrad Anker, Galen Rowell, Jimmy Chin, and me (l to r). **Jimmy Chin Collection**

Chapter Twenty-Two

The Better Angels
of Our Nature

The Chang Tang traverse was one of the most rigorous expeditions of my life. When I departed, my hair was brown, and when I returned, it was gray. But it was also one of the most fulfilling. It required the strength and skills I had developed as a mountaineer, especially the ability to keep putting one foot in front of the other. It required strategic thinking and planning. It required teamwork and avoiding conflict while under physical stress. The best part was that it wasn't about any of us on the team; it was about us using our lifetimes of accumulated skills to help save a species.

The goal was simple enough: to do our part to save the chiru from extinction. The strategy for reaching the goal, however, seemed like a moonshot. First, find the unknown calving grounds of the western population of chiru. Second, document the calving grounds with photographs and video. Third, use the visual assets to create as much media about the slaughter of the chiru as possible in the hope of persuading the Chinese to protect the calving grounds.

Less than a year after we returned from the Chang Tang, George Schaller published an article about our chiru sightings in a World Conservation Union (IUCN) bulletin. *National Geographic*, who funded both the expedition and much of the follow-up publicity, ran an article in the magazine on our adventure with my words and Galen's photographs, and made a TV show for their *Explorer* series with Jimmy's video. I wrote a book. NPR did a radio show. Jimmy, Conrad, and I went on a nation-wide lecture tour. And the author Jacqueline Briggs Martin published a children's book about Schaller's study and our rickshaw traverse called *The Chiru of High Tibet*.

Schaller then used the media to try to persuade the Chinese to create a protected area around the calving grounds before the poachers could get there first. The Chinese agreed. The Shar Kul Nature Reserve covers 1,300 square kilometers. For the first three years, until the Chinese could integrate the new area into their operations, Patagonia, Inc. and the Wildlife Conservation Society split the cost of field patrols. During the second year, a patrol turned back a group of poachers that were headed toward the calving grounds.

For the first time in the fifteen years of George Schaller's study, chiru numbers started to increase. The victory, however, was bittersweet because Galen wasn't there to enjoy it. A month after we had returned, he and his wife, Barbara, died in a small-plane crash. For the thirty days it took to follow the chiru I had shared a tent with Galen. At first, I couldn't accept the fact that he wouldn't be calling the next day to invite me to drive to the eastern Sierra for a trail run, a ski, or a climb.

* * *

Two years later National Geographic called to invite me to come to Washington, DC, to meet with the Dalai Lama. The society wanted several of us who had been part of environmental and cultural conservation initiatives in Tibet to make presentations.

"Make sure you keep it to a maximum of four minutes," I was told.

The meeting was in the old building on the corner of 16th and M Streets, in the high-ceilinged room where the society was started in the late-nineteenth century. His Holiness entered and nodded to us, and everybody bowed, and many clasped their hands. All the upper-level executives of the society were there, and the CEO of National Geographic presented the Dalai Lama with a bound collection of original editions of the magazine that had articles on Tibet, going back to Francis Younghusband's forced entry into Lhasa in 1904 and a story by Ilia Tolstoy, Leo Tolstoy's grandson, about his adventure as an OSS officer in World War II crossing Tibet in search of an alternative to the Burma Road after the Japanese closed the important supply line.

His Holiness lifted his hands in delight when he was presented the volume, and immediately started turning the pages. I could see some of his handlers getting nervous that he was spending so much of the limited meeting time looking at magazine pictures, but the Dalai Lama was too engrossed, especially when he got to Tolstoy's story about having an audience with him when he was only seven years old. His face lit up with excitement. The Dalai Lama told us how Tolstoy had presented him with a watch that was a gift from President Roosevelt. With a grin he reached in the pocket of his robe and pulled out the gold Patek Philippe pocket watch that he had kept his entire life.

Sitting at the long conference table, with His Holiness in the middle and the CEO of National Geographic opposite him, we gave our presentations. I had worked hard to summarize our rickshaw traverse of the Chang Tang, and the protection of the calving grounds, into a couple dozen slides, and it seemed to go well, as did the other three presentations.

"Your Holiness," the head of National Geographic asked, "what do you think?"

"I like Rick's trip!"

"Why?"

"He and his friends had a goal and a plan, and it included the Chinese because that was the only way they could get it done. And they did it."

After the last point, the Dalai Lama leaned forward and looked down the table at me and nodded. I gave a queen's wave in return.

"Rick," the Dalai Lama said, "are you doing any more trips like that one?"

How can you not be smitten with someone who said, "We need to learn to want what we have, not to have what we want."?
Rebecca Hale/National Geographic Society

"Are you kidding? That one almost killed me!"

I could see the others tense up, including the CEO, and I realized that maybe I should have addressed him as His Holiness. But the Dalai Lama grinned, and it was clear that he enjoyed the informality.

"That's too bad," he said.

"I tell you what. I'll do another trip if you come with me."

Everyone once again tensed, except for the Dalai Lama, whose grin widened.

"OK. I'll come with you. But you have to carry me in your rickshaw."

"Do you have any idea how bad that would look for both of us?"

We both laughed. His handlers whispered in his ear and he checked his pocket watch. It was time to leave. He stood and circled the room, quickly shaking hands. When he got to me, he took my hand without looking up and perfunctorily shook it and turned toward the next person. But then he looked up and the grin returned. He reached out and took my hand again and, gently leaning toward me, touched his forehead to mine.

* * *

If the Chang Tang trip had been both the most fulfilling of my career and the most physically demanding, that raised the question of what, now that I was in my midfifties, I was going to do for the next chapter of my life. I had worked in the second units of a few dramatic films, and I considered trying to make my own television drama or maybe even a feature film, but many of the people I had met working in the first units—the producers, directors, and some of the actors—were often ego- and money-driven; the opposite of the kinds of people I wanted to work with. I could write more books, but the kids were in college and Jennifer had retired after twenty years working at Patagonia, and she was not impressed with the royalty checks that I held up with pride whenever they trickled in.

Then Patagonia offered me a full-time job. The woman running their myriad environmental initiatives had left, and they wanted to know if I would take over. I wasn't sure. Yvon was one of my closest friends, and if I were to work for his company, I would have to make sure we didn't clash. For that matter, I wondered if I could work for *any* company. I had been self-employed my entire life. I asked Jennifer what she thought.

"You always say you like to try new things. Maybe you should try the one called 'having a regular job.'"

If I was going to have a "regular job," running Patagonia's sustainability and environmental initiatives was as good as it would probably ever get. I took the job. I had to study to get up to speed on the sustainability part, but the wildland conservation part was a natural fit. Every year or two, the company ran a campaign focused on an environmental topic of emerging importance, and I suggested for the next one the theme of connecting habitats through wildlife corridors. One of the main threats to wildlife is the fragmentation and subsequent isolation of habitats caused by human development: suburban sprawl, roads and highways, industrial farming, the draining of wetlands, overgrazing of grasslands, and fencing of open spaces. At the time I joined Patagonia, conservation biologists were becoming increasingly aware that wildlife was also threatened by habitat changes resulting from human-caused global warming, and connecting habitat fragments through corridors was seen as an even more important tactic against this threat.

My increasing understanding of the impact of climate change on wildlife habitat—as well as on the planet as a whole—was linked directly to my experiences spending time in nature. A couple of years before going to work at Patagonia, I had read an article in the newspaper with the headline "Large Ice Shelf In Antarctica Disintegrates At Great Speed." The piece described how a section of ice the size of Rhode Island had broken off the Larsen B Ice Shelf and floated into the Weddell Sea. The article quoted a scientist who said that there was no evidence that, since the last ice age ended 12,000 years ago, there has ever been open water in this area. In what sounded like a conscious effort to be seen as impartial, the article stated that while it was premature to conclude that the breakup was related to the buildup of greenhouse gas emissions in the atmosphere, experts were nevertheless increasingly challenged to find another explanation.

My mind returned to my dog-mushing trip down the Larsen. I recalled that first day, when we camped on the slope of the Seal Nunataks at an elevation high enough that we could look south, down the Larsen, for at least 200 miles. I remembered how on my last night with the expedition I lay in my sleeping bag and heard the ice crack, and how it didn't resonate like cracks do on glaciers, and how instead it was sharp and shallow.

Back then I didn't understand the significance of that crack the way I would a dozen years later. My growing awareness of the scale of the challenge of climate change took a steep jump the year after that trip, however, when Yvon had given me a book that changed the way I thought about our species' impact on the planet.

"Read this," he had said. "If you thought we had problems before, they're nothing compared to what we're going to have."

The book was *The End of Nature*, by the environmental thinker Bill McKibben, and the cover blurb, from *The New York Review of Books*, promised "a kind of song for the wild, a lament for its loss, and a plea for its restoration." The book posited that what then was called "the greenhouse effect" was an alteration of the self-regulating systems of Earth so fundamental that we could no longer think of nature as something operating apart from our species' activities. *The End of Nature* wasn't the first time I had heard about climate change. In the late eighties I had read NASA scientist James Hansen's testimony to Congress when he warned about the consequences of increasing atmospheric carbon. But this was the first time I had considered that, as McKibben put it, "our sense of nature as eternal and separate [from our human activity] is washed away, and we will [soon] see all too clearly what we have done."

I was astounded to consider that I was bearing witness in human time to change that until then had been measured in geologic time. Then, in 2017, I read that a chunk of the Larsen C—the largest section of the Larsen Ice Shelf—broke off, creating an iceberg that weighed a trillion tons and was nearly the size of Delaware. I then realized I was also bearing witness to the accelerating *rate* of change that had once been measured only in geologic time.

I thought of my friend Dave Foreman, the environmental activist, who had told me that the word *wilderness* comes from the Old English *will-deor-ness*, with *deor*, the word for deer, and, by extension, for wildlife. The idea was that the land, the *ness*, was willed by nature. But now nature was no longer self-willed but willed by us. We were in the driver's seat, steering a planet of marvelous and unfathomable complexity, and I realized it would require an act of hubris beyond my understanding to believe we could really know where we were going, much less how we might get there.

* * *

The concept of connecting habitat fragments through wildlife corridors as a way to mitigate the extinction crisis had been around for a couple of decades, so the goal of the Patagonia campaign was to increase awareness about corridors in the hope of building support for the idea among the general public, as well as influencing governments and landowners to

I proposed to my colleagues at Patagonia, Inc., we integrate the California state flag into the Freedom to Roam logo to express the irony of having a subspecies driven to extinction by development in the state that adopted that same subspecies as its totem.

support it. We called the campaign Freedom to Roam. For the next year the company published articles in its catalogs about the science of large landscape connectivity, about the politics of protecting wildlife corridors, and about building community to support the idea of human beings going about their activities in ways that gave their wild brethren freedom to roam. I knew we had chosen a good name when I had a meeting with several high-ranking Army and Navy officers in Washington, DC, to discuss creating wildlife-friendly buffers around military bases, the sensitive zones the officers referred to as being "outside the fence."

"This name is perfect," one of the generals said. "If we're talking to a landowner who leans to the right, we'll emphasis the 'freedom' part, and if the owner leans to the left, we'll focus on the 'roam' part."

At the same time that Patagonia was working to increase awareness about the need to protect wildlife corridors, I reached out to other organizations, including the National Wildlife Federation and the World Wildlife Fund, to get them to focus more on protecting corridors.

I had retained a position with the National Geographic Society that I had held before I started at Patagonia, serving on the Expeditions Council that advised the society on applications it received from adventurers seeking financial support for expeditions and other projects. The program had expanded to include an initiative called Young Explorers, which awarded small grants to adventurers, scientists, and conservationists ages eighteen to twenty-five, and reading the proposals came with the anticipation of finding a few whose imaginative creativity and excitement for discovery reminded me of my own passions—what some might call obsessions—when I was that age.

One evening I read an application titled "Path of the Pronghorn" from a twenty-one-year-old photographer named Joe Riis. For two years, Riis had photographed a population of pronghorn antelope that migrate between Grand Teton National

Park, where they summer, and Wyoming's Red Desert, where they winter, following a wildlife corridor increasingly threatened by development from ranchette subdivisions, fencing, roads, and highways. Joe's idea was to migrate with the pronghorn, following them on foot to photograph in detail the entire hundred-plus-mile migration corridor. It was reminiscent of my trip following the migration of the chiru, and my proposal to National Geographic was not only to give Joe a grant, but to allow me to go with him on his trek. After all, every twenty-one-year-old needs a mentor.

Joe had grown up outside of Pierre, South Dakota, and his dad worked for the state fish and game department. He had strong shoulders and hands and a courteous smile and an endearing self-deprecation.

"It's an honor to meet you, sir."

"Just call me Rick."

"Yes, sir."

Joe had read my article about following the chiru migration, and when I floated the idea of joining him on his trek he agreed enthusiastically. Even though I didn't mention it explicitly to Joe, I took seriously my opportunity to do what I could to help him toward his goal of becoming a *National Geographic* photographer. I call it an "opportunity" because I had learned from the Chang Tang traverse how gratifying it was to support someone coming up through the ranks. Jimmy Chin had worked hard and done a great job videotaping our rickshaw trip, and the result was a half-hour TV show on National Geographic's cable channel that led to other assignments for Jimmy as both a photographer and a filmmaker.

Joe estimated our walk would take nine or ten days. We started at Antelope Flats in Grand Teton National Park. The day was unseasonably warm, and because of hot weather the pronghorn had not yet started to migrate. After an hour, we saw a small group canter up a moraine and, once they sensed us, break into a gallop as they made their characteristic spitting sound. The animals stopped and resumed grazing, apparently content during the Indian summer to enjoy the fodder on the valley floor. Joe and I were also content, knowing that the weather over the next two weeks would almost certainly turn cold, triggering the migration.

At noon we stopped above the Gros Ventre River to have lunch. Due to the exigencies of my job at Patagonia, I had accepted Joe's offer to organize our trek, including buying provisions. He now removed from his rucksack a packet of flour tortillas. Opening a jar of peanut butter, he applied a thin coating to a tortilla and handed it to me.

"That was good," I said after I ate it. "What's next?"

"Next?"

"For lunch."

"That was lunch."

I shouldn't have been surprised: a Spartan diet was consistent with Joe's Spartan life. He lived in a rusted Toyota truck on a scrap of foam in the back bed, resting atop a life-sized cutout of a pronghorn attached to a stick that he held in front of him as he stalked his photographic prey. Whatever trickle of income he received from sales of his photographs he used to buy film, not food.

"I can give you a little more," he said, his inflection rising at the end, so it was more query than suggestion.

"That's OK. I'm fine."

By prearrangement we rendezvoused with a National Park Service biologist who was knowledgeable about pronghorn. She hiked with us for the rest of the afternoon. As she was walking back to the dirt road where she had left her vehicle, I asked her if she could deliver a note to two friends who lived in a town just outside the park boundary.

"Yvon and Malinda Chouinard," I said. "Do you know them?"

"I know where they live."

I knew that in a few days we would cross a dirt road before we climbed out of the Gros Ventre drainage, and my note

Joe Riis setting a camera trap at one of the pinch points along the Path of the Pronghorn. **Joe Riis Collection**

contained both directions to the road crossing and a shopping list for groceries.

At the end of the day, we pitched our tent on a ridgeline with a view of the full sweep of the Tetons. Joe made a packet of ramen noodles for dinner. After I finished my portion I was still hungry. The next day it rained, but it was still too warm to have any hope that it might turn to snow, which would spur the migration. Through the spruce forest we heard in the distance a passing ATV that we knew was most likely a hunter. It was hunting season, and we had to stay in the open as much as possible so hunters wouldn't mistake us for elk. Fortunately, that was easy, because the migration trail tended to follow any available meadow.

"Pronghorn like to be in the open," Joe explained, "where they can see predators."

Other than hunters, the pronghorn's main threat was mountain lions—but in the open, no mountain lion could hope to catch them. Pronghorn are the fastest four-legged animals in the Western Hemisphere, clocked at over fifty-five miles per hour. Evolutionary biologists speculate that pronghorn evolved to outrun cheetahs. About 30 percent larger than the modern cheetah, the American cheetah—not closely related to the African or Asian cheetah but similar-looking due to convergent evolution—went extinct in the Pleistocene overkill event 12,000 years ago when 80 percent of the megafauna in North America went extinct. American cheetahs have been recovered in the La Brea Tar Pits in Los Angeles, and learning about them had been part of the research I'd done following my walk across Tsavo.

Today, when I see pronghorn run, my mind goes to American cheetahs and the other animals that went extinct in the overkill, and from there to my conclusion that, whenever we have the opportunity combined with the technology—unless we evoke what Abraham Lincoln called the better angels of our nature—we'll hunt them and steal their habitats until all that is left are skeletons in a museum.

* * *

We flushed a group of mule deer bedded under a spruce. The trail rose and fell as we traversed folds in the hillside scoured by seasonal streams. We camped in a small grove of aspen with yellow leaves that brought welcome contrast to the gray sky and dark hillsides. As I sat on a log sipping coffee, Joe told me more about his background.

"My father's an avid hunter, birds and game, and our family life centered around hunting—that's how we got our food, or at least our meat. My grandmother Artemis also has had a big influence. She's ninety-six and she's never been to a doctor and never taken any medicine, not even aspirin. When she meets somebody new, she keeps a distance, studying them to make sure they're OK."

"You pick up any of those traits?"

"Well, I like hunting, you know, sustainable hunting. I grew up with it, and that's where my love for wildlife comes from." Then with a grin, he added, "But I've learned to get along with new people."

Now it was my turn to grin as I toasted Joe with my cup of joe. Despite our slim rations and Joe's slim budget, he had heard I liked coffee, and when he was shopping at the grocery, he had asked a clerk to recommend the best brand of canned coffee.

"So, I got you this coffee called Yuban," Joe had told me, pronouncing it "YOU-bn." I had not corrected him, and instead started calling it "YOU-bn" out of appreciation for this young man for whom I was growing fonder each day.

In the morning we traversed a barren hillside called Red Hills, one of several bottlenecks in the migration route. We stopped at a turn in the trail where the week before Joe had positioned a camera trap—only there was no camera, just the light beam and a counter. National Geographic had been slow equipping Joe for our trek, and he'd been trying to determine the best place for a trap once the cameras arrived.

"Pronghorn are so skittish and so sensitive to any movement that I figure camera traps are the only way to get good close-ups," he said. "Nobody's ever done that, and that's my dream: to get the first really intimate photographs of pronghorn."

When Joe had first been awarded his Young Explorers grant, senior photography editors at *National Geographic* wanted to send a seasoned photographer to cover his trek following the migration. I had gone ballistic, asking them how they could expect to bring up a new generation of photographers if they didn't give them a chance to take ownership of a project, especially a project that, in this case, Joe had proposed? They finally backed off and allowed Joe to photograph our trek himself.

Joe reset the counter and we continued hiking. I stopped to look at a bird through my binoculars.

"What is it?" Joe asked.

"Williamson's sapsucker."

"Who was Williamson?"

"A surveyor. One of the early guys in the middle of the nineteenth century trying to figure out the best route for the transcontinental railroad."

Joe looked at the bird through my binoculars.

"It's a male," I said. "The females have a brown head, not black and white like that one."

"That's cool. How did you get interested in birds?"

I told Joe about raising pheasants with my grandfather when I was a teenager, and how that had led to my dream of someday getting to the mountains and jungles of Asia to see the birds in their native habitats.

"Then for my twenty-fifth birthday my mother gave me a copy of the Audubon bird guide," I explained. "One day I was at my desk when I saw a hummingbird out the window. I looked it up in my new bird guide and identified it as an Anna's hummingbird. The bird guide said that during the mating season the male Anna's flies straight up, turns, and does a nosedive straight down, then pulls out and spreads its tail feathers to make a popping sound. The book said that sound was the hummingbird's mating call.

"A few days later, I was working on my car when my eye caught a hummingbird flying straight up and then straight down, and then I heard it. *Pop!* Just like the bird guide had said. Then a minute later I heard another *Pop!* I stood up and closed my eyes and listened. Every minute or so, from around the neighborhood and the hills, there were more pops, and I realized they had been going on all day, and all week, and all throughout the hummingbird mating season. Pops every minute or so—and all that time I had been oblivious."

Joe nodded, and handed my binoculars back to me, and we kept walking. Whenever I tell this story I usually add at the end how learning to listen for the pop of the Anna's hummingbird was the beginning of a lifelong effort to learn how to pay attention. With Joe, however, I felt I didn't need to point that out.

* * *

That evening we camped close to the end of the dirt road that would for the next couple of days be our last access to the outside world. In the morning we waited at the road's end, and I was relieved when one of Joe's friends arrived in Joe's old truck and delivered a bag of groceries from Malinda Chouinard. Joe unpacked the sack and handed the items to me to divide between us. Picking up a block of cheese, I saw him read the label. The price tag was still on it. He handed it to me. It was imported Basque sheep's milk cheese, and it cost more than I suspected Joe made in a week.

"That must be some pretty good-tastin' cheese," he said with his endearing grin.

If the trip was going to be successful—if it was going to reach the twin goals of bringing awareness to the need to protect the pronghorn migration corridor and, at the same time, advance Joe's career at *National Geographic*—we needed to be migrating with the pronghorn, and, so far, because the unseasonably warm weather had delayed the migration, we had only seen a few animals.

We crossed the crest of the Gros Ventre Range and descended into the Green River valley. For the next three days, we crossed private ranches that had given us advance permission to enter, with one exception. Because we wanted to continue to follow the exact migration route the pronghorn followed, and because that meant we had to walk across the holdout ranch, our only option was to wait until dark. The sky started to cloud up, marking the beginning of a dark night, as we squirmed under the barbed wire fence. We could have climbed over, but we wanted to crawl under because that's what the pronghorn had to do; because they have evolved to run fast, they have front leg bones that are

Using GPS tracks from biologists who studied the pronghorn migration, we walked the hillsides where the pronghorn walked and crossed the rivers where they crossed. **Joe Riis**

too lightweight and fragile for them to jump over fences without risking breaking a leg.

It was too dark to see easily, but we dared not turn on our headlamps for fear the ranch owner would spot us. Just past midnight, I fell in a badger hole but fortunately didn't sprain an ankle or knee. It was 3:00 am when we crawled under the fence on the opposite side of the ranch and set up our tent. It was starting to snow, and when we woke and looked out the tent's door, there was a foot of fresh flakes. We made coffee and continued our trek, flushing a sage grouse that exploded into the air, raising our pulse rates. We stopped every few minutes to look back. There were still no pronghorn. An hour later we turned again, and we saw them in the distance, a long line of animals coming toward us.

"I count over a hundred and fifty," I said, looking through my binoculars.

We crouched behind a clump of sagebrush, and I followed Joe's admonition to remain motionless because pronghorn can't process shapes as well as they can movement. The animals were walking in a single file, and soon they started to pass us, some pausing to browse on the sage. Two fawns left the line and started walking directly toward us. We remained frozen, and when the pair was only twenty feet from us, they suddenly stopped and looked directly at us, and then bolted back to their mothers. The full herd broke into a run, and once past us the animals regrouped and continued their migration.

By midday over 300 animals had passed us. Late that afternoon we arrived at the highway between Jackson and Pinedale. The pronghorn grouped behind the fence bordering the highway and in twos and threes crawled under it, ran across the road, then crawled under the opposite fence. A semitrailer approached and braked hard, nearly jackknifing. A doe panicked and tried to jump the fence, but her hind legs caught on the barbed wire. We were about to run to help her when she freed herself; we hoped she wasn't too injured to survive.

We counted 700 pronghorn crossing the highway. There were more close calls with trucks and automobiles, but fortunately no collisions. We had been walking for nine days, and had reached the end of our trek.

* * *

The following week Joe's cameras arrived, and he rushed back to Red Hills and captured the first close-up photographs of migrating pronghorn. National Geographic published them on its website, and Joe distributed them everywhere he could. Inspired by the photos, as well as by ranchers, hunters, conservationists, and others who rallied to the pronghorn's defense,

the Wyoming governor and state legislature, listening to the
better angels of their natures, authorized funds to build a wildlife bridge across the Jackson-Pinedale highway. Joe was there
to photograph the first pronghorn that crossed it; today all the
pronghorn migrating to and from Grand Teton National Park
have learned to use it. Joe went on to become one of National
Geographic's leading wildlife photographers.

After getting his camera traps from National Geographic, this is one of the images Joe captured of the pronghorn crossing the Red Hills in the Gros Ventre Mountains. **Joe Riis**

Chapter Twenty-Three

Laser Focus

The construction of the wildlife bridge over the Jackson-Pinedale highway was a collaborative effort, with many people coming together to safeguard the path of the pronghorn. But a big part of that effort came from Joe Riis, when he decided to buy film instead of food, and when he ended each day sleeping in the back of his truck on a foam pad atop his life-sized cutout of a pronghorn, and when he fell asleep thinking about how to reposition his camera traps to capture the first close-up photographs of his totem animal.

The word *obsession* gets a bad rap from its association with mental health, but when you look over the history of human achievement you realize much of it happened because one person had an obsessive laser focus on one goal. When we returned from the Chang Tang, George Schaller used the findings from our trip to convince the Chinese to establish a 1,300-square-kilometer nature reserve. The new protected area was adjacent to the existing Chang Tang Reserve, which had also been created as a result of Schaller's singular persuasion. Put together, the two protected areas were about the size of the entire country of Germany.

If there was a weakness to Schaller's accomplishment, however, it was in the low level of protection conferred by a nature reserve in China because it ended up not being enough to prevent the construction of hundreds of miles of roads to access new gold mines. Solving for outcomes like that was the reason Kris

Entering the Chacabuco Valley on the road trip with my family to Chilean Patagonia, in 2001. No one among us could have foretold that two decades later it would be a national park rated by Trip Advisor among the top ten parks to visit in Chile. **Rick Ridgeway Collection**

and Doug Tompkins developed their strategy around creating and expanding national parks in Chile and Argentina, the two targets of their laser focus.

"You look around the world," Doug said, "and national parks are the gold standard."

Kris and Doug were clear-eyed that it was going to be a long-haul strategy from initial purchase of private lands to fully fledged national parks. By the early 2000s, however, they were having some wins. Using a new foundation that Kris managed, they bought two estancias on the Atlantic coast north of the Strait of Magellan that in 2004 became Argentina's first maritime national park. Monte León National Park encompassed twenty-two miles of pristine coastline, safeguarding a rookery that was home to half a million penguins and another that was used by more than a thousand seals. The following year Chile created Corcovado National Park, just to the south of Pumalín, after Doug convinced the government to accept his offer of over 200,000 acres of land that he and Peter Buckley had purchased, so long as the government agreed to add about 500,000 acres of its own federal lands.

At the same time, Kris and Doug were working on an even more ambitious vision: creating a transboundary park in the central region of Patagonia that would be bigger than Yellowstone. Needing a name that had equal currency in both countries and at the same time was politically neutral, they called the potential project the "future Patagonia National Park."

* * *

Kris and Doug had had their eyes on the area for years, but the idea for the future park got a jumpstart in 2000 when my family and I, in a vehicle we borrowed from Kris and Doug, scouted the Chilean side of the potential project while Kris and Doug, in their other vehicle, investigated the Argentinian side. The genesis for the trip was Jennifer's and my interest in exposing our three kids more directly to what Aunt Kris and Uncle Doug were trying to do. As I developed the itinerary for the road trip, however, I realized we needed more time than the two-week break the kids had over Christmas. Some of their teachers had pushed back, and I had called Doug to tell him I wasn't sure we would be able to do the trip. I anticipated this would rile him, knowing his opinion of school since he himself had dropped out of the tenth grade and had never gone back. I was not disappointed.

"You go tell those teachers," Doug had replied, "not to let school get in the way of your kids' education."

We started the journey by spending three days with Kris and Doug in Pumalín, where Doug took the kids on a hike that included a stop at one of the biggest alerces in the park, a tree more than 2,000 years old.

"The idea is to someday give this tree and this forest and all these buildings and trails and campgrounds back to Chile," Doug told the kids. "That will expand the country's national park system, but, more importantly, it will raise it to a higher standard and that way increase the pride that people have in their parks. And the more pride, the more they'll want to protect their parks. See?"

The next day the kids helped me strap our gear on top of the SUV we had borrowed. We left Pumalín, driving south on the Carretera Austral, an 800-mile-long dirt road paralleling the crest of the Andes. Meanwhile, Kris and Doug left in their other car, crossing the border into Argentina. We planned to meet five days later at a remote border crossing in the center of the proposed park.

For the next three days we either camped in tents or stayed in small lodges. On the fourth day we turned off the Carretera Austral and followed a secondary road to the headquarters of Estancia Valle Chacabuco, a 173,000-acre sheep ranch on the Chilean side of the envisioned park.

Jennifer and the kids stayed in the vehicle while I went to the door of the ranch office and knocked. A middle-aged man with skin that looked like leather opened the door.

"I'm with my wife and kids," I said, gesturing toward the car. "I was wondering if we could get permission to camp on the estancia."

"Anywhere you want," he answered with a smile.

"Thank you. We really appreciate it."

"You German?"

"No, North American. California."

"California?" His face soured and he shook his head. "There, pure bad."

Then his expression sweetened. "But here," he said waving his hand at the surrounding hills, "pure good."

It was Christmas Day, and at seven in the evening we still had three more hours of daylight. We stopped at a reed-lined lake to admire five black-necked swans. A herd of guanaco stretched their camelid necks to watch us. I balanced my camera on a fence post to take some pictures while Carissa shot video with our camcorder. National Geographic's *Traveler* was interested in an article, and they needed video for the website; that seemed like a good opportunity for Carissa, who was interested in filmmaking.

We found a grassy flat next to the small river that meandered through the valley and set up our two small tents. Connor and I built a fire while Jennifer peeled bubble wrap off the bottle of Veuve Clicquot we had carried with care from California. I filled five metal cups, and we made a champagne toast to a perfect Christmas Day, which had started that morning with a half-day rafting trip on the nearby Río Baker, which flows out of Lago General Carrera, a natural body of water so large that it extends into Argentina, where it is called Lago Buenos Aires. Surrounded by glaciated peaks, the lake has a mineral composition that supports diatoms that give the water an aquamarine color; the Baker River has the same gemstone blue as it descends a canyon lined with beech forests.

"The river is flowing at about thirty-five thousand cubic feet per second," our rafting guide had said. "Do you know how much that is?"

"No," Connor replied.

"Do you know how much a gallon of milk weighs?"

All three kids shook their heads, so I offered that a gallon of milk weighed about eight pounds.

"How many gallons of milk have you carried at once?" he asked Connor.

"I guess two."

"Well, there are two hundred and fifty thousand gallons of milk flowing down this river every *second*."

That seemed to make an impression, as did the subsequent conversation about a proposed dam under study by the Chilean government that would submerge this section of the country's largest free-flowing river. If the dam and the park both became reality, future visitors would stand at the entrance to the new

"It's like the American West," Yvon Chouinard had said, describing Patagonia. "Only with no people." Well, at least with only a few people, including my family and me at our Christmas Day campsite next to the Chacabuco River. Rick Ridgeway

park and in one direction see thousands of acres of restored grasslands, and in the other a concrete behemoth on the order of Hoover Dam.

* * *

The morning after Christmas, I packed our tents while the kids, following the rule book from school campouts, scoured the campsite to make sure we would "Leave No Trace." Driving up-valley, I pointed out several lateral and terminal moraines, explaining how glaciers during the last ice age had bulldozed the valley so deeply that the Chacabuco was one of only two or three places in the southern Andes where the plants, insects, and animals from the wet windward side commingled with those from the dry leeward side, rendering the valley exceptionally biologically diverse and a place long coveted by Chile's national park service.

We arrived at the remote border checkpoint, and the guards greeted us with smiles. Inside the small office they were slow to process our papers, and I had the impression it was less because they were inefficient and more because they were lonely and enjoyed our company. Another car arrived—unusual at this outpost—and through the window I saw our kids waving.

"Your friends?" the guard asked.

It was Kris and Doug, arriving as planned. With paperwork completed, we followed them on the dirt road to a large estancia named poetically Sol de Mayo. Now that we were on the Argentinian side and in the rain shadow of the Andes, the landscape changed from hills forested with deciduous beech, bottomlands lush with bunchgrass, and wetlands rimmed with horsetail to ruddy cliffs with exposed strata bordering mesas that framed valleys whose bottomlands held spring creeks with banks that were tinged green. A cloudless sky opened like a great dome that pushed down the distant horizon, and I was reminded of parts of Utah, Idaho, and Montana but with no towns and few people. "Like the American West two hundred years ago," Yvon once said, describing this place on Earth that was still so open and so wild that it had inspired him to name his company after it.

The owner of Sol de Mayo greeted us warmly and invited us to pitch our tents on the lawn next to the main house. While it was likely he didn't know for certain the reason for Kris and Doug's visit, it was a safe bet he had a good idea because Doug's reputation preceded him wherever he went in Chile and Argentina. In hotels, restaurants, and on the streets citizens recognized him as the gringo buying up huge swaths of their two countries, and the conspiracy theories about his motivations continued to shadow him. Whether the owner placed any credence in any of that was hard to say, but from his gracious hospitality it seemed unlikely.

"We will have an asado tonight," he told us. "A big party, to welcome you to Argentine Patagonia."

With several hours before the party started, we drove around Sol de Mayo and some of the neighboring estancias. We had a picnic on a cobblestone beach overlooking Lago Pueyrredón, a deep-water lake over a hundred square miles in size that crossed the border where, on the Chilean side, it is known as Lago Cochrane. It had the same gemstone-blue water as Lago General Carrera, its sister lake to the north. Had these two enormous lakes been situated in Europe or in the United States, they would have been celebrated globally as being among the greatest natural wonders of the world.

"I'm starting to be able to imagine it," I said. "The south end of the park along this lake, the north end on General Carrera. In between, the Jeinimeni mountains and the Chacabuco Valley on the Chilean side, these plateaus and tablelands on the Argentinian side. It would be incredible."

"It'd be five stars," Doug replied, using his favored phrase to describe anything of superb beauty. "One of the great national parks. Not just in South America. In the world."

* * *

For the next three years Kris and Doug periodically checked in with the owner of Sol de Mayo, asking if he was interested in selling, but the affable Argentinian said he enjoyed the solace of country living and wasn't interested. Then without warning the owners of the Estancia Valle Chacabuco said they were selling. The asking price for the 173,000 acres, however, was more than Kris and Doug could afford, given the financial obligations of completing Pumalín as well as other projects already underway. Could Conservación Patagónica, the public foundation that Kris ran, raise the money from other philanthropists?

Kris had initiated conversations with potential contributors when another buyer surfaced. Kris had to decide whether to make an offer and hope during the escrow she could raise the gap money.

"I can't sleep," she told me.

Doug and Kris at the end of our scout on the Argentinian side of what someday could become a transnational Patagonia National Park. **Rick Ridgeway**

"Remember that note card above Doug's desk at Esprit?" I replied. "Commit, and then figure it out."

She made the offer, and the owners accepted. During escrow Kris worked through the days and into the nights to raise the money. Finally, the deal closed. The next year Conservación Patagónica bought another 22,000 contiguous acres. Kris hadn't given up the idea of someday extending the park into Argentina and creating a transborder peace park, like the Waterton-Glacier International Peace Park between Canada and the United States, but for the foreseeable future the focus would be on building out the Chilean side.

Two years later I visited again, this time bringing two potential donors who were, like me, in awe of the scale of the project—not just its size but the amount of work required to turn vision into reality. I watched Doug meet with architects to review designs for the buildings and campgrounds. I joined him and the foreman of a field crew as we adjusted survey stakes hammered into the ground every kilometer to plot the location of a future trail. When completed, the trail would enchain a series of alpine lakes just as a string links a collection of pearls.

Doug insisted that everything be of the highest quality, so the new park would, as he had once explained to my kids, raise the standard of the entire park system in Chile. The buildings were constructed from stone quarried from within the park, and workers made the roofs out of copper, another material indigenous to Chile; the park headquarters collectively would become the largest expanse of copper roofing in South America.

There was talk, even among Doug's friends, that his obsession was verging on madness. It reminded me of the article in *The Atlantic* a few years earlier that compared Doug's quest to *Fitzcarraldo*. On the surface there was perhaps some similarity to the rubber baron winching his steamship up a hill between tributaries of the Amazon in order to build an opera house in the middle of the jungle. I've been to that opera house in Manaus that inspired the story, however, and it's pretty cool. So is the trail that starts from just outside of the park headquarters, now officially called Sendero de Lagunas Altas.

* * *

In 2006 I had another chance to visit what then was still the *future* Patagonia National Park. I was working at Patagonia-the-company, and one of its surf ambassadors, Chris Malloy, proposed making a film inspired by the Fun Hog road trip that Yvon and Doug had made in 1968 from Southern California to Southern Argentina to climb Fitz Roy. Doug had convinced the others that they should make a movie "to pay for the trip." They bought a secondhand 16mm Bolex camera and anointed one of the team, who was a photographer, to be cinematographer. The resulting film, *Mountain of Storms*, remained unknown to all but a few climbing aficionados until nearly four decades later, when Chris got hold of a VHS cassette inside a beat-up sleeve labeled "Fitz Roy."

Inspired by the movie, Chris's idea was to have a group of young climbers and surfers repeat the trip, "not just climbing and surfing," he added, "but searching for the souls of the sports, in the wildest places on the planet."

We decided to make the film with Chris directing and me producing. We agreed that once our young climbers and surfers got to Patagonia, they would join Yvon and Doug, who would now, as old graybeards, show the younger generation that it's not just about the sports, or even about finding the soul of the sports, but about saving the places where you do the sports.

Then we agreed it would be more interesting if our young surfers and climbers could sail a boat to Patagonia instead of driving a van. But where to find the money to buy or charter a boat? Maybe we could find someone with a boat willing to sail south with our crew? I put the word out in the sailing community, and almost beyond belief, we learned there was a guy in Seattle who had grown up in southern Chile, and who had just bought a fifty-three-foot steel cutter that he was planning to sail back to his home in Patagonia.

Chris and I flew to Seattle. The boat was perfect, and the owner said he would take our crew if we helped with part of the costs. The owner also liked the idea of our film. He said that while he had never met Doug Tompkins, he was familiar with Doug's efforts to create new parks, and while he personally supported their creation, he also knew they were controversial.

"The idea of taking these ranches and converting them to parks, it's a message that's pretty hard for most Chileans to understand," he said.

"One of the ways Doug tries to explain it," I replied, "is by telling people that if you're on a path leading to a cliff and you get to the edge, what are you going to do? Take another step forward? Or do a one-eighty and turn around?"

"That might be a good name for your movie," he replied.

"How's that?"

"The idea of doing a one-eighty. That's pretty much our compass course to Patagonia. One-eighty south."

* * *

We had the boat, and we had the name for our movie. Our team and a cameraman departed from the Ventura harbor just as Doug and Yvon had left in the Ford van from Yvon's blacksmith shop in Ventura forty years earlier. The voyage on the cutter was going fine until 500 miles out from Rapa Nui the backstay broke and the mast crashed down onto the deck. Luckily, no one was hurt. Chris Malloy and I, along with some of the camera crew, flew to the remote island to film the crew jury-rigging a temporary mast. It took nearly a month, and put us behind schedule, but we knew the dismasting would also make an exciting element in our film. As Yvon liked to say, it isn't an adventure until something goes wrong.

The boat made it to Chile, and our crew continued to Pumalín, where they met up with Yvon and Doug. By then Doug's petition to the Chilean government to designate Pumalín an official nature sanctuary had been approved, and we filmed Doug showing our younger surfers and climbers around the future park, and then later, with Yvon, we filmed the two old guys sharing their views on the importance of wildland conservation with the young guys.

"Most people see nature as nothing more than a basket of resources," Doug said. "A cornucopia to benefit the human economy."

"They think we can live without nature," Yvon added. "Or they think they're better than nature because they can manipulate nature. They don't think we need free-flowing rivers because if the salmon are blocked, no problem, they can just farm the salmon."

"They delude themselves into thinking they can live in a glass box above nature," Doug added. "They don't see that civilizations are as fragile as life itself. Bang, one day you're dead. The Ottomans, the Romans, the Greeks, the Mayans. None of the globalists want to look at *that* possibility."

"Accepting that you're going to die," Yvon said, "that we're all going to die—that all societies have a beginning and an end—doesn't mean you have to give up on living, or that you have to become part of accelerating the end. Doug and I agree on that, but in other ways we're opposites. He is more bothered about the end of society and maybe mankind. I'm just a laid-back Zen Buddhist, saying 'I'll do what I can do, and then so be it.'"

"Well, my buddy Yvon," Doug said with a grin, "forgets that all good Buddhists have to take their bodhisattva vows and forgo enlightenment until all the world is enlightened."

* * *

While the theme of our film was to *save* the places where we did our sports, we still wanted to *do* the sports. There wasn't much surf on the Pacific coast of Patagonia, however, because a long chain of outer islands blocks swells. But there was a breach in the chain just south of Pumalín, and we suspected that it might be wide enough to let a swell through. If that were the case, there might be surfable waves somewhere along the coast of Corcovado, the new national park that Doug had by this time talked the government into creating. The park's namesake was the glaciated volcano that had been climbed only once when Doug had made the first ascent . . . solo. If we were right, we could surf waves that no one had ever ridden and climb a mountain that had only been ascended once, all in a place that had been saved by the guy who was one of the central characters in our film.

Theory became reality when the small fishing boat we had chartered to ferry our team of surfers and climbers rounded a point and we saw perfectly shaped four- to five-foot waves peel across a cove framed by a beech forest. The Corcovado volcano, with glaciers gleaming in afternoon sun, rose behind the cove in a perfect cone. We spent a day surfing the waves, and then departed to climb the volcano, an ascent we estimated would take a round-trip of four or five days. With the delay caused by the boat's dismasting, however, we were late in the season. We made good progress until we reached the plug of near-vertical rock that rose out of the top of the peak. When Doug had climbed the mountain, the summit plug had been sheathed in ice. Now the ice had melted, and the exposed rock was so loose we feared our foot- and handholds might break, or, worse, our anchors might rip loose. Less than 200 feet from the top, we had to turn back.

Chris Malloy and I were disappointed that we didn't have a successful climb for our film, and our climbers were disappointed they had come so close only to have to give up. We interviewed Yvon, who had been with the team as far as the base of the summit plug. Later, in postproduction, Chris would use Yvon's interview as voice-over in a scene that became one of my favorite parts of the film. The team, down from the climb, is surfing waves in the pristine cove with the glaciers of Corcovado gleaming above them. Over this footage the musical group Love as Laughter plays their classic song "Coconut Flakes." The song fades, and Yvon's voice-over comes up:

"When those guys got back," Yvon says, "they were pretty shot. Any mountain at certain times is safe and other times it's super dangerous. They were just there at the wrong time. Maybe they were disappointed, but it's like the quest for the Holy Grail. Well, who gives a shit about the Holy Grail. It's the quest that's important, the transformation within yourself."

* * *

From Corcovado we drove two days south to the future Patagonia National Park. The plan was for our climbers and surfers to join a team of volunteers taking down 500 miles of barbed wire fence that was no longer needed since the sheep and cattle that had inhabited the ranch for the previous hundred years were gone. When I had first visited the area with my family on our road trip eight years earlier, the grass on the hills was nibbled to stubble and in some places the stubble was gone, exposing bare ground that was in the process of eroding.

I knew that 300 miles of fence had already been removed by the volunteers, and that two of those volunteers were my children Cameron and Connor, whom I was excited to see. As we entered the park the transformation was remarkable. The grasses were

Chapter Twenty-Three

Hamming it up at our Base Camp on the Corcovado climb.
Timmy O'Neill on the right can legitimately be called ripped,
but for Yvon and me ... well, we can always pretend. **Jimmy Chin**

recovering; as the sheep had been moved out the guanaco had
moved in. When we arrived at the project headquarters, I hugged
Cameron and Connor, and then turned to hug Kris.

"How does it look?" she asked.

"It's taken me a minute to figure it out," I answered. "But it's
not how it *looks*. It's how it *feels*. And it feels *wild*."

Over the next week we filmed our guys doing their part to
remove the remaining fence. It was a personal treat to be in the
field, working with the volunteers and with my kids. Cameron
and Connor were both taking time off from college, and it was
fulfilling to see them taking care not to let school get in the way
of their educations.

We had nearly everything we needed to complete our movie and were close to a wrap. The days were still long, and after dinner I hiked to the top of a hill that provided an overlook of the future park's headquarters. Doug had replaced not quite half of the tin-roof ranch buildings with the copper-roofed structures for the new park. He told me it would take several more years to finish everything. The old building that was the office of the former ranch was still standing, and I remembered that day on the road trip with my kids when I had gotten out of the vehicle we had borrowed from Kris and Doug and asked permission to camp on the estancia.

What if back then I had been able to see into the future, to see what I was now looking at? That led me to think how the film had turned out in an uncanny way to reflect the changes in my own life. Like the surfers and climbers in our cast, I, too, used to focus on the sports, and it had been a long evolution to focusing more on saving the places where I did the sports.

Still, the heart of it all was the sports, because without the sports we wouldn't have been in the wild, and without the wild we wouldn't have fallen in love with the beauty of nature, and without the love of nature we wouldn't have made the commitment to save nature.

Still, it's too bad we didn't make it to the summit of Corcovado, I thought. *I know it's the quest that counts, and not the Holy Grail, but . . .*

Chris felt the same, and as we wrapped up the project, we had an idea. There was a triangular peak that rose from the center of the future park with a singular beauty that for years had caught Doug's eye. He and Yvon had tried to climb it the year before but had failed, not because the climbing was difficult but because Yvon—maker of some of the best climbing gear in the world—had brought the same boots he had worn twenty-eight years earlier on our attempt to climb Minya Konka. Kris and Malinda had driven Doug and Yvon to the start of the approach hike, but Yvon had only gotten a few feet before the ossified plastic uppers of his aging boots shattered into a dozen pieces.

We asked Doug and Yvon if they might be interested in giving it another shot, and they both agreed. The first day was a long walk on a stony ridge to the base of the peak. This time Yvon had new boots, but his crampons and ice ax still dated to the '70s. Doug was dressed in his trademark pressed chinos, white oxford shirt, sporty white newsboy cap, and neck cravat.

"Look, Doug's hiking in tennis shoes," I heard one of the climbers whisper in a tone of incredulity. "I mean *tennis* shoes. Like the kind you fucking play tennis in."

It took us most of the day to reach the end of the ridge and the base of the climb. We set up our tents. The sky was clear and there was no wind. We watched the sun set over the northern ice cap and the last light reflect off the great lake of General Carrera. Yvon made dinner, and it was still light when we finished our after-dinner tea.

It snowed during the night, but shortly after we left camp the weather cleared. There was still no wind. It was shaping into a perfect day for a climb. We traversed a short glacier, then climbed a steep bergschrund. We did not rope up. We were all within our levels of skill. We reached a ridge that we knew led to the summit. There were a few places that were fifth class, but no one called for a rope.

It was midafternoon as we made the last steps to the summit. It was warm and clear, and we could see the breadth of the new park. We were the first people known to have stood on top of the mountain. The peak had no name, but in the years ahead the Chilean government would grant Doug's request to officially designate it Cerro Kristina, acknowledging Kris's central role in the creation of the new park.

When the filming was complete, Doug, Yvon, and I sat on the summit, and Jimmy Chin, whom we had hired as part of the camera crew, took our picture. It's the photo that's on page 8, opposite the prologue. I didn't know it then—although the three of us were getting old enough that we were starting to think about such things—but the first ascent of Cerro Kristina would be the last ascent for the Do Boys.

We used proceeds from our film to support protesters opposing
the dams on the Río Baker and adjacent rivers in the campaign
they called Patagonia Sin Represas. Illustration courtesy of
Shepard Fairey/obeygiant.com

That Unmarked Day
on Your Calendar

A few years after we climbed Cerro Kristina, the Do Boys gathered at the future Patagonia National Park to paddle kayaks down the Río Baker to the ocean, to celebrate Doug's seventieth birthday. This time Nadine Lehner joined us, a young woman who worked for Kris and Doug as general manager of the new park.

"It's about time you guys have a Do Girl on one of your trips," Kris had teased us, a rejoinder that was not entirely in jest. Nadine was an outdoor athlete extraordinaire, and as the rest of us were at ages where we had begun frequently to refer to ourselves as "the geezers" we had no illusion that Nadine was likely the strongest member of our birthday celebration. Over the decades, we had never consciously excluded women from our trips but neither had we included them with anything you could call "affirmative action." Looking back on it through the frame of today's frequent mix of women and men in adventure sports it was a gap, but if we were guilty of anything, it was a sin of omission rather than commission. Nadine was a natural addition to our posse, and we all enjoyed having a Do Girl on the Do Boy descent of the Río Baker.

Two years later it felt like time for another Do Boy adventure, and we decided to do another kayak trip, this time along the roadless north shore of Lago General Carrera, the giant lake that is the headwaters of the Río Baker. For Jib Ellison and me, the timing was perfect since we were going to be in the area anyway, as part of our jobs. In addition to our mutual passions for outdoor sports, Jib and I had both been working in corporate sustainability; me in my role at Patagonia, and Jib in a consultancy that had been among the main catalysts for Walmart choosing to reduce its environmental footprint. We were both involved in a coalition called the Corporate Eco Forum, which hosted an annual field trip for sustainability professionals; each year the trip was staged in a different, wild part of the planet.

Jib and I had proposed to host the upcoming trip at the future Patagonia National Park, and the Eco Forum enthusiastically accepted our idea. Jib and I welcomed to the park eight professionals from Fortune 50 companies like Apple, Tiffany, Disney, and Boeing. Jib and I set aside part of a day for Doug to talk to the group about what he called the environmental predicament. We anticipated that some members of the group might find his views challenging, if not aggravating. Doug was famously dismissive of the sustainability efforts of most big companies, efforts that he considered greenwashing— motivated more by increasing sales than decreasing impact. Furthermore, he was convinced the system of capitalism, based on annual, compounded growth, was creating technologies with what he called an "autonomous intrinsic logic" that was forcing society into a perpetual overshoot of the planet's ability to sustain life.

"If the current development model is so good," Doug had written to many of us in one of his frequent diatribes, "how did it produce the extinction crisis? Answer that for me. If you don't think the biodiversity crisis is the Mother of All Crises, then just what is?"

Doug was halfway toward finishing the last building, a visitors center that promised to be unlike any visitors center in any national park in the world. The exterior, designed to suggest

The entrance to the visitors center at Patagonia National Park. **Rick Ridgeway**

the shape of a church, was near completion, but the interior was a jumble of table saws, tools, and stacks of lumber. Still, Doug had the floor plan and the displays designed in his head.

"When you enter here," Doug told the group, "we'll have big photos of the park and the wildlife on the walls of the entry. Then, here in the center, there'll be a 3-D model of the park."

We stood in a circle in the open building, rays of light streamed through the high windows reinforcing the feeling of being in a cathedral, and I had the thought that future visitors would come here to worship the wild gods of the world.

"We're building it so you have to follow a prescribed path," Doug continued. "The first room here is what I call the Predicament Room, because it will describe the human predicament we are facing: too many people using more of the Earth's resources each year than the Earth can replenish. We use the word *predicament* because predicaments don't have solutions, at least not easy ones. So, we'll have displays talking about the outcomes of overshoot: climate change, ocean acidification, freshwater eutrophication, things like that. And, of course, the explosion of the world population.

"Now follow me. This next room is where we see the grand-daddy of all outcomes of overshoot, the extinction crisis. The walls here will be high, and there will be hundreds of pictures, or maybe models—I'm not sure yet—but hundreds of depictions of species. All kinds of animals and insects in their full glory. Except for one little problem. They're all extinct, all extinct because of one reason, and that one reason is us."

We followed Doug through the next rooms.

"We'll have a section here on the beauty of nature," he continued, leading us through more rooms. "You would hope people see and appreciate beauty, but we want to make sure they understand why it's so important: because beauty is what leads to love of nature, and, as Kris says, you don't save what you don't love."

We followed Doug into the last room.

"This room will be a little different, see, because we're calling this the Activist's Room. It's where we're going to pause to think about what we've just seen. Think about it and think whether we want to *do* something about it. So, there will be displays about how we can get involved. How *you* guys can get involved. See, it's going to be over to you. *We've* messed it up, and *you've* got to fix it."

To drive the point home, Doug walked us out of the final room and through what he said would be a narrow hall that would require people to exit one at a time.

"Right here, we want everyone to stop before they leave. We're going to put a full-length mirror on this wall, so we can all stand for a moment and look at ourselves."

After the tour I watched Doug walk away, his step jaunty and fast, as it always was, dressed in his pressed and creased chinos, as he always was, with his white newsboy cap.

"That went well," Jib said, his voice a mix of surprise, relief, and amusement.

"Doug's changed," I replied.

"How so?"

"It's been slow. The last twenty-plus years, since he married Kris, little by little, year by year, he's become more inclusive. Just now, for example, the thing that was different was his use of pronouns."

"Pronouns?"

I told Jib the story of how, thirty years earlier in Bhutan, Doug had told me he would never be friends with John Roskelley because John used too many imperative verb conjugations, and Doug felt that signaled a certain inflexibility in John.

"So, it's not verbs, but pronouns," I told Jib. "Just now, Doug was using more plural pronouns than I can ever remember. It wasn't 'I' and 'me,' but 'we' and 'us.'"

I made a mental note to see if I could get John and his family to come down to visit the park. John had dedicated the second half of his career to politics, becoming a supervisor of the county around his hometown of Spokane and a leading advocate for regional environmental protection. I knew that if I could get them together, this time they *would* be friends, and it wouldn't just be because John had become an environmentalist.

* * *

The young executives from the Corporate Eco Forum left to return home, and we spent the day preparing for our paddle along the north coast of Lago General Carrera. In addition to Doug, Jib, and myself, Yvon had come down to join us, as well as a rafting friend of Jib's, Lorenzo Alvarez Roos, and Weston Boyles, the son of Edgar Boyles, who had been Jonathan Wright's friend and who had been on Minya Konka with us when Jonathan died. Malinda and Jennifer had also come down, and they would stay behind and visit with Kris while we were on our outing.

We organized our food into breakfast, lunch, and dinner bags, divided the community gear—tents, stoves, and fuel—into parcels of equal weight, and packed our boats.

"I'll take the sat phone," Jib said.

Malinda and Kris had insisted we take a satellite phone, even though both Doug and Yvon grumbled about bringing technology into the wilderness. Early the next morning, we drove a van to a lakeside eco-resort, where we chartered a boat to ferry us and our gear to the opposite shore, which was for a long stretch uninhabited. We spent the next two days paddling easterly along the shoreline under a clear sky with only light winds. It was a combination uncommon enough in Patagonia that we noted it, saying to each other every hour or two, "Boy, are we lucky with the weather."

We had four boats: Doug and I paddled a double kayak, Jib and Lorenzo were in a second double, and Yvon and Weston were in single kayaks. The only annoyance was that the rudder in Doug's and my boat wasn't working properly, but with no wind it was easy to steer using only our paddles.

We had budgeted five days, with the goal of arriving in Puerto Ibáñez, the only sizeable town on the north lakeshore, where we had arranged a van to take us back to the park. With good conditions, we made good time. On the second day we camped in a sheltered cove near the outflow of the Avellano River. We decided to spend the next day hiking up the Avellano Valley. Doug had flown over it many times in his beloved two-seat Husky, and he had long wanted to see it from the ground. Most of the valley was owned by one family, and if they were ever interested in selling, it might be a conservation opportunity.

We left the next morning after breakfast and soon, in Do Boy fashion, everyone had gone their own way navigating through a forest of stunted Antarctic beech. I was keeping loose track of the others' positions, and soon crossed course with Jib and Yvon.

"Weston and Lorenzo are over there," I said.

"Where's Doug?" Jib asked.

Jib Ellison takes a self-portrait of the Do Boys crossing
Lago General Carrera. **Jib Ellison Collection**

"I think he's behind us," I answered. "Maybe wait here until
he catches up?"

We were on top of a small rise, high enough we could see
over the tops of the beeches, which were more bush than tree.
A hundred yards ahead I noticed movement. An animal? A ran-
cher? I focused my binoculars and saw the top of a white cap
moving up and down. Its owner, alone and walking fast, was
not pausing to look back.

"Doug's not behind us," I said. "He's in front. *Way* in front."

Three hours later we stopped at an overview to have lunch.

"It's five stars," Doug said, borrowing my binoculars to look
up valley.

"Think you might make an offer?" I replied.

"I don't know. There's so much we've already bitten off. But look at this place. It *should* be a park!"

"Maybe you should commit, and then figure it out," I said to Doug.

"Yeah, listen to my own advice."

That brought to mind a conversation I'd had with Doug a few months earlier, when I told him how, back in the 1980s, when I had seen that maxim on a note card pinned to the wall behind his desk at Esprit, I had taken it to heart and applied it to my own life.

"Oh, that?" he had said, grinning mischievously. "I got that one from Napoleon."

By midafternoon, we were back in camp, and with the sky clear, the wind calm, and the air temperature mild we dove in the lake, surfacing with loud whoops: the water was thirty-nine degrees Fahrenheit. We made a pasta dinner and sat around the campfire telling stories. In the shoreline shelter of low cliffs, the air was calm, but at higher elevations clouds had formed, and the strong winds shaped them into the saucer forms emblematic of Patagonia. As the sun set, we watched the lenticulars turn deep orange, and the snow on the peaks turn a deep pink that complemented the deep blue of the deep lake.

We sat silent, other than an occasional comment about beauty, the beauty of nature and the beauty of the untamed world that had become a foundation for all our lives. The beauty that manifested in the sports we followed, where, as Yvon once said, the cleanest line was the most graceful route you took up the rock face of a wall or down the water face of a wave. For Yvon and Doug, the beauty of the natural world had influenced the designs of the products their companies created. The design team at Patagonia conducted field trips to wilderness to seek inspiration for the palettes of upcoming seasons, and at Esprit the beauty of nature had been integrated not only into the dresses and shirts and accessories, but into all the marketing, photography, imagery, and even architecture of its headquarters and stores. Doug had now taken his sense of design—more refined than the rest of ours—into the creation of the buildings he was constructing in his new national parks.

* * *

That night we could hear the wind blow through the trees atop the ridges bordering our cove. In the morning the temperature was brisk, and we added extra layers before setting off; Doug pulled on a puff jacket over his long-sleeved button shirt and also wore his cravat and cap. We made oatmeal for breakfast, and Yvon fiddled with the troublesome rudder on the double kayak that Doug and I shared, while Doug, using lake sand as abrasive, scrubbed the soot off our cooking pot until it shone like new.

"That rudder should work a little better now," Yvon said.

With gear in our boats, we pushed our crafts partway into the water, slipped into our cockpits, fastened our spray skirts, and, using our paddles as staffs, pushed off the gravel lake bottom. As soon as we left the cove, we felt the force of the westerly wind, but it was blowing on our backs, so it aided our speed through the water. About three miles ahead we could see a point protruding into the lake; we rafted our four boats to make a plan, and decided to paddle directly to the tip of the point, where we could then tuck into its lee.

As we paddled into the bay, our four boats began to separate. Despite Yvon's efforts, our rudder continued to malfunction, and Doug and I slowly fell behind as the wind continued to strengthen and the waves increased to three feet. We caught a steep wave and surfed down it with exhilarating, yet frightening, speed.

"We need to be careful," Doug yelled from the rear cockpit. "This rudder is still screwed up."

"OK," I yelled without turning my head for fear of losing my concentration and missing a stroke.

The larger waves were now four feet, and the wind, while still increasing, was alternating direction, with some gusts descending from the Avellano Valley and hitting our beam instead of our stern. I could see Jib and Lorenzo in their double kayak ahead of us, and also Yvon and Weston, in their singles; all three boats were making better time as we struggled to keep our boat aimed at the point.

The others reached the point and then disappeared into the safety of its lee. Doug and I had about 200 yards to go before we, too, would be there, and none too soon. Our boat began to accelerate down the face of a wave, turning to the left and crosswise to the waves. Doug, his feet on the rudder pedals, pushed hard to get us back on course, and we both pulled as hard as we could on our paddles. The boat corrected, and we continued to fly fast over water increasingly white with wind-blown caps. Another wave started to lift us as the boat pulled again to the left, and though I dared not turn my head, the wave was big enough that I could hear its breaking crest just before it hit us.

* * *

Through the gemstone blue I could see from my position, upside-down and underwater, that the surface was just out of reach. My first thought was that I had to pull loose my spray skirt. But the weight of my body was enough to free the skirt, and in a second, aided by my life jacket, I was on the surface, one hand on my paddle and the other on our turn-turtled boat. Doug surfaced, and somehow he still had his white cap on his head. We looked at each other, and I could see in the set of his eyes that he had the same thought I did: in a matter of seconds everything had changed, and now we would be fighting to stay alive.

"Let's turn the boat over," Doug yelled.

I moved to the bow, and on a one-two-three we flipped it upright. We worked our way back to our respective cockpits. A yellow dry bag that held my journal was floating near the boat, so I retrieved it and threw it in the cockpit. We were on opposite sides of the boat, and on another one-two-three we pulled ourselves back up on top of the boat.

"Now try to straddle," Doug yelled.

We both sat up, straddling the boat. We still had our paddles, and, struggling to maintain balance, we started to dig our paddles into the water. With the wind fully on my torso, I felt the cold even more than when I had been in the water. In only two more seconds, another wave hit and again the boat turned over.

"Let's try it again," I yelled.

Once more we flipped the boat, crawled on top, and sat up— only to be knocked over again. It seemed like our only option, so we tried it again, and again the waves knocked us over.

"The wind is taking us away from the point," I said.

Doug didn't answer—there was nothing to say. Our situation seemed not just grim but near hopeless. Even though the profile of the upturned kayak was not that far above the water, it was exposed to the wind enough that it was propelling us even faster toward the center of the lake than the current alone. The point was still close—maybe a couple hundred yards—but we were quickly being carried away from it.

"Maybe we could swim?" I yelled.

"You think?"

"I don't know. We're being pushed out fast."

"Any sign of those guys?"

"No. They might have kept going."

We held onto the boat. We had been in the water for a few minutes. How much longer did we have? Fifteen minutes? Twenty? A few yards away I could see the dry bag with my journal, the journal I would add, when the year ended, to the shelf of journals I had kept since I was twenty-five years old. But it was too far to retrieve. Would anyone ever find it? Would anyone ever read the entry I made last night, about the beautiful sunset?

"Maybe we *should* try and swim," Doug said.

"That might be our only chance."

We both let go of the boat. I started to stroke, but it was difficult with my life jacket. I turned over and backstroked. That worked better, although the waves kept washing over my face. I stopped to catch my breath and saw Doug on his back trying to use his paddle to backstroke. Maybe I should have kept my paddle? I looked around but couldn't see it.

Concentrate on swimming. Backstroke is best. Kick, pull with my arms. Another wave, close my mouth. OK, now swim, hard. Another wave . . .

I hadn't closed my mouth in time, and I coughed to force the water out of my throat. When I caught my breath, I decided to try the breaststroke again, but it was difficult with the life jacket.

The life jacket. Why isn't it working? Shouldn't it be keeping my head higher? Try holding my breath and stroke with my face in the water. Two strokes, three. Up for a breath. Back down. Two strokes, three. Up, breathe.

But a wave hit just as I lifted my head, and again I breathed in water and had to cough it out. I looked for Doug. He was farther away, and he no longer had his paddle. Maybe the idea hadn't worked? That was just like Doug, trying to use his paddle as though his body were a boat. Always thinking, always trying something new.

Backstroke. Pull with my arms. Kick. Kick. Wave. Close my mouth. Breathe. Kick, stroke.

Another wave washed over me, and again I had to cough out water. I looked toward the point. It was about the same distance, no farther but no closer. We were holding our own, but that wouldn't be enough. We had to swim harder. I returned to the backstroke, but each time I came up to breathe the waves washed over me and I had to cough out water. I couldn't see Doug anymore. I looked at the point, and there were people standing on it. Two, maybe three. Jib, Lorenzo, Weston, Yvon. Did they see us? I waved but they didn't wave back. I yelled, but then realized with the distance and the wind that yelling was futile. I waved again, but again no one waved back. Then they disappeared. Had they seen us?

Maybe they saw us. But have to keep swimming, have to get close to the point. Backstroke is better. Stroke, stroke, wave, close my mouth, stroke, stroke, wave. . .

I stopped to cough out water. The life jacket didn't seem to be working. I was starting to drown. The point was there, still the same distance. How much longer did I have? Ten minutes? I rested my head against the life jacket and looked across the lake to the peaks, white snow against cerulean sky. So, this was the day. December 8, 2015. The day on the calendar, the day that had always been on the calendar. Always unmarked, until now.

I looked around. The peaks were so beautiful. And this time, unlike the avalanche, when everything was whirring by, this time I could pause and enjoy the beauty. This time, it was peaceful. I turned over, face in the water, eyes open. The gemstone blue. Fathomless. The blue world. The blue beauty of the blue world.

Get my face out of the water! What am I doing? Giving up? I never give up.

I yelled as loud as I could, *No!* And again, *No!* The yelling forced the water from my throat and made it easier to breathe. With everything I could muster I yelled *No!*

Then I turned and swam. I made two strokes, three, then stopped to catch my breath and stroked again. Whenever I swallowed water, I yelled *No!* and that cleared my throat. I wouldn't stop swimming until my body couldn't swim any longer.

Then I saw them, my friends, in their boats. Two boats coming toward us. I stopped and waved and saw one of the boats turn toward me. Our friends were coming to rescue us. We were going to make it! We were going to live!

As the one boat got closer, I could see it was Jib and Lorenzo in the double kayak. In another minute they were alongside me.

"We can't carry you on top," Jib said. "Hang onto the back loop."

I grabbed the rope loop on the stern of the boat with my right hand and felt the water move by me as Jib and Lorenzo started paddling toward the point. I closed my eyes and focused on my hand, on keeping my grip on the loop.

"You OK?" Jib yelled.

"Yes. What about Doug?"

"Weston has him."

Weston has Doug, I thought. *All we have to do is hang on and we'll get out of this alive.*

Keep your grip. Fingers folded, tight. It's taking so long. We must be there by now?

I opened my eyes and saw the shoreline. I picked a rock and focused on it. We were moving past it, but very slowly. I closed my eyes again so I could focus on my grip.

It's taking so long. But I'm still OK, even kind of comfortable. Is that Jib calling to me? Don't try to answer, just focus on your grip. It's taking so long.

I have a vague memory of rocks under me, and then being pulled over rocks. Or was I trying to walk? I'm not sure, but the next clear memory was both what I saw and what I felt. It was fire. Fire burning in front of me. Fire, and the feeling of warmth on my face.

* * *

"Are you OK, Rick?"

It was Jib's voice. I was in a sleeping bag and he was in it with me, holding me against his body. I shivered violently, my body convulsing.

"Yeah. Where are the others?"

"Yvon's down the beach, but close. He's OK. We called a helicopter, with the sat phone. It's here and it picked up Lorenzo, to go find Weston and Doug."

I was shivering again and closed my eyes in the comfort of knowing that help had arrived, that Doug and Weston would be OK. I told myself that shivering was my body's way of regenerating

heat. Heat. Warmth. I kept my eyes closed. The insides of my eyelids were orange and red, the colors of fire, of heat, of warmth.

I breathed consciously, deep, even breaths. Several minutes passed, and I could feel my shivering condense into waves, and between the waves I could feel warmth returning to my body. Then I heard a voice talking to Jib. I didn't know who it was, but I could just make out the words.

"We have Weston, back with Yvon," the voice said.
"What about Doug?" I heard Jib ask.
"Doug is dead."

Lenticular clouds over Lago General Carrera. **Linde Waidhofer**

Chapter Twenty-Five

The Only Synonym
for God

Jib asked me if I had recovered enough for him to leave. I told him I had, and he left with whoever it was that had told us Doug was dead. I lay in the sleeping bag in front of the fire. Ten or twenty minutes passed—I wasn't sure—when I heard a helicopter land and take off, and a few minutes later I heard Weston calling my name. He was standing next to the fire, shivering.

"What's going on?" I asked.

"The helicopter dropped me off. Lorenzo and Jib are in it, taking Doug's body to the hospital in Coyhaique."

"Get in the bag with me."

Weston crawled into the sleeping bag and I held him. He was shivering uncontrollably. I was still having spasms myself, but I was breathing more easily, and thinking more clearly. I realized that the voice I hadn't recognized, the voice that told Jib and me that Doug was dead, must have been the helicopter's pilot or copilot.

"Jib called for the helicopter on the sat phone," Weston explained. "They pulled me ashore, with a tow line. I had Doug on top my boat. By then he was unconscious." He paused, then said, "I did everything I could to save him."

He was crying, making his paroxysms of shivering more intense. I held him. Another fifteen minutes passed.

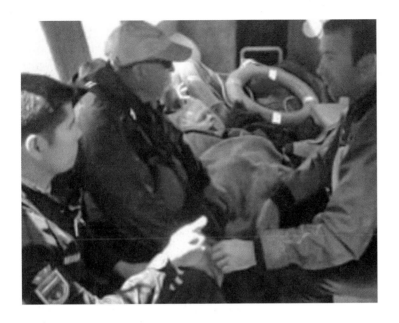

Crossing the lake in the Chilean Navy launch after our rescue.
I was still recovering from hypothermia, and one of the crew
had wrapped me in a blanket. **Armada de Chile**

"We should try and get back to Yvon," Weston said. "You strong enough to paddle in the double?"

"How far?"

"A kilometer. Maybe two."

I stood, and my legs held. Weston also stood, and he seemed to have improved a little. We walked slowly down the cobbled beach to Jib and Lorenzo's kayak—the one they had used to rescue me—and grabbed the paddles. We turned the boat around, launched, and started paddling toward Yvon, staying just off the shore. Then we saw a gray patrol boat approaching.

"Chilean Navy," Weston said.

It pulled alongside our kayak, and a crew member helped Weston and me aboard. We then headed toward Yvon's position, and once we had him in the boat we started across the lake toward Chile Chico, a small town on the south shore, on the border with Argentina.

"You better?" Yvon asked.

"I'll be OK."

We were quiet, sitting in the small cabin, staring blankly at the floorboards. It took an hour to cross the lake. The police drove us to the hospital, where we were examined. We were told the helicopter that had taken Doug's body to Coyhaique, the nearest large town to Lago General Carrera, was on the way back to pick us up and take us to the eco-lodge where our adventure had started five days earlier.

The helicopter arrived and we climbed in and took off. The wind was so strong it barely made headway and it took over a half-hour to cover the sixty-mile distance to the eco-lodge. When we landed, we walked slowly to the dining room. It was warm, but even then, I stood next to the wood-burning stove. Our hosts set bowls of hot soup on the dining table. I looked at my soup. Steam was rising off the bowl, and I could feel the steam against my face, and smell it. I looked at Yvon. He and Doug had been best friends for sixty years. They had both established companies that had become the most iconic brands in outdoor sports. They had become leaders in the global movement to save what is left of the wild parts of our beloved home planet. As Yvon liked to say, they both had started as juvenile delinquents, all their lives succeeding by staying true to their maxim that you didn't have to worry about breaking the rules if you made the rules.

Yvon picked up his spoon and sipped his soup. Was he reliving some of the stories? There were so many. One of my favorites was when they had first met, in 1960. Yvon had been drafted and was stationed at the Presidio in San Francisco. Doug would show up at the gate on his motorcycle with his pack and climbing gear. He would go to the pay phone and dial Yvon's commanding officer.

"This is Major So-and-So. Where is that Chouinard?"

"I don't know, sir."

Yvon Chouinard and Doug Tompkins sharing a gourd of maté during an interview in the Pumalín Sanctuary during the filming of *180 South*. **Frame grab from the film *180 South***

"Well, find him. He's supposed to be here at the gate. Tell him to get here right now, and make sure he has a pass to leave!"

"Yes, sir!"

Yvon took another sip of his soup, and then looked up. Our eyes held.

"This soup's good," he said. "You should eat some."

* * *

A van picked us up and drove us to Coyhaique. Doug's body was in a small boutique hotel, in a room next to reception. The core members of Kris and Doug's Chilean team arrived, and we all helped Kris with the immediate logistics, including planning a memorial service. Since it would be difficult for people to travel to the future park—six hours on mostly dirt roads from the nearest commercial airport—the group decided to fly Doug in his casket north to Puerto Varas, a small city where the Tompkins Foundation was headquartered. After holding a vigil and wake for three days, we would fly the casket back to the park for Doug's burial.

At the headquarters we positioned Doug's open casket in a downstairs salon, and for the next three days hundreds of people filed past. Hundreds of articles appeared in newspapers around the world, and dozens of appreciations aired on television and radio.

In the evenings, Jennifer slept with Kris, holding her through the long nights. Jib and I slept in the salon, next to Doug in his casket. Before we went to sleep, we placed our hands on his cold forehead to say good night, and again, when we woke, to say good morning. Friends arrived from Europe, from North America, from across South America. On the third day, in the back garden, we had a private service.

Many of us spoke, but none with the power Kris summoned when she stood from her seat in the front row, walked a few steps, and turned to face the audience. She wore a long-sleeved black dress and a single strand of pearls. She had on a light-colored lipstick, and her gray hair was held in a barrette (when her hair had begun to gray, she had wanted to dye it, but Doug had been strongly opposed). She looked at her notes, then looked up, but did not speak. She took a long breath, exhaled, and straightened.

"My husband and I were a pair, but we were much more together than the two of us apart. We were the loves of each other's lives, but also we were in love with all things wild."

She stopped and breathed again, pursed her lips, and nodded her head as though she were having an internal conversation with one voice saying *I can't do this* and another, stronger voice saying *Yes, you can.*

She told us that although she and Doug lived in isolated places, they did not live alone, but had their teams and their teams' families working alongside them, such that they became one extended family. She and Doug had their friends who visited from all parts of the world, everyone connected by the common passion of preserving and protecting nature.

"Doug died doing what he loved. Out on the water, with his closest friends, with Yvon, his lifelong friend, with Jib, with Rick, who nearly died as well, with young Weston, who fought with Doug to the end. All of them, all of you, all of us, we are all fighters, and, like Doug, we will move forward, working harder, faster, working with more clarity than ever before."

* * *

We flew the casket in a private plane offered by a wealthy Chilean supporter from Puerto Varas to Cochrane, the nearest airstrip to the future Patagonia National Park. It was a cloudless day, and as we flew south I could see Corcovado, the namesake mountain of Corcovado National Park, which Doug had also created with his Esprit friend and partner Peter Buckley, who was with us in the plane. Corcovado was the peak that Doug had climbed in the winter, reaching it solo, the first human known to stand on top of the pointed summit. We flew past Yanteles, the peak Doug and I had climbed, also a first ascent—the place where everything we could see looking north to the horizon was land Doug had purchased as part of what would soon become Pumalín Douglas R. Tompkins National Park.

We flew close to the glaciers surrounding San Valentín, the highest peak in Chilean Patagonia, and through the cockpit window all we could see was ice. Kris was in the copilot's seat so she could see the ice cap, the summits, the fjords, the grasslands, and the wildlands she and her late husband had protected. Now, as we approached Cochrane, we could see Cerro San Lorenzo with its great east face, the face that for twenty years Doug had reminded us was the unfinished project of the Do Boys.

"I don't know," I had said only the year before, when the conversation about climbing the east face had come up, as it did every year. "At this point in our lives we might be the Done Boys."

"Speak for yourself!" Doug had replied.

A van was waiting for us at Cochrane's airstrip. We loaded the casket and drove to the park headquarters, where some of the staff transferred Doug into a simple casket that the carpenters had made of wood from his beloved alerce trees—wood gathered from natural deadfall. Like all construction in the future park, Doug had overseen the restoration of the small cemetery where some of the gauchos and their families had been buried. Many of the team who had worked on building the new park, along with others who were his close friends, exchanged places as we carried the heavy casket past the new lodge to the cemetery and

lowered it into the grave. Then, one by one, we tossed handfuls of dirt over the casket.

There were many locals attending the burial, the locals who Doug had recruited into supporting his vision, and who had been part of the campaign Patagonia Sin Represas—Patagonia Without Dams—to prevent the construction of the dam on the Río Baker at the entrance to the park, the same proposed dam that my kids had learned about years before on our family road trip. It was a campaign that had succeeded in large part because of Doug's financial and creative support, a campaign

Corcovado, the namesake peak of the surrounding national park created by Doug Tompkins and his Esprit partner and close friend Peter Buckley. Corcovado, the peak Doug climbed solo with no rope, the first time anyone had reached the summit. **Jimmy Chin** that culminated in one of the largest civil society protests in the country's history: 30,000 people gathered in front of the president's residence chanting, "Patagonia Sin Represas!"

When the grave was filled, one of the locals, a middle-aged woman who had been central to the campaign, stood and raised her fist above her head. "Patagonia Sin Represas!" she shouted. She raised her fist again and shouted, "Patagonia!" and the crowd took up the refrain, "Sin Represas!" Again, she raised her fist: "Patagonia!" And again, the crowd raised theirs: "Sin Represas!"

* * *

Those of us close to Kris worried that Doug's death might be a potentially fatal amputation, and it was our hope that the work that remained to convert the various protected areas she and Doug had created over the last thirty years into officially designated national parks would save her. In the months that followed, Jib, through his sustainability consultancy, worked with Kris and her executive team to put all the projects into a strategic framework with a financial structure that gave Kris and her team a map of how to work effectively toward their ultimate goal of getting their land turned into national parks in Chile and Argentina.

The strategic plan, more than a hundred pages long, included timelines to get all projects converted to parks within five years. To a degree that surprised us all, Kris rallied her team of more than 300 people and they began to deliver each milestone ahead of schedule. As we had hoped, the long days filled with meetings, phone calls, strategy sessions, and fundraisers were giving her a purpose that in turn was giving her the strength to continue.

But I knew that even with long days filled with hard work, the nights were even longer. During the three days immediately following Doug's death Jennifer had slept with Kris each night, holding her in her arms, and in the months and years

Kris Tompkins in the backcountry of Patagonia National Park. **Jimmy Chin**

that followed, that intimacy continued. In addition to her work, Kris also found both reprieve and solace in the time she spent in nature among wild creatures. She increased her travel, and many of her trips were to other protected areas around the world where she could learn by example how wild areas were safeguarding wildlife, or, in some cases, how rewilding efforts were addressing areas where some of that wildlife had been extirpated.

Jennifer accompanied Kris on all of these trips, to the Pantanal in Brazil to see jaguars; to Africa, to be close to elephants, rhinos, and especially lions; to India, where Kris and Jennifer were with guides who knew how to interpret the calls of the wild creatures in the forests when those creatures alerted one another a tiger was approaching.

Going to India to see tigers was the first of these trips, and they left less than two months after Doug died. For Kris, it had been a fantasy for decades to see a tiger in the wild. For the first two days, she and Jennifer traveled in a safari vehicle through a national park known for its population of tigers, but there were no tigers. Then on the third day the safari vehicle slowed and stopped, and the guide pointed to a gully that was more of a gulch. There was a large female tiger, moving stealthily through a trickle of water. Instead of raising her binoculars, however, Kris sank to the floorboard of the vehicle and curled into a ball. Having found the great cat she had dreamed of finding, she could not confront it. Kris would tell me years later that she recognized that the impulse of most people would have been to encourage her to sit up to see the tiger they had come so far to see. Jennifer, however, scooted across the bench seat and placed her knee into the small of Kris's back, and pressed her to the floorboard so that she could not rise even if she wanted to.

Jennifer was discreet about her many journeys with Kris, even with me, but she shared enough that I realized she wasn't trying to keep Kris from looking into the face of the tiger, but rather she was accompanying her until she was *ready* to look into the face of the tiger.

"She never tried to pull me back," Kris told me years later. "Jennifer instead went with me to the edge and stood by me so that together we leaned over and looked into the deep dark well."

Eventually for Kris the deep well became more mystery than allure, and she learned how to turn away from the dark and face the light.

"I realized that marriages never end," Kris said. "They transform."

* * *

One of the principal challenges of getting the protected-area projects in Chile converted to national parks had always been winning support from the government. While at a glance it might seem easy to convince a government to accept a donation of private lands into the country's public lands, the reality was more complex, and it was compounded by Kris's intention to require the government to add public lands that had no or little protection to the proposed national parks. The challenge was more pressing because the president of Chile, Michelle Bachelet, who was supportive of Kris and her timeline for creating the parks, had less than two years remaining in her term-limited presidency. Even with the president on board, there was still the challenge of persuading the legislature and cabinet ministers to support the land transfers.

At each hurdle, Kris found a way over. It wasn't that she worked harder—she and Doug had always worked hard—but that she worked with an attitude that she had nothing to lose. Instead of simply asking the government to match her donation acre-to-acre, she told them she wanted the leverage to be ten-to-one: for every acre she donated, the government had to add ten.

Kris made it clear this request was nonnegotiable. It was a request, however, that was considered by most with the respect due a widow who despite her grieving had, as soon as her husband was interred, changed out of her black dress and into her work dress. That respect was strengthened even more when Kris had decided to bury Doug not in the United States, but in the small graveyard a short walk from the new stone-walled and copper-roofed headquarters of the *future* Patagonia National Park. Doug's headstone was among the headstones of the gauchos and their family members who had died generations before while working at Estancia Chacabuco. For many Chileans, her decision was confirmation that the couple had really meant what they'd said from the beginning, that they were buying these lands and restoring them and constructing park infrastructure with the intention of giving it back to their host country.

* * *

Less than a year after she buried Doug, Kris signed a protocol with the government that mapped the details of the transfer. Ten months after that, we gathered in front of the restaurant of the future Patagonia National Park to witness Kris Tompkins, standing next to Chilean president Michelle Bachelet, sign an agreement to create five new national parks and expand three more. Kris was donating a million acres, and the government was adding a little over ten million, for a total larger than five Yellowstones combined. It was the biggest conservation achievement by private individuals in history.

The five new parks included Pumalín, now known as Pumalín Douglas R. Tompkins National Park, and Patagonia National Park, now no longer the future Patagonia National Park. After the ceremony, we gathered for lunch and wine in the living room of Kris's house, overlooking the park's headquarters. Jennifer was with me, along with Yvon and Malinda and the core members of Kris's conservation team—most of them Chileans and Argentineans—and other key Chilean supporters.

After lunch, after the president and the others had left, Kris sat alone on a cushioned bench in the living room, looking through the front window. A herd of guanacos was in the near distance, grasslands and wetlands in the middle distance, and mountains and glaciers occupied the far distance; all of it was now conferred the highest level of conservation protection in the

The Chilean president Michelle Bachelet signs the protocol with Kris Tompkins that would eventually create five new national parks and expand three more. **Jimmy Chin**

country. She was like Christina in the Andrew Wyeth painting, only on the inside looking out at a landscape through a window portioned into multiple panes framed with precisely joined hardwood. I had once asked Doug why he had designed the windows in the house—along with the rest of the park buildings—with multiple panes. He said it was because they were more beautiful and less industrial than single-pane picture windows, and they framed the view in a way that made you think about the parts of the landscape and the beauty of those parts aggregating into a beauty greater than any part alone.

Robinson Jeffers, poet laureate of the Do Boys, wrote:

> *Integrity is wholeness,*
> *The greatest beauty is*
> *Organic wholeness, the wholeness of life and things,*
> *The divine beauty of the universe. Love that, not man*
> *Apart from that.*

We decided to allow Kris some time alone, so I descended the hill past the native cushion plants and the califate, ripe with purple berries. I stopped and picked a handful. Approaching the new park headquarters, I passed the large wooden sign hand-carved with relief lettering that spelled "Parque Patagonia." There was a rectangular space of wood between "Parque" and "Patagonia"—Doug had designed it that way, so that someday, when the moment arrived, workers could take the sign back to the shop and carve out the third word, "Nacional," avoiding the need to make a new sign.

"No Detail Is Small," read the sign above Doug's desk at Esprit.

I passed the restaurant, the administrative office, and the visitors center. The exhibits inside were now near completion, and they were true to Doug's design. His design philosophy was informed by his belief in deep ecology, that to save ourselves we humans need to live in harmony with our fellow wild creatures, to protect the wildlands that they need not just to survive but to thrive, and to protect the solace we humans need to remind ourselves where we have come from, because only then can we have the vision to imagine where it is we need to go.

I crossed the small creek flowing between the park's buildings and walked down the gravel road toward the small cemetery, imagining in years to come how pilgrims will walk this same path, coming here to the ends of the Earth to think deeply about how to save the Earth. I walked to the cemetery and opened the gate under the arch made so beautifully of hand-joined hardwood and sat on the grass in front of Doug's headstone.

Under his name, carved into the stone, were the words, "Birdie and Lolo." I imagined future visitors would wonder what the names meant, but I knew they were Doug and Kris's nicknames for each other, their terms of endearment. How proud my friend would be to witness what his wife Birdie had achieved.

I took the handful of califate berries I had carried down the hill and sprinkled them over his grave.

"He who eats the califate," I said, repeating a local saying, "returns to Patagonia."

I left the grave and walked back toward the gate of the small fence framing the cemetery. There, carved into a wood panel on the back of the arch over the gate, was the last of the many signs Doug left us. It was another of his favorite sayings, this one from John Muir.

No hay sinónimo para Dios más perfecto que la Belleza.

There is no synonym for God more perfect than Beauty.

Doug Tompkins's headstone in the small cemetery at the Patagonia National Park headquarters. **Rick Ridgeway**

Epilogue

What if I had died along with Doug? My wife, Jennifer, would then have lost two husbands to boating accidents. Would she have recovered? Would she have had the strength to be the life ring that saved Kris? And after saving her, to support Kris as she turned tragedy into resolve with an alchemy nothing less than astonishing?

I never imagined that Jennifer would die before me. Jennifer, however, never felt that way. It wasn't that she had a conviction she would die first, but rather a deep understanding that none of us knows when our life, or the lives of those around us who we most love, will end, and that the ending can take us by surprise. We all know this, of course, but how many of us have the wisdom to go about our daily rounds integrating this awareness into all our actions, into all our decisions, whether those decisions are matters of consequence or matters of inconsequence, to find plea-sure in the commonplace, to integrate into our lives what it really means to, with profound awareness, live fully in the moment?

We got the news of Jennifer's cancer on her birthday, as she turned sixty-nine; we were only four months apart in age. For the next eight months, her mantra was "It is what it is." It became a source of strength through acceptance for our whole family. It was an acceptance of fate, or of plight, but it was also

Jennifer Ridgeway (standing) and Kris Tompkins on safari in East Africa, three years after Doug Tompkins died. **Kris Tompkins Collection**   413 a refusal to permit plight to eclipse spirit. We were in and out of hospitals, and every time we were in, it was only a matter of a day or two before Jennifer became the favorite of the nurses and doctors, and it was because she kept her spirit, even in the cancer ward.

Much of that spirit was propelled by the daily arrival of the kids and the grandkids, everyone taking their turns to hold Jennifer's hand—Ama's hand, as the grandkids called her—all of them encircling the matriarch. Family, her family, the family she had birthed and nurtured, inspired, disciplined, and loved all those years, years that had so many months when I was gone and she was the one with two full-time jobs, one at the company and the other at home.

She never permitted her plight to eclipse her spirit. I remember one day a psychiatrist came to her hospital room to assess her mental condition, to make sure she wasn't suicidal.

"Is there anything that makes you angry?" the doctor asked.

"Yes!" Jennifer answered emphatically.

"What?"

"Racism!"

"Oh, well . . . that's probably OK."

"And there's another thing!"

I could tell she was—to use a phrase she always favored—getting worked up.

"What's that?" the doctor asked.

"Intolerance of immigrants. That really makes me angry."

* * *

Our three children and I decided to limit the attendees to only those whose lives had been touched directly by Jennifer. That came to a little over 400 people. We held the service at Patagonia's auditorium. The employees Jennifer had mentored over the decades had hung on the walls her favorite photos from the Patagonia catalogs she had produced during her years as photo editor.

I stood at the door to welcome friends. I hugged Tom and Meredith Brokaw. Tom was too distraught to speak. Jib and Marci Ellison. If it wasn't for Jib, who had pulled me ashore, I would have died first. Dan and Rae Emmett. Dan, my mentor, who was always there to guide me with advice and by example. Yvon and Malinda Chouinard. Yvon, who had been with me in the avalanche, when we both had died and been reborn. Jimmy Chin, an adopted son for Jennifer and me both.

Asia Wright and her husband and their two children, ages eight and six. After our trip to find her father's grave, Asia had reset her relationship with her mother, and married a man who, like her, had a successful career in advertising and marketing. Asia, an adopted daughter for Jennifer and me both.

John Roskelley, there without his wife, and we both knew why. I was deeply grateful he came. Only weeks before, their son Jess had been killed on a difficult climb in the Canadian Rockies. Jess, the little boy who, with my little daughter, had gone camping with us all those years ago. John and I held each other tightly.

Laurel Peacock arrived, Doug Peacock's daughter. Our oldest daughter and Laurel had been high school classmates.

"Where's Doug?" I asked.

Laurel said he had been stopped by the TSA in the Bozeman airport and prevented from boarding because he had tested positive for explosives. We both laughed and we knew that Jennifer would have laughed too.

"Hayduke lives," I said as I hugged her.

* * *

I walked to the stage and paused in front of the poster-sized photograph of Jennifer, framed in a garland of marigolds, aware that 400 people were looking at my back, and more aware that Jennifer was looking at me, with her glowing smile, and past me to all her friends.

"We're all here, Bella," I said out loud. "All here for you."

At the podium I opened my notes, looked at our hundreds of friends, and, slowly putting on my reading glasses, gave my remembrance:

"In October 1981, I was having dinner with Jennifer in a small restaurant in Little Italy in New York when I asked her to marry me. It was not an expensive restaurant, and despite my dirtbag lifestyle, she accepted. This was less than six months after we had met, and Jennifer decided there was also no reason to wait before we married, so she set the wedding date for Valentine's Day. 'That way,' she told me, 'you'll never forget your anniversary or Valentine's.' Then, raising one eyebrow in the way I would later come to know very well, she added, 'Will you.' Despite being a dirtbag, I recognized the subtle distinction in the way she said, 'Will you.' It was not a question."

I then told our friends how Jennifer and I had met in Kathmandu at the Yak & Yeti, how I told her I was there to complete the story on Sagarmatha (Mount Everest) National Park for *National Geographic* that Jonathan Wright and I had started but never finished because, after the avalanche, he had died in my arms; I told them how Jennifer had then revealed that her husband had died when they were hit by a tidal wave while sailing their yacht off the coast of New Guinea; I told them how, after we married, I read her *The Little Prince*, and how the Little Prince had talked about "Matters of Consequence," and how distinguishing matters of consequence from matters of inconsequence became the axiom of our marriage, a marriage that endured for nearly forty years.

"One afternoon in the hospital room," I said, "Jennifer and I were listening to the classical music channel on the television when Dvořák's 'Going Home' began to play. I was standing next to her bed, and I reached down and held her hand as we listened to the words. When the song finished, she looked at me and said, 'If this doesn't work out, I want you to play that at my funeral.'"

I took off my glasses, looked at our hundreds of friends, and asked them to hold the hands of those next to them. A choir then sang "Going Home."

> Morning star lights the way,
> Restless dream all done.
> Shadows gone, break of day,
> Real life has begun.
> There's no break, there's no end,
> Just a-living on.
> Wide awake, with a smile,
> Going on and on . . .

* * *

For thirty of our forty years of marriage, Jennifer and I lived in the same house in Ojai, a historic Spanish Revival designed by Paul Williams, the first successful Black architect in America; we could feel his noted advocacy of self-reliance imbued in the walls. Jennifer had painted those walls with the colors of the palette of Provence favored by the Impressionists. Doug Tompkins, noted for his design aesthetic, told many of his friends it was his favorite house in the world. For my part, I told Jennifer, "Su casa es su casa."

A friend built a small box for Jennifer's ashes out of wood from a live oak dead-felled on a neighbor's property; the corners were perfectly mortised and tenoned. At my request he inlaid an old worn tile that Jennifer had bought in Mexico depicting Our Lady of Guadalupe on the front of the box. Mexico was Jennifer's favorite country, and Mexicans her favorite people, and while she was not religious she did believe in spirits. And she believed that some of those spirits were guardians, and that Guadalupe was her guardian. I don't feel Guadalupe abandoned her, but I do feel it is possible—in the way that most things are possible—that Guadalupe may be accompanying her. For me, there is no way to know, and therefore no way to give the consideration currency, but I welcome it not because it provides comfort but because it evokes mystery.

I don't believe in the idea of closure. It is a misguided response to death. It is healthy to face toward, rather than turn away from, the gap left by the death of someone you love, even as you face the pain of no longer hearing the voice of the one you loved in your ears while you continue to hear the voice in your mind.

Love is the truest balm against the pain of the loss of love.

Avoiding closure made it a little more challenging to address a desire to simplify my life, or at least to cull the accretion of Jennifer's belongings that over the decades had grown like barnacles on the hull of a boat that now needed a good scraping. Her twenty-year collection of back issues of *Gourmet* magazine was easy to let go, even if back-breaking to carry to the recycle bin. Not so easy was her exquisitely curated wardrobe, each piece evoking the image of her body inhabiting it, each piece still bearing her smell. I told myself each piece had years of useful life left and should be worn by a daughter or friend; there was a mitigating comfort in thinking of the clothes as having a "life."

Jennifer wasn't the only one who over the decades had accumulated stuff. In the garage, which had always been used to house stuff instead of automobiles, I faced two rows of three-ring binders, each with paperwork from an expedition whose identity was recorded on the spine: Everest 1976, Minya Konka 1980, Borneo 1983, Aratitiyope 1992, Queen Maud Land 1998, Chang Tang 2002. Forty binders from thirty-five years of adventures. I went through each one, keeping photographs and a couple of maps too sentimental to toss. In the K2 binder I found a letter from Fritz Wiessner, written to me after he had read my book on our ascent of K2, describing the final pitches of his attempt in 1939 when he had to turn back, just short of the summit, because his companion lost confidence. I sent that to the American Alpine Club, for the permanent collection in their library.

I filled the bin and wheeled it down the driveway. The next morning, out the open window, I heard the garbage truck approaching. Coffee in hand, I walked to the street. The truck arrived, the remote-controlled forks grabbed the bin, and I watched the binder pages fly into the huge dumpster behind the cab, like one of those scenes in a period black-and-white movie where decades of calendar pages scroll by in a blur. The truck lowered the bin and drove away.

I walked back to the house, empty garbage bin in one hand and coffee in the other. I paused to listen to the birds in the live oaks. They were not the songs and calls of the usual residents that spend the winter in my area. No, these were the songs and calls of the warblers—the Wilson's, the hermits, the Townsend's—the birds that pass through twice a year on their eternal departures and returns. The spring migration had begun.

Jennifer and me on safari in East Africa, three years after we married. Rick Ridgeway Collection

Acknowledgments

This book started during a long layover in a bar in the Santiago airport. Timmy O'Neill and I had been in Patagonia National Park with Jimmy Chin, who was making a film about Kris Tompkins. Timmy, Jimmy, and I were halfway through our first round of beers when I started telling stories, including some of the ones in this book, like the K2 climb.

"We had to walk one hundred and ten miles each way to Base Camp, with four hundred and fifty porters," I told them.

"Four hundred and fifty porters?" Jimmy asked incredulously.

"Three hundred and eighty to carry our stuff. Then fifty more to carry food for the three hundred and eighty. Then a few more to carry food for the guys carrying the food."

"Do you have photos?" Jimmy asked. "You need to start an Instagram account."

"Hashtag old school," Timmy added.

They took my iPhone and by the time we finished another round I had an Instagram account and had posted my first photo along with a story caption. Soon I had a few thousand followers.

Timmy and Jimmy, thanks for kick-starting this project, and Jimmy, it was a "proud-father" moment when I watched you and Chai walk to the podium to get your Oscar for *Free Solo*. You've come a long way since we pulled our rickshaws across the Chang

Tang (or, as Malinda Chouinard tells her friends, "when Rick and his buddies pushed shopping carts across Tibet").

My daughter Cameron Tambakis, in her mother's footsteps, is a photo editor at Patagonia, and when she and her photo department pal Eugénie Frerichs became two of my followers, they talked me into converting my Instagram account into a book. Cameron and Eugénie, a hug to you both. To my other daughter Carissa Tudor and her husband, Dwight, for coming up with the title.

When I finished writing the book there were fifty stories. Here I need to thank Elizabeth Hightower Allen for helping me get it into shape. To Liz Grady, for helping gather permissions. And the Patagonia Books team: Karla Olson, John Dutton, Christina Speed, Annette Scheid, Jane Sievert, Sonia Moore, Sus Corez, Rafael Dunn. And my agent Susan Golomb, and her team at Writers House: Susan, I have more ideas for more books, so hang in there with me.

* * *

And you, dear reader, you may have noticed that there are only twenty-five stories in the version of the book you just read, and not the fifty I mentioned above. That's because when I finished the first version I sent it to Candace Davenport, to make sure it was OK with her to tell the story about the time we got arrested together and thrown in jail in Panama.

I hadn't talked to Candace in over four decades. I knew she had a successful career as a lawyer in the Bay Area. I did an internet search and found a photo of her holding a hawk that she and some fellow birders had mist-netted to band and release. Using a phrase I had learned from my kids, I said "Yessss!" when I saw the photo.

"Rick!" Candace exclaimed when we connected by phone.

Her voice sounded just the same. I told her I had three kids and four grandkids. I explained how my beloved Jennifer, after thirty-eight years of marriage, had died of cancer. Candace told me she had two kids, and they were long out of the nest, and she and her husband still lived in the Bay Area.

I told her about the book, that I wanted her to read the jail story, to make sure it was OK.

"Can I read the whole book?" she asked.

Two weeks later she sent a text saying she had read the manuscript and was ready to talk. I was nervous. What if she didn't approve the jail story? Or worse, what if she didn't like the book?

I called her, and after some cordial small talk she told me she liked the book. If we had been FaceTiming she would have seen me exhale a silent whistle of relief.

"But who did you write the book for?" she asked.

"What do you mean?"

"Who do you want to read it?"

"I don't know. Climbers, outdoor people, maybe conservationists. I haven't thought about it."

"What do you want them to learn from it?"

I wondered if maybe Candace had been a trial lawyer. I told her I hadn't thought about that either.

"Well, I think you need to think about it. Because you have fifty stories that are trying to be a memoir, but to be a memoir you need more focus, and you need to be more open. About yourself."

I told her I needed a couple of days to think about it. By the next day, I realized she was right. For one thing, the book was so long it was more doorstop than memoir. I called her and said I had emailed the Patagonia Books staff to tell them I was delaying publication while I did a rewrite.

"I'll help you," Candace said.

"Candace, you're a lawyer. Where did you learn about editing?"

"I keep forgetting—we haven't talked for a while. In addition to law, for the last thirty years I've had a parallel business as an authors coach."

So, dear reader, if you enjoyed the book, don't thank me, thank Candace Davenport.

Other Books by Rick Ridgeway

The Boldest Dream

The Last Step

Seven Summits (with Frank Wells and Dick Bass)

Below Another Sky

The Shadow of Kilimanjaro

The Big Open

About the Author

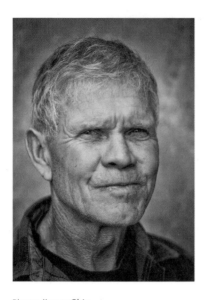

Photo: **Jimmy Chin**

By the time he was thirty, Rick Ridgeway had gone on more adventures than most people do in an entire lifetime. Called "the real Indiana Jones" by *Rolling Stone* magazine, Ridgeway doesn't shy away from unknown territory. In fact, he seeks it.

Ridgeway is recognized as one of the world's foremost mountaineers. He was part of the 1978 team that were the first Americans to summit K2, the world's second-highest mountain, and he has climbed new routes and explored little-known regions on six continents.

Ridgeway is also an environmentalist, writer, photographer, filmmaker, and businessman. For fifteen years beginning in 2005 he oversaw environmental affairs at the outdoor clothing company Patagonia. Before joining Patagonia, he was owner/president of Adventure Photo & Film, a leading stock photo and film agency. He has authored six previous books and dozens of magazine articles and produced or directed many documentary films. He was honored by National Geographic with their Lifetime Achievement in Adventure Award and was awarded the Lowell Thomas Award by the Explorers Club.

Ridgeway serves on the boards of Tompkins Conservation, the Turtle Conservancy, and One Earth. He lives in Ojai, California.

GREENLAND

Somerset Island, Nunavut **13**

NORTH
AMERICA

9 *Mt. Rainier N.P., Washington*

9 *Grand Teton N.P., Wyoming*

Jackson Hole, Wyoming **5**

22 *Red Desert, Wyoming*

Pacific Ocean

Atlantic Ocean

4 *Panama City, Panama*

14 *Aratitiyope, Venezuela*

21 *Queen Maud Land*

SOUTH
AMERICA

12 *Larsen Ice Shelf*

ANTARCTICA

8 *Vinson Massif*

6 *Aconcagua, Chile*

15,17 *Pumalín N.P., Chile*

24,25 *Lago General Carrera, Chile*

23 *Patagonia National Park, Chile*

11 *Magellanic Fjords, Chile*